Nothing Succeeds Like Failure

A volume in the series

HISTORIES OF AMERICAN EDUCATION

Edited by Jonathan Zimmerman

A list of titles in this series is available at cornellpress.cornell.edu.

Nothing Succeeds Like Failure

The Sad History of American Business Schools

Steven Conn

Cornell University Press
Ithaca and London

First published 2019 by Cornell University Press

Library of Congress Cataloging-in-Publication Data
Names: Conn, Steven, author.
Title: Nothing succeeds like failure : the sad history of American business
    schools / Steven Conn.
Description: Ithaca [New York] : Cornell University Press, 2019. | Series:
    Histories of American education. | Includes bibliographical references
    and index.
Identifiers: LCCN 2019006302 (print) | LCCN 2019009534 (ebook) |
    ISBN 9781501742088 (pdf) | ISBN 9781501742095 (epub/mobi) |
    ISBN 9781501742071 (cloth : alk. paper)
Subjects: LCSH: Business education—United States—History. | Business
    Schools—United States—History. | Master of business administration
    Degree—United States—History.
Classification: LCC HF1131 (ebook) | LCC HF1131 .J694 2019 (print) |
    DDC 650.071/173—dc23
LC record available at https://lccn.loc.gov/2019006302

For Bruce Kuklick and Mike Zuckerman
Teachers, mentors, friends

CONTENTS

Nothing Succeeds Like Failure

Introduction

The Beast That Ate Campus

Each month when my colleagues and I gather for our faculty meeting we assemble in a slightly cramped seminar room and deposit ourselves into an array of mismatched furniture. Some of us sit in rolling office chairs whose wheels don't quite roll anymore, but if you get there early enough you might get to sit on the sofa—one whose springs are shot in the middle causing those perched on either end to list gently toward each other. There are two stacks of stackable chairs, and one lucky person can occupy, throne-like, an upholstered wing chair. It is the kind of genteel shabbiness that one might expect to find in a humanities department—four-legged analogues to many of us: rumpled, frayed around the edges, a tad misfit.

As it happens, the furnishings are hand-me-downs from the business school.

In a gesture of environmental responsibility (reuse, recycle!) or in an act of campus charity (alms for the campus impoverished!) the business school's used furniture wound up in the history department several years ago when their offices were redecorated with newer, better seating. One suspects that no business school bottoms sit on busted springs in any business school couch.

So we joke about this each month among ourselves because it all seems so emblematic of campus dynamics these days, so perfectly apropos. The business school growing ever bigger and ever wealthier while humanities departments shrink and suffer and starve, grateful for the leftovers tossed at us by our business school betters. Furniture as a metaphor for higher education today. I described all this to an old friend who teaches history at the University of Denver. She laughed too and then told me that her entire department, along with other humanities and social science departments, occupy a hand-me-down building. No longer good enough for the business school there, it had been passed on to them after the sparkly new B-school palace had opened and those faculty relocated to what are surely very comfortable new chairs.

The chuckles come with more than a little bitterness, needless to say. Those of us who regard the arts and sciences as the heart of higher education often view the business school with anger, contempt, and envy in varying measure. We, many of us at any rate, are suspicious of the teaching and research that goes on in those increasingly extravagant buildings; we can't believe how much money these schools attract from alumni donors and corporate "partners"; and even beyond the equivalently extravagant salaries our peers in the business schools draw each year, we are jealous of all the students who choose their classes rather than ours.

That isn't new. Students have always flocked to business schools, just as soon as they opened on campuses. And in some sense universities opened them in response to that student demand. By 1900 roughly 20 percent of U.S. college graduates were headed into some sort of business career; 30 percent of those graduating from Harvard, Yale, Columbia, Princeton, and the University of Pennsylvania.[1] Three of those Ivies would open among the earliest business schools; Yale would join them later. (Princeton still has not opened a business school.) If college graduates were choosing the business world, as opposed to the ministry or the law or teaching, then universities felt increasingly compelled to provide them an education for that choice. In 1915, business degrees accounted for 3 percent of the 19,000 bachelors of arts degrees awarded that year. That quadrupled to 12 percent by 1928. By 1950, business degrees constituted roughly 18 percent of all BAs awarded; by 1970 American universities were granting more than 120,000 BAs in business every year.[2] And by 2018 there were roughly 13,000 business schools on university campuses all over the globe.

Most of all, many of us simply don't believe that teaching business techniques constitutes the real work universities ought to do. We may not quite believe in the disinterested search for truth the way our predecessors once did, but we bristle at the idea that a university ought to promote profit making as a goal unto itself. "I have had English professors at the Faculty Club tell me that the School of Business should not be in the University," recalled Berkeley's Ewald Grether, who served as dean there in the mid-twentieth century, and he was surely not the only B-school dean to hear such complaints.[3] Develop a new cancer treatment drug in a university lab, and no one would argue that the research constitutes a public good; teach students in an upper-division marketing class new ways to sell drugs to consumers more aggressively, and that starts to feel as if the university has become a subsidiary of Big Pharma. That last is not just a hyperbolic hypothetical, as we are learning more and more that the prescription opioid epidemic in the United States began with aggressive and dishonest marketing campaigns. How many of Purdue Pharmaceutical's pill pushers majored in marketing at some American business school?

This uneasiness is hardly new either. In fact, it has been expressed by various observers almost from the moment business schools started to appear on campuses in the late nineteenth century. In 1918 Thorstein Veblen summed up this animosity when he lacerated business schools in his characteristically caustic way. Unlike other professional schools, Veblen wrote, which "may be serviceable to the community at large," the "business proficiency inculcated by the schools of commerce has no such serviceability, being directed singly to a facile command of the ways and means of private gain."[4]

Business schools, however, at the outset and then repeatedly across the twentieth century, promised more and better than that. With a college training, future businessmen would learn that private gain was subsidiary to larger social goals, though business schools have always been a little vague about what those goals might be. The keynote speaker at a 1920 Illinois Chamber of Commerce gathering told the assembled businessmen that "the modern business man with a university education . . . will regard business as a public service enterprise, to justify itself, not by profits but by the social service rendered."[5] People guffawed at that idea then, just as many chuckle at it now.

So my faculty colleagues and I, at universities all over the country, hunker down on our beat-up furniture and stare over at the Oz-like castles built for the business schools. We don't quite know what goes on behind the curtains, but we are convinced that it isn't good. We are just as convinced that if they had their way, business schools would simply swallow up everything else on campus. Whether we want to admit it or not, the business schools have triumphed.

In the second half of the nineteenth century, American higher education underwent two nearly simultaneous revolutions in a way and to an extent that no other nation did. Two dates mark this twin transformation as conveniently as any: 1862 and 1876. In 1862, President Abraham Lincoln signed the Land-Grant College Act, known usually as the Morrill Act after its principal author; in 1876, Johns Hopkins University enrolled its first students. Both events are well known, and so I review them only briefly.

Through the Morrill Act, the federal government created a funding mechanism for higher education in each state by ceding federal land to the states for this purpose. The initial formula was straightforward. Each state would be granted thirty thousand acres for each member of Congress from that state, and the state could, in turn, sell, rent, or otherwise use that land to fund higher education. Some states, like Massachusetts and New York, attached their land grant to existing schools—Massachusetts Institute of Technology and Cornell University, respectively. But most opted to build new institutions with the money. Sixty-eight colleges and universities can trace their roots back to the original 1862 Morrill Act; more opened, especially in the South, after the 1890 version of the act.[6]

There is no question that the Morrill Act has been astonishingly successful at providing access to higher education to the kinds of people who, especially in the late nineteenth and early twentieth centuries, would not have been considered college material—what the act called "the industrial classes." Whatever small gripes people may offer about it, the Morrill Act stands as among the very greatest efforts of democratization in the history of the nation. Or of any other Western nation—there was no European equivalent to the land-grant university.

Beyond changing the constituency of *who* got a college degree, the Morrill Act also changed the nature of *what* could be studied in college. The language of the act stipulated "such branches of learning as are related to agriculture and the mechanic arts." The "A&M" of Texas A&M and Florida A&M. In other words, the Morrill Act wanted to promote college education for future farmers and engineers, and indeed it can be credited with creating those as academic fields in the first place. Practical education for a practical people at a time when higher education was still dominated by denominational colleges, often with the purpose of producing ministers. At the same time, however, this new education was not supposed to neglect "other scientific and classical studies" that had been at the heart of the liberal arts curriculum since at least the eighteenth century.

At one level, then, the Morrill Act promoted a remarkably expansive view of education, liberal and practical all at once. In this, Justin Morrill, the act's author, hearkened back to Benjamin Franklin, who believed that students should learn "everything that is useful and everything that is ornamental." At another, the Morrill Act embodies a central tension in American education between the liberal and the practical. However easy it might be to pair the useful and the ornamental in theory, in practice the two have often elbowed each other as they cohabit on campus.

That tension came into sharper focus almost immediately when Johns Hopkins University was opened in 1876. If the land-grant university is a pure product of American egalitarianism, Hopkins represented a European import product. By the mid-nineteenth century a new version of what a university could be had developed in Europe, most especially in Germany.[7] German universities invented our modern conception of academic research and of graduate training, and after the Civil War a small trickle of Americans who wanted that cutting edge education started making their way to Germany in order to earn a doctorate, a degree not yet readily available in the United States. Hopkins brought that model to the United States and dedicated itself to graduate training. It was built from the ground up to be a research university.

Antebellum colleges, many as I mentioned still tethered to their denominational origins, taught students what was already known. The new, dynamic research university would be a place to discover the things that we didn't. As late as 1866 Harvard faculty member John Fiske could write that the "whole duty" of a university was to train the "mental faculties" of its students so that they might pursue "varied and harmonious activity." It should also give students "the means of acquiring a thorough elementary knowledge of any given branch of science, art or literature."[8] But that broad, general—

"harmonious"—education would soon yield to an emphasis on research, specialization, and the professionalization that grew from both. Older colleges—Yale, Penn, Princeton—moved in that direction in the last decades of the nineteenth century. In 1890 Harvard had formalized its graduate programs in a graduate school. By 1900 roughly three hundred doctorates were being granted each year.[9]

Schools of business grew up as part of both the Morrill Act and this new conception of the research university. With the exception of the Tuck School of Business at Dartmouth College, the first collegiate schools of business were attached to some of the most dynamic, ambitious universities of the age: the University of Pennsylvania, the University of Chicago, Berkeley, Harvard, the University of Wisconsin. In fact, the 1868 Organic Act passed by the California legislature creating the University of California specifically includes "commerce" as an area of instruction for the new university. Business schools, like intercollegiate athletics, are woven into the DNA of modern higher education, and neither is going anywhere. My view that the arts and sciences are the heart of the university, therefore, is merely that: my view. It doesn't really reflect the history of higher education over the last century and a half.

And at the end of the nineteenth century nothing seemed more urgent than education for business, because business schools arrived on campuses amid another revolution in American life. The rise of industrial capitalism and large-scale corporations transformed the nature of the U.S. economy profoundly, and while the modern university was itself shaped through the philanthropy of those industrialists, business schools connected campus to the world of business even more directly. As Richard Hofstadter and C. DeWitt Hardy noted in 1952, "Clearly the emergence of the business school as a flourishing center of specialized training came on the heels of the bureaucratization of American business, which was a well-established trend by 1900."[10]

Here then were the two new directions, broadly speaking, in which American higher education ventured after the Civil War: economic utility and social openness; rarified research and the creation of an intellectual elite. Practicality versus purity; educated everyman versus highly trained expert. Of course, the dichotomy I am delineating here was never as clean and stark as I am suggesting. The relationship between knowledge seen as pure and that seen as practical has always been more fluid than that. Americans have always wanted the former to lead to the latter. Indeed, Charles Thwing complained in 1928 that U.S. universities had not quite mastered the German model because the "tendency of American methods is to promote the application of scientific truth without a proper acquaintance with the truth itself."[11] Still, I think the frictions I've laid out here—between teaching what we know and creating new knowledge; between practical education and that which is merely intellectual—remain to this day in U.S. higher education. Even an intellectual as accomplished as Barack Obama once asked why on earth anyone would major in art history.[12] Business schools, perhaps more than any other development on U.S. campuses over the last century or so, are caught in the middle of those tensions and have embodied them from the very start.

Professionalization was perhaps the most significant consequence of trying to square the circle between research and access. The professionalizing impulse began in earnest after the Civil War, and it continues to this day. As a consequence, a whole host of new fields were created that now required a college credential for practitioners. This has been the trajectory of nursing and engineering and teaching. Harvard and Michigan became the first two universities to offer college training for dentists shortly after the Civil War (and Michigan became the first to offer graduate degrees in for that profession in 1980). Now college degrees in dental hygiene have become quite common as have any number of other degrees in subjects that once never required them. Occupational therapy, say, and turf management and optometry. Indeed, one way to tell the story of the American university is to chart the more or less continuous rise of the "practical arts" on campus and the relative diminution of the traditional liberal arts as a consequence.[13] In this sense, business schools are absolutely of a piece with the way higher education transformed in the late nineteenth century and on its cutting edge. Medical schools predate the Civil War and so do law schools; history and math and philosophy were all taught at American colleges from the very beginning. Business, therefore, was just one more subject spawned by the proliferation of professionalization unleashed by the modern university, a proliferation that continues apace.

So was agriculture, and the two make an interesting comparison. The Morrill Act, in effect, created the ag school, and plenty of people at the time wondered why farmers would possibly need a college degree. Farmers learned to farm through experience and the accumulated wisdom of traditions passed on, and they had done so for thousands of years. Similar skepticism greeted collegiate business schools—business should be learned through on-the-job experience!—and they have not succeeded in quelling that skepticism. Writing fully seventy years after the first American business school launched, Hofstadter and Hardy observed that "business schools are still bedeviled by the problems of whom to teach and what to teach."[14]

And yet schools of agriculture have developed into thriving places that marry pure research with practical application—in fields as diverse as botany, genetics, entomology, hydrology, and soil chemistry, among others—in the best combination. Norman Borlaug graduated from the agricultural college at the University of Minnesota in 1937. He finished his career teaching in the ag school at Texas A&M. In between, he developed several new varieties of high-yield, disease-resistant wheat in Mexico, Pakistan, and India that revolutionized food production in those countries. He won a Nobel Peace Prize for his work in 1970.

Business schools, however, cannot make the same claims, either to academic success or to public utility. In my travels through the history of American business schools, the refrain I have heard has been remarkably consistent. In two-part harmony, people on campus seem consistently disappointed with the intellectual integrity and rigor of what constitutes a business education, while business leaders themselves have complained across the decades about the quality of the graduates of those programs. And although business leaders have repeatedly asserted the centrality of the private sector in solving social problems, no one associated with a business school has ever won a Nobel Peace Prize.

In fact, the skepticism and suspicion with which many of us on the more traditionally academic side of campus hold the business schools has existed from the very beginning and has not relented over the years. In 1913, to take one example, Edmund James, the former dean of the Wharton School and by that time president of the University of Illinois, recalled that Penn's faculty "were opposed to the whole purpose" of a business school, "thinking that the future business man might acquire his education in the so-called commercial college, or he might succeed without any education at all." Thirty years later, things had not improved much. A. L. Prickett, the dean of Indiana University's business school, in a Delta Pi Epsilon lecture in Chicago, told the crowd, "I do not know a college campus in *this* country today where the collegiate school of business is *completely* 'accepted.'"[15] Forty years after that, the literary critic and English professor Paul Fussell acidly noted that an "important class divide falls between those who feel veneration before the term *executive* and those who feel they want to throw up," capturing nicely the disdain with which at least some faculty view the ethos of the business schools.[16]

And in the other direction, businessmen and corporate leaders have continually complained about what business schools have taught or have failed to teach. In the mid-1980s, the American Association of Collegiate Schools of Business, funded by a long list of corporations, undertook a study on the state of U.S. business education. The study concluded that "members of the corporate world, by and large, are neither highly satisfied nor highly dissatisfied with the quality of university-based management education in this country."[17] Hardly a ringing endorsement of the products coming out of U.S. B-schools.

In this sense, business schools have become the Rodney Dangerfields of American higher education—loud, crass, more than a little buffoonish.[18] They have gotten little respect from the rest of the university and not much from the private sector either. And yet like Dangerfield himself, they keep doing what they do, despite the fact that few people think they do it very well.

In truth, we don't mix and mingle much. Certainly those of us in the arts and sciences have little understanding of and even less to do with what goes on inside those posh B-school buildings. And business schools don't have much to do with the rest of us either. As a member of the history department I might teach my classes in the physics building, over in the art building, or indeed anywhere the registrar decides to put me. Business school classes, however, are all taught nowadays in the business school compound itself, lest the business school students (and faculty) have to slum it on other, less well appointed parts of campus. In their history of Harvard's business school (insufferably smug even by Harvard B-school standards), Thomas McCraw and Jeffrey Cruikshank wrote of one dean that he "remained very cautious . . . about collaborations with other parts of Harvard, let alone other universities." Instead, "the real teamwork went on within the confines" of Harvard's business school building itself.[19] After all, if the gods already reside atop Mount Olympus, where else would they want to play?

In this, however, business schools have also tracked the larger trends at American universities. Historians don't have much professional interaction with our engineering or medical colleagues either. I have never taught a class with anyone in the education school (though at least I teach in that building all the time), nor has anyone there ever invited me to visit one of their classes. Until quite recently, classes at Ohio State University were taught on a quarter schedule, except at the law school, which was on semesters. A fundamentally different rhythm of academic time. Business schools are no different in having become just as "siloed"—in the current noun-turned-into-verb locution—as every other unit on campus.

While at one level business schools stand as of a piece of the way American universities have grown and evolved since the end of the Civil War, they stand apart from the rest of higher education in three, interconnected ways. First, and I've hinted at this already, they have consistently disappointed even their most enthusiastic boosters—failing to develop a definition of professional business education, failing to develop a coherent, intellectually vibrant body of knowledge, unable to agree on what the raison d'être of business schools ought to be—to an extent simply not true of any other academic pursuit.

Despite this, of course, business schools have flourished on U.S. campuses and continue to do so (and this certainly sets them apart from humanities departments and even some social science ones on many campuses right now). I have more to say about that success in chapter 6, but here I want to note a second distinction between business schools and the rest of the university, one that Veblen noticed a hundred years ago. The subtitle of Veblen's extended meditation on higher learning is "A Memorandum on the Conduct of Universities by Business Men."[20]

The late nineteenth-century revolutions in higher education fostered a change in how universities were funded and governed. Just as private institutions began to seek and accept large sums from the new class of wealthy industrialists, those institutions came to be governed more and more by that same class of businessmen. (Trustees at the new state universities were often political appointees and often politically connected businessmen as a result.) Boards of trustees during the denominational nineteenth century had been populated, fittingly enough, with clergymen.[21] By the turn of the twentieth century, the ministers were out and businessmen took their seats. The takeover of college boardrooms was complete enough by the First World War that Veblen could write:

> It is not simply that experienced businessmen are, on mature reflection, judged to be the safest and most competent trustees of the university's fiscal inter-

ests. The preference appears to be almost wholly impulsive, and a matter of habitual bias. It is due for the greater part to the high esteem currently accorded to men of wealth at large, and especially to wealthy men who have succeeded in business, quite apart from any special capacity shown by such success for the guardianship of any institution of learning.[22]

One doesn't have to be as caustic as Veblen to recognize that, for the businessmen who now presided over higher education, a business school on their campus might hold a special place in their hearts.

Finally, business schools serve as the handmaids to corporate capitalism in the United States in a way that no other campus enterprise does. More to the point, what they teach, and what their students seem to expect, is an uncritical, even incurious approach to that system. Universities as a whole promise that they are places of inquiry and critical thinking, and while they may often fall short of that ideal, the ideal remains. Except at the B-school. "The things taught and the way they are taught," Martin Parker has concluded after over twenty years teaching in business schools, "mean that the virtues of capitalist market managerialism are told and sold as if there were no other ways of seeing the world."[23] Business schools are the only places on U.S. university campuses that implicitly promise students: no hard questions asked.

So I ask some hard questions in this book. As I realized that I didn't know much about what went on in the business schools that have been on every campus of which I've been a part, I discovered that we don't know much about their histories either. That isn't altogether surprising. Histories of institutions can be a bit dull to read—or to write for that matter. A number of the gilt-edged business schools have commissioned their own histories, but these are usually a combination of coffee-table production and hagiography in equal measure. Still, given how ubiquitous business schools have become on campus over the last century and a half, and given that they have always aspired to shape the course of American business and by extension the whole of American society, their history deserves more critical attention.[24]

This book is not a comprehensive, begin-at-the-beginning, end-at-the-end history of American business schools. That task is too big and too daunting for a single volume, and I am not the historian to undertake it. Instead, this book examines what I see as a set of crucial and largely unasked questions about the role of the American business school and how it has, or has not, changed over time. These pages measure what business schools have aspired to be against what they have, in fact, become.

Chapter 1 does begin at the beginning, though, and asks why educational leaders and businessmen in the United States thought it was a good idea to establish business schools in the first place. The answer often offered at the time was that American business itself had grown so big and complex by the turn of the twentieth century that a new university-level education was now required for the new world of managerial work. As we will see, however, the more powerful rationale was that businessmen wanted the social status and cultural cachet that came with a university degree. Having decided to open collegiate business schools, universities faced a first-order problem: What, exactly, constituted a university-level curriculum in business? Chapter 2 traces the debates over those questions and their implications. The problem of what students should be taught sat at the fault line that defines business schools in the first place. To what extent should students learn academic subjects, and to what extent should they learn what amount to vocational skills useful to their prospective employers? Viewed one way, the entire history of business schools can be described as a pendulum swinging back and forth between these two.[25]

Whatever else people might think ought to be taught at business schools, everyone agreed that economics should be a core part of the education. Except, as it turned out, the economists. Chapter 3 drills into the unhappy relationship between business education and the developing academic discipline of economics. Chapter 4 examines the question of who has, or hasn't, gotten access to business education. Periodically, at almost regular intervals, a study appears documenting that women and people of color remain woefully underrepresented in the corporate world, particularly in its upper echelons. There are undoubtedly many reasons for this, but in chapter 4 I reveal the role business schools themselves have played in creating these disparities. Indeed, business schools have not even kept up with medical and law schools in enrolling women and minorities in their programs.[26]

Whatever the relationship between business and the economy, both have experienced periods of crisis that have had all sorts of ripples throughout American life. Chapter 5 examines how business schools have responded to these crises. Or haven't. What is striking is how little impact economic downturns have had on the practices of business schools. That was as true during the 1930s as it has been since the financial meltdown that began in 2007. And chapter 6 brings the story to the present to look at what has changed and what has stayed the same in business schools across the United States. On the one hand, the growth of the finance economy since the 1980s has meant that what goes on in business schools has aligned more perfectly with the corporate world than at any other time in the preceding century. Shareholder value became the mantra chanted in classrooms and boardrooms. On the other hand, business schools continue to evade the ethical issues raised in and by the business world, and they have avoided much by way of accountability for what they teach.

I have never fully understood that line from the old Bob Dylan song, "there's no success like failure" ("Love Minus Zero/No Limit," for those who don't remember), but in many ways that line sums up the history of U.S. business schools that follows. They have largely failed, even on their own terms, much less on other, broader social ones. For all their bold talk about training tomorrow's business leaders, as institutions they have largely been followers. "In reviewing the course of American business education over the past fifty years," wrote one observer, "one is struck by its almost fad-like quality."[27] That was in 1957.

Despite their repeated insistence that they are places of innovation, and their mantra-like chanting that they teach "outside-the-box thinking," business schools have consistently exhibited a remarkable conformity and sameness. Don't take my word for it. A study done by the American Association of Collegiate Schools of Business in 1988 found "a distressing tendency for schools to avoid the risk of being different. . . . A 'cookie cutter mentality' does not seem to be too strong a term to describe the situation we encountered in a number of schools."[28] Finally, while honest people can disagree over whether business is better off for having business schools, the schools have provided scant evidence that Veblen was wrong in 1918. Business schools don't appear to have done much to transform business into something more noble than mere moneymaking. Indeed, by the late twentieth century, they stopped pretending they could. The story that follows is one of unfilled promises and unmet aspirations across nearly 150 years. Failure, simply put. Yet, take any measure you please, business schools have made a tremendous success of all these accumulated failures.

Chapter 1

THE WORLD BEFORE
(AND SHORTLY AFTER) WHARTON

Getting a Business Education
in the Nineteenth Century

In the beginning there was Wharton.

Or more properly, the Wharton School of Finance and Economy at the University of Pennsylvania, and when it was founded in 1881 it became the first business school in the United States. All the more than six hundred business schools founded in the nearly century and a half since descend from Wharton. Wharton began and Wharton begat.

The origin story of U.S. business schools is familiar enough and almost folkloric inside that world. Joseph Wharton made a great deal of money in the metals and mining industry in the mid-nineteenth century. (Wharton has been inducted into the Mining Hall of Fame.) In 1881 he made a gift of $100,000 to the University of Pennsylvania to establish a school with his name on it. He called it his "project," and happily for historians he wrote a detailed rationale to explain what he wanted to do and why.

First, he reviewed the history of higher education as he saw it. "The general conviction that college education did little toward fitting for the actual

duties of life any but those who purposed to become lawyers, doctors or clergymen," he wrote to the university's trustees, "brought about the creation of
many excellent technical and scientific schools." He went on, "In the matter
of Commercial education there was formerly a system of instruction in the
counting-houses of old-time merchants which may fairly be compared to the
system of apprenticeship to trades." With the old system of apprenticeships
on the wane, Wharton concluded, "the existing great universities, rather than
an institution of lower rank or a new independent establishment, should lead
in the attempt to supply this important deficiency in our present system of
education." [1]

In supplying that deficiency, Joseph Wharton launched U.S. business
education. Or so the story goes.

In fact, this foundational tale of American business schools glosses over
another chapter in the history of education in the United States. After the
Civil War, schools of business (or commerce, the more common term in that
era) dotted the American landscape in places large and small, including in
Wharton's own Philadelphia. While it is certainly right to say that the Wharton School was the first business school barnacled to a university, it was
hardly the first school to teach business.

Joseph Wharton was well aware of these places, and in his letter to Penn's
trustees he dismissed them out of hand. As he described the demise of the
old training system built around apprenticeships, he noted, "Nor is their deficiency made good by the so-called Commercial colleges." Joseph Wharton
had twin goals in mind when he wrote that check for $100,000. He wanted
to establish a new experiment in higher education, and he wanted that experiment to supplant those dozens and dozens of schools that already taught
business. Founding the Wharton School was both an educational endeavor
and an exercise in creating distinctions of prestige, drawing the line between
those few who would train for business as part of their university education
and the many who learned their business skills at one of those "Commercial
colleges."

So in this chapter we revisit that world of commercial education before
the Wharton School was founded, a world that lasted well into the twentieth century.

Business Education as a Proprietary Business

Let's start with the figure: 269.

That's the number of U.S. commercial schools and colleges tallied by the Frenchman Eugène Léautey as part of his survey of commercial education around the world. He published this vast tabulation in 1886, just a few years after the Wharton School opened its doors, and he divided that number into two categories: business colleges (165) and commercial colleges (104). The difference, according to Léautey, was that the former taught *practique*, while the latter included *théorique* as well.[2]

In fact, the phenomenon that Léautey documented had been around since before the Civil War and probably dates back to the 1830s (there is some dispute over who founded the first of these schools and where).[3] These "colleges"—for example, the Iron City Commercial College in Pittsburgh—were by and large proprietary, founded by an individual or partnership and run for a profit, and they filled a need that became increasingly urgent in the middle decades of the nineteenth century. "We know it is easy to pick flaws in almost any system of education," a writer conceded in 1844, "but we appeal to all thinking men if the training young boys receive, who intend to follow trade as their occupation, is not necessarily incomplete and shallow?" In calling for more deliberate "mercantile education," this writer complained that "little care and expense is bestowed upon the lad who is destined for the store, because the parent hopes that his education will some how or other be completed by running of errands, doing up parcels, and going to the post-office."[4] Enter the commercial college.

More broadly, these schools responded to the same changes in the U.S. economy that prompted the founding of collegiate business schools by promising to prepare young people for work in the emerging white-collar world of industrial capitalism. "Since so large a proportion of our youth select mercantile occupations, for a livelihood," a writer for *Hunt's Merchant's Magazine* noted in 1858, "that branch of popular education should possess its halls of learning and practice, its cultivated and experienced professors, its regular courses of instruction, and its diplomas and degrees of dignity."[5] They were also of a piece with the dynamics of higher education at that moment as well. Beginning about 1850, many of the smaller denominational colleges tried to modernize by adding coursework in engineering, by opening separate schools of science, by offering training to new teachers, and by adding courses in business to their classical curriculum.[6]

By the 1890s, most of these colleges had given up their experiments with professional training and graduate degrees, but proprietary schools of business continued to thrive. The growth of these educational establishments paralleled almost precisely the growth of the industrial economy as it accelerated after the Civil War. Of the eleven institutions that Léautey counted in Michigan, for example, two predated the war. Many were purely local, like the Archibald Business College in Minneapolis, founded in 1877. But others were what we might call now franchise operations: Bryant & Stratton had locations in many places, as did the Spencerian Business Colleges and the Eastman schools.[7]

Messrs. Bryant and Stratton had both graduated from Folsom Business College in Cleveland, and their successful entrepreneurial venture suggests that they received a pretty effective education there. In fact, by the Civil War there were apparently enough Bryant & Stratton schools that the two men convened a national meeting of their operators in New York in 1863, again in 1864, and in Chicago in 1865. They brought their group together once again in 1866 in Cleveland, and *Harper's*, reporting on the convention, called the success of the business college movement "unprecedented." The magazine continued, "Through individual institutions and admirable text-books the sphere and limit of business education have been as clearly defined as those of law, medical, and theological schools."[8] Textbooks, however, don't seem to have been the primary purpose of these conventions. The goal appears to have been to exert monopoly control over a growing and lucrative market. Bryant and Stratton had grand ambitions of opening one of their schools in every city with ten thousand or more people, and in so doing they hoped to drive out their competitors.

By 1866, however, Bryant and Stratton had overreached. The franchisees, unhappy with the terms of their contracts—and gathered in one place where they could share their frustrations—rebelled and founded their own organization, which they called the National Union of Business Colleges.[9] Bryant and Stratton never achieved their monopoly dreams, though at one point there were fifty Bryant & Stratton colleges around the country.

Students who enrolled in one of these business or commercial colleges often already had jobs and thus attended classes at night. They studied a curriculum suited to the demands of the late nineteenth-century business world: stenography and shorthand; business writing; bookkeeping; commercial geography, perhaps; and business law. Whether or not they attended a Spencerian College, students undoubtedly learned Spencerian script, the penmanship style that predominated in the United States until at least the 1920s. The style was developed by business college founder Platt Rogers Spencer and disseminated in his *Practical Penmanship* book. Most of us would recognize it today: the Coca-Cola logo, still ubiquitous around the world, is done in Spencerian script.

Students might have learned bookkeeping from the popular and widely distributed *Modern Bookkeeping* written by David Lillibridge. Born in Connecticut in 1839, Lillibridge served with the Eleventh Rhode Island Infantry during the Civil War. After the war he made his way to Lincoln, Nebraska, where he operated the Lincoln Business College and Institute of Penmanship, Shorthand, and Typewriting. The National Union of Business Colleges adopted his *Modern Bookkeeping* as their recommended textbook, and in turn Lillibridge became president of that organization.[10]

When Léautey divided his count of business schools between those that taught only the practical and those that added theory, he might well have been thinking of the Theoretical Department of the U.S. College of Business and Finance or the Theoretical Department at the Eastman National Business College in Poughkeepsie. As the "Student's Guide" to the former explained, students would "gain a thorough knowledge of the *principles* of Bookkeeping and an appreciation of the duties of an Accountant, which must form the basis of all further advance in the ACTUAL BUSINESS DEPARTMENTS." The explanation was much the same in Poughkeepsie: "In this THEORETICAL DEPARTMENT, you will lay the foundation for your more extended and practical course of study in *actual business*."[11] Nelson's Business College in Cincinnati promised even more of that "practical" education inasmuch as "one of the advantages which it enjoys [is] the privilege of having its students allowed on the floors of the Chamber of Commerce and other trade bodies. Regular transactions are carried on by the students exactly as in the ordinary channels of business." Nelson's wanted to make it clear that theirs "is the only business college in the United States enjoying this privilege."[12]

These schools were quite proud that they offered a practical education. They provided "a technical but not a liberal education," as James Hodges put it in 1887, and that was seen as all to the good, especially when compared to the education on offer in America's colleges in the mid-nineteenth century. Hodges described the contrast in a way that sounds entirely familiar to any student telling his parents he's going to major in English: "A youth comes from college with a good record and enters a counting-house. His classics, his higher mathematics, his philosophy and history, which he has learned so zealously, seem to be of no use to him at all, and of that which he needs he knows next to nothing."[13]

They also prided themselves on their democratic access. Stressing its egalitarianism, a promotional brochure of the Eastman School in Poughkeepsie from the 1880s claimed, "Students enter any week-day in the year with equal advantage. There are no examinations at commencement. No particular qualifications are required on entering. . . . Few who apply themselves will be longer than three months and many who have had previous experience will complete it in less time." The same brochure declared, "Eastman college does just what it claims to do, and we defy any one to show to the contrary." Education for the aspirational masses, and by 1886 Eastman claimed to have taught 25,000 students.[14]

In this sense, we can see the rise of these business colleges as a tacit indictment of what passed for higher education in the United States in the mid-nineteenth century. Far fewer students attended those institutions of higher education, and what they learned had remained largely unchanged since the eighteenth century or, indeed, since the Middle Ages: classics and classical languages; ancient philosophy; and theology, often of a denominationally specific variety. Moribund in the eyes of some, irrelevant in the eyes of more. "The university of the past," according to General R. D. Mussey, "was for the thinker; the college of today is for the actor."[15] He was speaking to the graduates of the Washington Business College on June 18, 1873, and he made it clear that actors, not thinkers, were what the world needed.

No one drew the distinction between business colleges and higher learning more sharply or critically than James Garfield. Garfield had been in attendance at that gathering of Bryant & Stratton operators in Chicago in 1865. Four years later the future president, a sitting member of the House of Representatives from Ohio, delivered a commencement address to the graduates of the Bryant & Stratton College in Washington, D.C. He called his talk

"Elements of Success," and in it Garfield sounded remarkably like many contemporary critics of education. "Business Colleges my fellow-citizens," he told the crowd gathered in June 29, 1869, "originated in this country as a protest against the insufficiency of our system of education." Warming to the topic, he went on, "As a protest against the failure, the absolute failure, of our American schools and colleges to fit young men and women for the business of life." Garfield wanted "every college president in the United States" to hear him when he charged, "Take the great classes graduating from the leading colleges of the country . . . how many, or rather, how few, of their members are fitted to go into the practical business of life?" And just to make sure the point was not lost on those assembled, Garfield railed, "*These Business Colleges furnish their graduates with a better education for practical purposes than either Princeton, Harvard or Yale.*"[16] (For his part, Garfield graduated from Williams College in 1856 and seems to have done all right.)

Others also recognized the need to draw a distinction between the education provided by business colleges and the education young men received at U.S. colleges and universities and in so doing define the identity and purpose of the business colleges. For some, business college graduates with their practical know-how would come to the rescue of the college boys who were not prepared for life in the real world of business. "The relations of our system to this class of people," said one speaker at the fifth meeting of the International Business College Association in Cincinnati in 1873, are "important as a means of promoting their welfare and saving them from serious ills that they too often bring upon themselves in consequence of business incapacity." And like James Garfield, General Mussey underscored the anti-elitist, small *d* democratic mission of business colleges in his 1873 commencement speech. "The vocations of university graduates—law, medicine, theology—have had in the popular mind heretofore a certain exclusiveness attached to them. They have been called the learned professions." At a moment when perhaps fewer than 5 percent of college-age men attended a liberal arts college, he told—or perhaps reassured—the graduates that the "lesson here tonight is that business has its dignity."[17] That word again, "dignity." Businessmen craved it and they wanted to be treated accordingly.

As proprietary operations with largely local or regional clienteles, these business colleges made money for their owner-operators. In this sense, they took from and contributed to the local economy. And they weren't necessarily as venerable or as durable as Harvard, Yale, and Princeton, creating instead a landscape of business education in a given place that shifted and changed. For example, the Spencerian College students attended in Detroit after the Civil War had actually been founded in Albion, Michigan, in 1860. Ira Mayhew, the school's director, moved it to Detroit in 1866. In 1885 it merged with Detroit Business University. It was joined in the city by the Detroit Business College, which opened its doors to students in 1903. The Detroit Business University formally incorporated in 1905 and seems to have swallowed up the Gutchess Business College of Detroit. The Business Institute of Detroit, founded by A. F. Tull and L. C. Rauch, started enrolling students in June 1906.[18] Proprietary commerce colleges were no more immune to mergers, acquisitions, and closures than the business world for which they prepared their students.

All of which is to say that well before Joseph Wharton approached the trustees of the University of Pennsylvania about his "project" there was a vibrant world of business education already present in the United States. One way to measure the success of these business colleges at doing what they did is to notice that for some years Wharton stood alone as a business school attached to a university. It would be nearly two decades before any other university established its own business school. In the last two decades of the nineteenth century, no one else seems to have felt compelled to compete with the proprietary business and commercial colleges.

Proprietary Schools under Attack

Which is not to say that all was right in the world of these business colleges.

The rapid proliferation of these schools in the post–Civil War era, and the explosive growth in their enrollments, led to concerns over just what was being taught and how. In fact, the organizational umbrella under which Bryant & Stratton tried to gather its outlets was, beyond trying to maximize market share, an attempt at curricular standardization and quality control. The National Union of Business Colleges, in breaking away from Bryant & Stratton, worked even more strenuously to raise standards, especially by lengthening the course of study and making the work more rigorous.

What evidence we have suggests that some of these measures were successful. In a report written as part of the U.S. effort at the Paris Exposition of 1900, E. J. James found that "increased popularity [of the schools] led to higher fees, longer courses [and] to the preparation of printed texts." And the demographic seems to have changed too: "Students were no longer adults wearied by daily labor; the commercial school began to draw young men and boys looking forward to employment; day classes largely took the place of evening instruction; school equipment improved and gradually these institutions grew into the apparently permanent places in public favor which they enjoy today."[19]

All that James reported might have been true, except that last bit. By 1900 business and commercial colleges found themselves under increasing scrutiny and attack. They might continue to attract students by the tens of thousands, but a new generation of educational reformers and commenters didn't think they deserved public favor at all. In a 1910 promotional brochure, the Peirce School of Business in Philadelphia advertised itself by responding, if only indirectly, to the criticisms of the academic programs at business colleges. Peirce noted proudly that "the school has for many years published its own textbooks." Further, the brochure boasted, "these books have been written by various members of the faculty." Peirce was also proud that because its teachers taught only one subject "each instructor . . . becomes a specialist in that subject."[20] By highlighting this, Peirce wanted to lay claim to having a legitimate faculty and a rigorous academic program of the sort that increasingly defined the university. We can't know just what the quality of teaching was at these proprietary schools. There was no system of credentialing or review or any formalized system of teacher training for them that I have discovered. Still, in the 1890s students at Duncan's Business College in Davenport, Iowa, were taught business mathematics by a young man saving up money to attend Harvard. William Ernest Hocking did save up the money, went to Cambridge to study with William James and Josiah Royce, and became one of the most distinguished American philosophers of the first half of the twentieth century. Certainly not all the teachers at these proprietary schools went on to join the Harvard faculty, but his story cautions that we should not dismiss the quality of instruction at these places out of hand.

By the turn of the twentieth century, however, even those who didn't find anything sketchy or nefarious in the operation of these business schools complained that the education they offered taught mere technique. As W. J. Ashley put it in 1903, "For years past every large American city has had its 'commercial college,' where tens of thousands of industrious youths of both sexes have acquired the arts of bookkeeping, shorthand and typewriting."

All well and good, and Ashley acknowledged that "many of their pupils have risen to important positions." But Ashley insisted that this success "has been the result of their native qualities rather than the instruction they received." Of that instruction, Ashley concluded, it "has been adapted only to make them efficient servants to their bosses." C. W. Haskins asked the question somewhat more pointedly: "America, the great business country, invented the term 'business education'; and under it hundreds of business colleges have for half a century been teaching—what?"[21] Speaking to the National Education Association in 1914, Brigham Young University's Earl Jay Glade agreed with Ashley that "the graduates of these schools were unprepared for anything other than subordinate clerical positions." He went on to vent his frustration with the world of proprietary business schools. He reminded his audience that "during the greater part of the past century, the most prominent exponent of business education in the United States was the so-called business college." They surely already knew this, but he pointed out that there wasn't even any real agreement about what a "business college" was: "The use of this term has caused so much annoyance in educational circles, particularly in the compilation of our statistics, so much, in fact, that some states have entirely forbidden its usage except when employed in harmony with the accepted meaning of the term."[22]

If some critics complained about the academic integrity of the business colleges, other Progressive-era reformers cast a suspicious eye on these colleges precisely because they were moneymaking enterprises. For those who saw the profit motive as anathema to genuine education, "the school which enrolls students regardless of any definite preparation, without aptitude for the subjects offered, giving no attention to immaturity, so long as they pay the tuition charged . . . has indeed no function in our modern civilization." Function or no function in U.S. civilization, by the First World War these schools continued to attract impressive numbers of students. A 1914 report by the U.S. Bureau of Education counted over 1300 such schools around the country (recall that Eugène Léautey had counted 269 in 1886). At the 700 whose enrollment it tallied, the bureau found 168,000 students. "In Chicago," the report noted, "the enrollment in the private commercial schools is greater than the combined enrollment of all the public high schools in that great city."[23]

Many in the business world (and even outside it) continued to believe that only experience in business could train young men for a life in business, but there was a broader feeling that the new, complicated world of industrial, corporate capitalism was creating a new kind of managerial worker, and that worker, in turn, required a new kind of education. And if older proprietary schools weren't the answer, the question, then, was how best to provide it. Several alternatives appealed to educational and business reformers during the Progressive era, and I want to look at them briefly.

A Business Education by Other Means

Proprietary schools were not alone in the task of educating American youth for mercantile occupations. Mercantile libraries, founded at the same mid-nineteenth-century moment as the proprietary schools in cities around the country, including New York, Philadelphia, Cincinnati, Boston, Baltimore, and Charleston, offered an opportunity for learning to those young people looking to work in the new world of business and who had the motivation to teach themselves. In addition to an education, of course, the libraries also offered themselves as alternatives to the temptations that beckoned in any of those cities. "It is not merely capable and intelligent *merchants* that they have assisted to produce," *Hunt's Merchant's Magazine* boasted in 1853, "for, besides being mercantile seminaries, they have proven excellent schools for the formation of general character."[24] The mercantile library in St. Louis opened its doors in 1845, and the merchants who founded it hoped it would be a refuge "where young men could pass their evenings agreeably and profitably, and thus be protected from the temptations to folly that ever beset unguarded youth in large towns."[25] It survived until 1998, at which point it was absorbed by the University of Missouri at St. Louis. The Mechanics Library on Post Street in San Francisco continues to serve patrons to this day, as it has since 1854.

A product of the mid-nineteenth century, the mercantile library got a Progressive-era update from Newark's pioneering librarian and museum founder John Cotton Dana. Early in the twentieth century he added a "business branch" to his library operation. He started the project in 1911 when "letters were sent out by the library to the 2,100 manufacturing concerns in the city, asking for either their catalogues or a description of their products." What came back from that mailing formed the core of the new branch, which Dana opened "on the ground floor of the principal office street, near the center of the city." Patrons could visit the library to learn about the city's businesses and their products, or they could use the library as a reference service.

By 1913 the business branch was answering roughly 1000 questions each working week.[26]

It is even harder to know what impact these mercantile libraries had on those who came to read their books than it is to gauge the pedagogical quality of what went on in the classrooms at one of the Spencerian Colleges. But they do attest to an important civic impulse to build institutions that offered an education to anyone willing to walk through the door. And at the turn of the twentieth century, mercantile libraries were not the only such institution designed to provide a business education.

By 1911, the Peirce School of Business had its own handsome building in the 900 block of Chestnut Street in Philadelphia. In addition to classrooms, the building housed a library and a commercial museum exhibiting "commercial history and geography."[27] You'd be hard pressed, I suspect, to find a museum in any of the hundreds of business schools on American college campuses today. In fact, the museum at Peirce was the second museum of commerce (at least) in the city. About two miles west of Peirce's building, the Philadelphia Commercial Museum had opened in 1897, and it was a huge and sensational operation.[28]

The Philadelphia Commercial Museum sprang from the mind of a University of Pennsylvania professor. William Wilson, like so many millions of Americans, took a trip to Chicago in the summer of 1893 to attend the World's Columbian Exposition. Like those millions, he was dazzled by what he saw on display. Unlike those other visitors, however, Wilson returned with his own vision.

Wilson lamented that these world's fairs brought so many and so much together for a time and then vanished. While several museums did grow out of world's fairs—the predecessor to the Philadelphia Museum of Art, for example, was founded in the wake of the 1876 centennial, and the Field Museum in Chicago was an outgrowth of the 1893 fair—Wilson quite rightly noted that the primary objective of these fairs was economic: the displays in Chicago might have been vast and various, but the overriding purpose of these world's fairs was to promote business. He proposed a museum of commerce to institutionalize what was otherwise temporary. After all, displays of economic progress and development were really the heart of these fairs—why not extend their usefulness permanently?

Wilson negotiated with fair officials to take material back with him to Philadelphia. Once the fair had closed, they obliged, sending exhibits by the boxcar load. He pursued this strategy with subsequent world's fairs as well. Wilson received four hundred tons of stuff from the Central American Exposition held in Guatemala in 1897; another five hundred tons came from the Paris fair in 1900. By 1900, a scant three years after it opened, the museum housed more than two hundred thousand samples of foreign manufactured goods in addition to what the University of Pennsylvania provost William Pepper called "the most extensive collection of natural products in existence in any country." The English traveler W. E. Hoyle visited the Commercial Museum at about that time and wrote, "[It] impressed me as much as anything I saw on the American continent, not excepting the Falls of Niagara or the Congress Library."[29]

Another of those who found themselves impressed by the Philadelphia Commercial Museum was Carl Plehn. Originally from Germany, Plehn was the first dean of the College of Commerce at the University of California at Berkeley. Begun in 1898, Berkeley's was the second collegiate school of business in the country, and Plehn came to Philadelphia early in the summer of the following year to investigate what Wilson was up to. Back in the Bay Area at the end of 1899, Plehn told a dinner gathering of San Francisco business leaders about what he found: "One Sunday afternoon last June, I found myself sitting on the veranda of the suburban residence of Director Wilson. . . . Hour after hour slipped away unperceived as he revealed to me his plans for the perfection of American commerce." He then called on the assembled group to build a similar museum: "I now propose that this association and all other good men interested in the progress of California," he intoned, "join with the university in a serious endeavor to establish here a similar organization. Your museum," he continued, "should be affiliated with the Philadelphia Museum. The authorities of that institution have already promised that if an organization similar to theirs is established out here and so constituted as to guarantee that it will be carried on in the proper spirit and not be devoted to private gain or personal advantage, that they will give us all the information they have accumulated or may accumulate in the future."[30]

As a faculty member at Penn, Wilson taught botany, and while a eulogist described his move into the museum world as midcareer dissatisfaction with "the herbarium and the paraphernalia of species naming," Wilson certainly brought a nineteenth-century botanist's view to his new institution. Wilson wanted to treat commerce as a form of natural history, to create a taxonomy of the world's business and trade. Visitors to the museum started with a history lesson on commerce that made the case—and not very subtly—that it was commerce that drove civilization and progress. Later on, visitors saw commercial products arranged in two systems. In one set of displays, like objects were grouped together—wool, for example, or canned foods. In the other, exhibits were arranged geographically—all the products of West Africa or Argentina—thus creating a dual system of what the museum called "geographic" and "monographic" exhibits. Visitors could thus learn what in the world could be bought and sold and where those things could be traded. Wilson attempted to create a natural history museum, only with commerce rather than fossils or stuffed birds as the subject.

Like all museums of the era, the Commercial Museum saw itself as an educational institution first and foremost. More specifically, Wilson wanted his museum to teach U.S. businessmen how to compete more robustly in foreign markets. As Wilson himself put it in 1899, "The Philadelphia Commercial Museum is endeavoring to increase foreign trade of the United States . . . with every nation of the world."[31] Those who made it to Philadelphia could see for themselves what the nations of the world were buying and what they were selling. For those who couldn't visit the museum in person, Wilson established the Bureau of Information inside the museum.

The bureau provided three services to businesses. It published reports, it provided information about a whole range of commercial subjects, and it offered a translation service for those businessmen who might not command the languages they needed to do business overseas. It gathered "all Consular Reports, Statistical publications, publications on Commerce, Navigation and Survey, with maps and official journals from all the different Governments, which show the possibilities of increased commercial relations." The bureau indexed and culled "five hundred current journals on Trade, Commerce and Finance from all the countries of the world." These, the museum reported, "are regularly received and are open to consultation in the Reading Room."[32]

The Commercial Museum also sponsored international conferences on trade and business. In 1897, and again in 1899, government and business leaders from many countries, especially from Central and South America, came to Philadelphia for largely self-congratulatory sessions about the role of trade and business in promoting peace and prosperity. The four-day conference in 1897 served as the museum's official debut, and President William McKinley came up from Washington to open the proceedings.

In the event, the Philadelphia Commercial Museum functioned for roughly two decades as a precursor to the federal Department of Commerce, which was created in 1903 by President Theodore Roosevelt. It was a modest operation initially, overseeing such things as the Geodetic Survey and Fisheries and Steamboat Inspection. Just before the First World War, the department's Bureau of Foreign and Domestic Commerce had a measly budget of $60,000. George Cortelyou served as the department's first secretary, and shortly after he was sworn in he traveled to Philadelphia to tour the Commercial Museum. Writing afterward, the secretary announced that the museum "deserve[d] the thanks of this community and the recognition . . . for what they have contributed to the fund of our information upon commercial topics." "Some day," Cortelyou mused, "the new Department of Commerce and Labor may find it advisable to have closer relations with these museums."[33]

It wasn't a school in a formal sense, but the Commercial Museum provided an education to men who did business and who wanted to do more of it. Taken together, its exhibits, its Bureau of Information, and its international conferences did not amount to a structured curriculum, but they certainly conveyed information to those who wanted it. The Philadelphia Commercial Museum was the only one of its kind built in the United States. Those businessmen in San Francisco did not, in the end, take up the call to build a museum companion to Berkeley's College of Commerce. But as the Peirce School's brochure suggests, museums and the object lessons they taught might well have been features of some of the proprietary business and commercial colleges. A section of a 1904 treatise on commercial education included this advice on how to establish a commercial museum: "Collecting a commercial museum is a local problem, and when completed the museum should represent the commercial interests of the region."[34]

When Berkeley's Carl Plehn returned from Philadelphia, he imagined a partnership of some sort between the Commercial Museum there and a new one in San Francisco. But his vision that the museum and Berkeley's College of Commerce would work in tandem did not, strictly speaking, come from his visit back East. The Philadelphia Commercial Museum sat less than a quarter mile from the Wharton School and the University of Pennsylvania campus. And while William Wilson started his career as a member of Penn's faculty, I have found no evidence that the museum ever interacted with the school. Whatever a collegiate school of business might become, museums were not going to be part of that future.

DIY Education for American Businesses

In September 1908 the Court of Common Pleas in the City of Philadelphia received an application to charter the "American University of Applied Commerce and Trade." John Wanamaker reported this news in the pages of the *Annals of the American Academy of Political and Social Science*.[35] Wanamaker was in a position to know: the application and the "university" were his.

For large-scale business enterprises at the turn of the twentieth century that worried about the skills of their workers—that were dissatisfied perhaps with the education provided in the public schools or that likewise found graduates of the proprietary establishments not adequately prepared for work—there was an obvious alternative: in-house education. Companies could teach the workers they employed themselves. As J. W. Dietz summarized "industry's point of view" about different educational tasks, "Train citizens. Let the public school do it. Buy trained help. Let the other fellow do it. Educate in business. It's our own job."[36]

Wanamaker, as he told his readers, had been doing this for about a dozen years already under the auspices of his "school store." By the time Wanamaker wrote, it had produced 7,500 graduates trained by a faculty of twenty-four teachers, "some of whom are instructors in the daily schools of Philadelphia." He continued, "In the curriculum you will find classes in reading, writing, arithmetic, English, spelling, stenography, commercial geography, commercial law and business methods."[37]

Wanamaker, perhaps the king among the great department store princes of the late nineteenth century and a devout, conservative Methodist, conceived of his school as fulfilling his sense of paternalistic responsibility. "The idea of the commercial institute," Wanamaker wrote, "came long ago to the writer with a realization of the full and sacred obligations of employer and employee." As it happened, Wanamaker wrote his article while he was building his new flagship store in the center of Philadelphia. So proud was he of his institute that he was incorporating it, literally, into his new building: "I may be permitted to say here," he concluded, "that my confidence and firm belief in the value of the commercial institute and its relation and ap-plication to the laws of business has led me to build it into the new Philadel-phia store building in stone and iron and cement. Yes—there will be special classrooms, a library and reading room, a gymnasium and swimming pool for the use of the students."[38]

The end result of this in-house schooling was straightforward, according to Wanamaker. It enabled "those who are doing the day's work and earning a living to get a better education to earn a better living." If he were around today, Wanamaker might market his institute as a place where theory and practice come together. Instead, he described his institute as combining edu-cation and career advancement. "The two have marched along shoulder to shoulder," he wrote, "study assisting labor, and labor in turn illuminating book knowledge." This union of schooling and work experience led to an increase in his employee's "earning capacity," increasing the employee's "value to his employer and to himself." Wanamaker had not, at least until this ar-ticle, discussed his institute publicly, but he insisted that it "has been the pivot about which the organization of the store staff swings, for it largely deter-mines the positions of the younger people, their wages and their advance-ment." It was a simple equation: do well in Wanamaker's school and do well in Wanamaker's store. Otherwise "habitual low marks" would "result in a change of names on the payroll."[39]

Wanamaker claimed that his was "the first actual 'school of practice' of business methods, giving daily opportunities to obtain a working education in the arts and sciences of commerce and trade." I will take his word for it. However, just four years after Wanamaker published his essay, enough com-panies and corporations were interested in the idea of running their own education and training programs that they formed the National Association of Corporation Schools.

The organization seems to have come together at New York University and included forty-eight businesses. Among them was the National Cash Register Corporation, which probably explains why the group's first meet-ing took place in NCR's hometown, Dayton, Ohio, in 1913. The following year, they held their second gathering in Wanamaker's Philadelphia over three days in June. *Outlook* magazine lauded the effort, casting it as the op-posite of the "sentimentalism or pseudo-philanthropy" that it saw as perva-sive in educational reforms. "The corporations which are banded together in this effort to educate their own employees," the magazine declared, "are frankly and openly committed to the principle that it pays the company in dollars and cents to educate its workmen in order to increase their efficiency."[40] Through educating their own workers, U.S. businesses could do well by doing good.

New York's National City Bank certainly thought so. At roughly this same moment it established its own educational programs to train its clerks and accountants. By 1916, the bank employed an estimated one thousand clerks at its Wall Street headquarters. Of those, approximately seven hundred had gone through the bank's school. As National City's F. C. Schwedtman described it to the National Education Association, the bank established its school because the college boys the bank had begun to hire were simply not working out. "After one year's experimenting with college men," Schwedtman told the group, "we find it necessary in defense of our ledgers and for the general efficiency of the bank to put the students thru our elementary course of penmanship and banking arithmetic."[41] Perhaps those young college men would have been better off attending Bryant & Stratton after all.

Initially, the National Association of Corporation Schools spread its tasks among twelve committees. The inventory of those committees gives a good sense of how these businesses saw their educational needs: special-training schools; advertising, selling, and distribution schools; retail salesmanship schools; office work schools; unskilled labor; trade apprenticeship schools; public education; employment plans; safety and health; allied institutions; vocational guidance; and administration and supervision. At its Philadelphia meeting the association committed itself to three broad objectives. It wanted to develop the efficiency of the individual employee, to increase efficiency in industry, and to influence the course of established educational institutions more favorably toward industry.[42]

Having businesses themselves take over the task of educating their own employees through corporation schools seemed to some like an updated version of the old apprenticeship system, its "logical descendant" as one reporter covering the Philadelphia convention described it. That system, of course, wasn't coming back, nor could it, because the "coming of big corporations and the sub-division of labor . . . left no place to learn a trade." That fact had been obvious for some time. The economist Simon Patten stressed the point in 1905 when he wrote that "the [apprenticeship] system has been well-nigh destroyed by large-scale production and the differentiation of its processes." Recall that that destruction of the apprenticeship system had been one major reason Joseph Wharton founded his school in the first place. The reporter covering the convention told readers of *Survey*, "There was no expectation at the convention that corporations can escape all educational burden with respect to their employees. It was taken for granted that the corporation school has come to stay, that it is as necessary an instrument to industrial efficiency today as the apprentice course was one hundred years ago."[43]

Surveying this situation in 1922, Leverett Lyon saw the inherent problem with corporation schools as educational institutions. "The corporation school, because of the profit motive, cannot be counted on to give 'general education' or unbiased instruction regarding social institutions such as trade unions, governmental regulations, and tariffs; nor can it, because of the uncertain loyalties of employees, be expected to make even its special training any broader than necessary," he wrote. But at the same time, he acknowledged that he was impressed by what he found at these training centers: "One of the most interesting things about the corporation-school movement is the thoroughly professional attitude which is taken, by its best representatives at least, toward the technical phases of their work."[44]

In the event, the National Association of Corporation Schools did not last long. Even as Lyon wrote in 1922, the association merged with the Industrial Relations Association, and in 1923 the new organization changed its name to the American Management Association. That did not mean the end of such educational ventures, though. Large corporations—the only ones, really, with the capacity to undertake such endeavors—continued to run their own training and educational programs across the twentieth century and still do. *Nation's Business* featured one Taco Industries of Cranston, Rhode Island, in a 1956 article as a company that, working with the American Management Association, had created its own management training course. On this route, Taco Industries bypassed business schools altogether.[45] Perhaps the most famous of these in-house operations, and probably the one most often the butt of jokes, is Hamburger University, run by McDonald's and located in Oak Brook, Illinois. Laugh if you will, but since Hamburger U opened in 1961, more than eighty thousand McDonald's employees have gone through its programs; today, some of those courses can be applied toward college credit. McDonald's founder, Ray Kroc, believed that the best way to train people for the work in his business was to do it himself, and he was convinced that his school would generate loyalty from his employees and would be the mechanism for those employees to advance through the organization. Somewhere in the Methodist hereafter, John Wanamaker smiled.

Let the Schools Take Care of It

"The organization and work of the National Association of Corporation Schools," wrote Charles Bennett shortly after the group's Philadelphia meeting, "has been looked upon with interest by educators generally, and possibly with suspicion by some. . . . Was this new organization indicative of a lack of faith in the schools and a desire to separate or what?"[46]

What, indeed?

Those Progressive educational reformers who distrusted the proprietary business colleges, because for-profit education inevitably led to scandals of one sort or another, wanted to expand the mandate of the public schools to include a wider range of business education and vocational training. They didn't want for-profit proprietary colleges simply to be replaced by schools run by even more for-profit corporations.

The suspicion Bennett reported, however, was probably misplaced. Most corporate leaders didn't really want to get into the educational business in more than a perfunctory way. Jane Stewart reported from the National Association's Philadelphia meeting, "We will have little need of these [corporation schools] when our public school system as a whole does the things of which it is capable and when all the forces of the community begin to look upon vocational education as having a distinct bearing on each of them."[47] Why go to all the hassle and expense of running your own schools if the public schools could do the job for you?

Here the interests of corporations and those of educational reformers overlapped. The latter pushed hard to move "practical" education into the public schools, through business courses and vocational training, and the former were just as enthusiastic to see that happen, especially if they could take a hand in shaping the kind of education and training students would receive. When *Survey* reported on the National Association of Corporation Schools Philadelphia meeting, it found participants being encouraged over and over to "reach out and modify established educational institutions. Again and again speakers urged those present to go back to their own towns and use their influence to make the public school what business men think it ought to be."[48]

This appears to be exactly the direction corporations took when they went back home from their gathering. In 1917 Albert James Beatty studied the relationship between public schools and corporation schools for his dissertation at the University of Illinois. He wanted to answer the question "In what way can the corporation school and the public school be mutually helpful in the solution of the problem of vocational education?"[49] That such education was a necessity went almost without saying, as Beatty reminded readers. U.S. society was already "fully awake" to the need. What remained was to figure out how best to fulfill it.

By the early part of the twentieth century the federal government had certainly become interested in the problem. The *Seventeenth Annual Report of the Commissioner of Labor* came out in 1902, and it ran to 1300 pages. The report surveyed—and it was subtitled—"Trade and Technical Education." While the first 300 pages were devoted to the United States, the rest took stock of countries around the world much as Eugène Léautey had done fifteen years earlier. The table of contents presents an interesting snapshot of occupations at the turn of the twentieth century and which of those had generated some sort of educational training: brewers' schools, dairy schools, and barbers' schools. Some were clearly the products of private philanthropy, like the Young Men's Christian Association Schools; others, like industrial schools, included some that received state support. It took a chapter each to review "industrial schools in the South for the colored race" and "industrial schools in the South for whites."[50]

Both public schools and corporation schools did certain things well, Beatty concluded. But corporation schools could never solve the problem of vocational education because corporation schools could never become universal, and universal education was a bedrock principle for a democratic society. As it was, Beatty calculated, corporation schools reached less than 0.5 percent of workers. Likewise, corporation schools were free to pick and choose those employees who received their education and those who would not. "This selection," Beatty noted, "is one feature which has for the past decade arrayed the American Federation of Labor against any form of privately controlled vocational education."[51]

Beatty found a happy medium in the creation of partnerships between corporations and public schools, and he concluded that "co-operative trade and continuation schools" held the most promise for the most students. In Beatty's view, these would "combine all the points of superiority of the public secondary schools and technical schools and of corporation schools which have been found in the matter of instruction, methods, motives, lesson materials, and curricula." These partnerships were already up and running in many places, Beatty found. In 1915, for example, The R. Hoe Printing Press Company in New York "has recently entered into an agreement whereby the city Board of Education supplies all teachers for the academic work of the apprenticeship school." So had General Electric in Schenectady. Beatty reported that the National Cash Register Company, one of the founders of the National Association of Corporation Schools, was now "working in cooperation with the Dayton High School, and Mr. Adkins, for the Company, pronounces the work a success."[52] Clearly, conference goers had heeded the advice dished out in Philadelphia and returned to their communities, reached out to the existing schools, and modified them to "make the public school what business men think it ought to be."[53]

So given an educational landscape that included proprietary schools, commercial museums, mercantile libraries, schools run by businesses themselves, and an expanded role for the public high schools in training students for jobs, what role did collegiate schools of business see for themselves? What niche did they expect to fill? After all, John Wanamaker was quite confident that a graduate of his store school "receives a degree which is in effect a combination of what Harvard College calls the degree of 'Masters of Business Administration' with a certificate of a certain number of years' actual experience in the business world."[54] In the midst of a dynamic educational world, what market, as the folks in business schools today might ask, did these collegiate business schools want to capture?

Profession Envy

At one level, the answer was simple, and we've heard it already. These schools would train the new managerial class necessary to run the U.S. corporate economy. Those enterprises had grown so large, so complex, and so quickly that they required an entirely different kind of education to understand and operate. For many, the changed nature of business itself meant that only universities could provide the necessary training. "Modern business is becoming more complex," wrote Edmund James, a Wharton School professor in 1901, "and requires a higher order of talent and a higher degree of preparation in order to succeed than ever before." A few years later, Cheesman Herrick, a Wharton alum who became director of commercial education at Philadelphia's Central High School, echoed this belief, if somewhat more laconically: "Business in these days is essentially a new occupation and requires a preliminary training more extensive and thorough than formerly was necessary." The University of South Dakota's Woodford Anderson laid out the issue succinctly in 1900: "The problem before us now resolves into two distinct questions: (1) Should young men receive higher commercial education? (2) Should this higher education be given in colleges and universities in preference to special schools?"[55]

At the University of Chicago, Leon Marshall, dean of the College of Commerce and Administration, which had also opened in 1898, shortly after Berkeley's, drew a more specific occupational distinction between the clerical and the managerial to justify the need for such a place as he now directed. Gesturing first toward the world of proprietary colleges, Marshall wrote, "It has long been accepted that it is possible to train men for the routine tasks of business." He went on, "It has not been so universally accepted that it is possible to train men for the responsible positions of industry—for those executive positions whose occupants are called upon to settle the great questions of business policy."[56] "The call of the hour is for efficiency in affairs," announced Earl Jay Glade, the head of the commercial department at Brigham Young University. "Only the highest type of man power is commensurate with the situation. Today this type of power cannot be generated thru apprenticeship in business and public life alone. . . . It is largely upon our educational system that we shall have to rely."[57] Never mind that none of the titans of industry, or robber barons if you prefer, at the turn of the twentieth century, the ones who built and ran these huge new enterprises, had been trained in business schools—not Carnegie, Rockefeller, Armour, or any of the rest.

But beneath the demands allegedly created by size and scope, and not very far beneath, either, was an even simpler answer to the question of why collegiate schools of business: professional status. Businessmen wanted more respect, and they thought a specialized college degree, from a collegiate business school, would give it to them.

Recall that this profession envy was woven into the DNA of the Wharton School. Wharton founded his school in part because he recognized that college education trained men for the professions, "those who purposed to become lawyers, doctors or clergymen."[58] And in the last quarter of the nineteenth century, these three constituted the vast majority of the professional world. Remember that by the turn of the twentieth century only a few hundred Americans held doctorates in an academic discipline. In 1900, over ten thousand degrees were awarded in theology, law, and medicine.[59] Wharton wanted businessmen to join the professional ranks as well.[60]

Ostensibly, professional prestige had also been the aspiration of the proprietary business schools well before the Wharton School opened. When *Harper's Weekly* reported on the convention of Bryant & Stratton franchises in Cleveland in 1866, the journal editorialized that, thanks to Bryant & Stratton, "the sphere and limits of a purely business education have been as clearly defined as those of law, medical, and theological schools." The writer went on, "It is becoming almost as necessary that a young man, in fitting himself for business, should graduate at one of these Colleges" as it is for anyone going into one of the learned professions.[61] By the turn of the twentieth century, however, only higher education proper was seen as conferring the necessaries to turn business into something on a par with law, medicine, and the ministry.

It wasn't strictly an educational imperative that drove the enthusiasm for business schools, therefore. Rather, businessmen themselves, tired of being looked at down the noses of the college educated, wanted the cultural cachet (and resulting respect) that came with a degree. Higher education for business would, ipso facto, make business something intellectual rather than merely clerical. When William Wilson, the Penn botanist turned museum impresario, officially launched the Commercial Museum, he did so by hosting the National Export Exposition in 1899. He invited Harvard's Charles Norton to speak, and though he was speaking at a museum, Norton chose to discuss higher education. "I can hear the objection of the old-fashioned merchant," Norton told the assembled, "to this whole project of a commercial school." And he offered his rejoinder: "In answer I can only say that I believe commerce and industry in their higher ranges to be eminently intellectual pursuits, and that I know of no other intellectual calling for which a professional school is not now provided."[62] The logic of the argument here is not airtight. Without offering any evidence about the "intellectual" nature of business dealings, Norton declared that they were and thus, as a result, concluded that higher education was a necessity for businessmen.

Intellectually rigorous or not, higher education conferred the social status that businessmen wanted. "Quite beyond its mere economic value," Henry Stimson told readers of the *Forum*, "when its advantages are understood, ambitious business men will demand for themselves and their associates the privilege of living in the spacious air which is now looked upon as the special prerogative of the men of the professions." Such a college credential would go a long way to making business socially equivalent to the other learned professions. "The country now has well-supported schools for the training of men in war, medicine, law and technology," J. Laurence Laughlin noted in 1902, "but it is quite within the truth to maintain that no one of these interests has as much influence upon the actual work and welfare of the people as those connected with ... the wider field of trade and industry." Therefore, he told his readers, "leaders and the public must be given instruction until they can think clearly on these subjects of every day concern."[63] "In fact, the business man is beginning to have a professional pride in being able to say something of real value," George Wharton enthused, "similar to that of the physician who addresses his medical society."[64] A certificate from one of the Bryant & Stratton franchises might be well and good for a clerk. But a degree from, say, Dartmouth College's Tuck School, founded in 1900, allowed the holder to breathe altogether more "spacious air."

One advantage that many saw to a college education in business, as opposed to an education at a proprietary school, was that it wouldn't be only an education in business techniques. "What seems to me the defect of these colleges [the Bryant & Strattons of the nation]," wrote James Hodges, "is that they are too narrow. Every merchant should know his business well ... but if he knows nothing but his business, though he count his gains by the millions, he is only a dealer in merchandise."[65] Only a business education provided by colleges and universities would ennoble the merchandise dealer into a true professional, though Hodges seems to have missed the ironic paradox here: colleges promised to turn business education into professional training precisely by teaching things other than business.

C. W. Haskins drew the same distinction with slightly different language. "The aim of the universities" in establishing business schools, he wrote in 1902, "is an exalted one, that their courses lead to a professional career, that their students look not to office utility, but to the brain-work and responsible activities of business life." Woodford Anderson was even more taxonomic in distinguishing between what kinds of graduates came from the proprietary schools and what kinds came from the new collegiate business schools. "The business school prepares a man for bookkeeping, stenography, or routine office work," he wrote, while "the commercial high schools prepare men to be business managers and local buyers and sellers." Reaching his crescendo, he concluded, "The higher commercial schools should fit men to be financiers, corporate managers, foreign agents, and consuls."[66] Brainworkers—executives—breathing rarified air, doing things beyond mere merchandise dealing: only higher education could produce these kinds of businessmen. The course catalog from Syracuse University's business school in the 1920s put the goal of a business education clearly and concisely: "To dignify the business career as a profession."[67]

If higher education in business would turn businessmen into professionals, then Henry Stimson clarified another reason why that was important in the first place. "The rapid development of the business life of our country and the wide diffusion of wealth in the business world," he observed, "have brought into the field a large number of young men destined to become the successors of their fathers. . . . The question now is, How can this large number of favored young men most successfully fit themselves, not only for the local administration of business, but for the wider competition in the markets of the world, and to take charge of some of the largest trusts that have ever been known?"[68]

Looking back on the occasion of the Wharton School's twentieth anniversary, Edmund James acknowledged that a little bit of higher education might not be such a good thing for a life in business, noting, "There is undoubtedly some danger that the young men who spend from seven to eight years in the study of Latin, Greek and mathematics, or even in the study of French and German, and natural science, may acquire, if not a taste for literary callings, at least a distaste for mercantile life." Quickly, though, he reassured his readers. "But this does not prove that the pursuit of a higher course of study, which should be related more closely to their future work would have the same effect. The study of the history and methods of insurance, for example, in all their different aspects, need not of itself destroy all interest of young men in the business of insurances as a practical career." In any event, James continued, the purpose of higher education for businessmen wasn't really about the utility of Greek or the seductions of the literary life. Instead, business schools responded to the demands of "successful business men desiring that their sons should succeed them in business" and who also wanted their sons to "become educated men of the world." These fathers wanted the status that came with a college degree, but many "felt that the old curriculum did not offer the sort of thing which they wished." Why not, therefore, create a hybrid so that "their sons could . . . be learning something bearing on their future business while acquiring a liberal education."[69] In his essay "The Gospel of Wealth," Andrew Carnegie argued that inherited wealth constituted something almost immoral and advised his fellow plutocrats to give it all away, just as he had. Stimson and James, by contrast, argued that higher education was necessary to train the next generation to handle the inheritance of privilege effectively. There is an interesting commentary here on the nature of social mobility and status. Businessmen who had grown rich without the benefit of a college education in business wanted their sons to do better, not strictly in economic terms, but in the world of cultural capital. Collegiate business schools would provide that capital.

In fact, there was no other choice, as some commentators saw it. If business was really to become a profession, it needed the sort of professional training and credential that only universities could provide. George Brett, president of Macmillan Corporation, didn't see any other way around it when he wrote in 1912, "Much as we may dislike the idea of piling university on university, school on school, when so many institutions already exist, we shall be obliged to establish separate colleges of commerce unless we can prevail upon some of the many higher institutions already existing to give us facilities of the broadest and most extensive character for this important subject of higher commercial education."[70]

As he wrote, those "higher institutions" were about to do just that. Many commentators in the early years of the twentieth century called the arrival of business education a "movement" and cheered its coming. Brigham Young's Earl Jay Glade trumpeted in 1913, "The history of education has seen only a few movements of this magnitude."[71] Writing in 1903, Frank Waldo wondered why it should arrive when it did. He offered several thoughts, including the familiar one that "commercial men" get the same kind of education "which the farmer enjoys in the agricultural colleges." He concluded by saying, "Whatever the cause of its origin, the idea of commercial education has arrived." However, he did note another factor worth pausing over for a moment: "It may be that the fast-changing conditions of commerce," Waldo wrote, "which have in prospect a vast foreign trade, are demanding a differently trained class of employees from those of other days, when local, or at least domestic, trade was all-important."[72]

There is no question that economic opportunities served as a major motivation for U.S. imperial expansion at the end of the nineteenth century. The acquisition of the Philippines provided U.S. companies with a stepping-stone to unlimited Chinese markets, at least in the fevered commercial dreams of U.S. business leaders. Taking full advantage of those markets, however, required more than just a new geopolitical position. It required training and education, and according to Henry Stimson, the Europeans already had it. Surveying the commercial education available in Germany, Stimson told his readers, "It is not surprising that German merchants should be found coming to the front in many Oriental markets, or that foreign governments are in some instances selecting their consuls exclusively from graduates of these schools." Putting it bluntly, Stimson told Americans, "The expansion of the United States into the tropics has given a new importance to the question of commercial education."[73] When the United States launched its war against the Spanish in 1898, the Wharton School had been joined by two others—Chicago and Berkeley—as the only collegiate business schools in the country; by the time Stimson wrote in 1900 those three had been joined by three more. By the outbreak of the First World War, that number would roughly quadruple, and that doesn't count the more than two hundred colleges and universities offering coursework in business.[74] Imperialism—and the perceived need that conquering world markets required a higher education—was, therefore, one reason for the growth of collegiate schools of business as the nineteenth century became the twentieth.

A Better Type of Businessman

At the same time, Progressive-era education reformers saw business schools on campus as a way to train a more responsible and civic-minded class of business leaders. The story of how Progressives tried, with varying degrees of success, to rein in the worst excesses of large-scale industrial capitalism is a staple of introductory U.S. history courses. The breakup of corporate monopolies by Teddy "Trust-Buster" Roosevelt; the social melioration provided by dozens of settlement houses and embodied by Jane Addams; the use of government regulatory power exemplified by the creation of the Food and Drug Administration to protect ordinary Americans—all these exemplified the era of Progressive reform. Yet as much as many Progressives were suspicious altogether of the bigness of business and were distraught over its effects on American life, some thought that business could be reformed and that the education of businessmen in colleges provided the best, most efficacious way to do that.

The University of Illinois at Champaign-Urbana opened its Commercial Building in 1913 (a few years ahead of opening its business school). Among other things, the new facility included the office for the new professor of railway administration and a statistics lab on the second floor. To mark the occasion the university threw a conference and gathered some of the leading figures in the worlds of higher education and of business. University president Edmund James gaveled the grand event to order, and fitting that he should. Before he came to Illinois he had been director of the Wharton School and was among the most enthusiastic advocates for collegiate business education in the country.

Among those invited to speak at the conference was Harry Wheeler, president of the U.S. Chamber of Commerce. The chamber had been created in 1912 at the urging of President William Howard Taft, who saw it as a counterweight to the labor movement, and Wheeler already saw that the real action for business would happen in Washington and in collaboration with politicians. "The true progress in business administration," he told the conference, "comes from a knowledge of the relation of business to government . . . to find the relationship that exists between legislation and business." Even so, Wheeler insisted that civic duty, not profit making, now constituted the primary goal for business enterprises: "Organizations, originally established for the purpose of stimulating trade, have broadened the scope of their action until today their work is largely civic and secondarily commercial." It was a logical turn of events, as Wheeler saw it: "After all, only as civic conditions are ideal can commercial conditions be made ideal." Writing in 1904 Herrick, the director of the Commercial School at Philadelphia's prestigious Central High School, pointed out that "commercial education is not solely an academic question," because "it directly concerns public welfare." He went on to make this equation: "No other epoch has had so many business men in public life. . . . The deduction is obvious; if busi-

ness men are to rule the world, let education set for itself the work of form-
ing a better type of business man."[75]

Over and over again university administrators, faculty, and other commentators expressed the earnest belief that higher education could reform—
indeed, redeem—the otherwise avaricious and amoral behavior of U.S.
business. Some sort of ethical imperative was at the center of most of the early
business schools when they were founded, including Wharton, Harvard's
graduate school of business, and Northwestern's business college.[76] Willard
Eugene Hotchkiss, who had a long career in several university business
schools, put the matter bluntly in 1918: "What the public really wants from
business, then, is a contribution to national welfare." And if that might ran-
kle certain businessmen, he went on to insist, "the efficiency ideal in [no] way
conflicts with the ideal of moral responsibility and service." Higher education,
Hotchkiss believed, would teach the businessmen of the future those ideals.
The University of Pennsylvania's Simon Patten made the prospect sound
vaguely religious when he wrote, "Higher business education instills in young
men a spirit that uplifts their profession or trade." Woodford Anderson at the
University of South Dakota saw this connection in even more utopian terms:
"When colleges and universities educate men especially for business, commer-
cial evils will disappear and prosperity will become permanent."[77]

The work here was heroic, at least according to William Carey Jones.
Writing in 1900, and to mark the opening the year before of Berkeley's new
college of business, Jones trumpeted, "The university that establishes a department of commerce throws itself right upon the battle-lines of the contending
forces." On the one side, Jones offered, was a "strangling conservatism." On
the other, "far-reaching revolution." The stakes could not be higher: "Universities have contributed much to emancipation of thought and to political
freedom," Jones reminded his readers, "but real political—not to say general social—freedom cannot subsist together with economic enslavement. A
university that supports a college of commerce undertakes the work of economic emancipation."[78] Jones was one among many Progressives who saw
the rise of large-scale industrial capitalism as a fundamental threat to U.S.
workers and therefore to U.S. democracy. In his view, and it was shared by
others as well, collegiate business schools stood on the front lines of protect-
ing Americans from the tyranny of unrestrained capitalism.

This belief that American higher education could save American freedom
from the predations of American business speaks to an almost poignant faith

in the socially transformative power of education, and one could be forgiven a certain skepticism. "I realize," National City banker F. C. Schwedtman told a crowd almost sheepishly, "that to provide students with means for earning a livelihood possibly should not be the strongest object, and certainly not the only object, of our schools and colleges." Certainly, he opined, "high ideals, good citizenship, and individual and collective happiness are higher motives for teacher and pupil." But, he confessed, "judging from my experience . . . 99 out of 100 have studied, not so much for the love of knowledge, not so much for the sake of high ideals or ultimate happiness, but primarily and principally for the purpose of greater or more rapid success in making a living."[79] Anyone who has taught college students can nod his or her head at that. Schwedtman seemed to take the juxtaposition for granted and therefore put his finger on the problem for which higher education might provide a reconciliation: high ideals on the one hand; making a living on the other.

For some, the kind of skepticism voiced by Schwedtman ran even deeper. Martha Owens reported frankly a conversation she had had to readers of the *Chautauquan* in 1895: "An eminent dry goods merchant in New York who employs several hundred bookkeepers, clerks, and helpers said to me, 'I would rather have a graduate of an ordinary business college for a bookkeeper or clerk behind my counter than a graduate of the best university.'" Twenty years later, Ernest Draper was no less blunt. "College men are notoriously lax in their habits," complained Draper and he wasn't finished: "Many of them are extravagant. . . . The college man is generally conceited. He has an exalted opinion of his ability. . . . He feels that he knows too much to learn a business 'from the ground up.'" Even Harvard's business school seemed sensitive on this subject. As it got under way in the early years of the twentieth century, the B-school's leaders did not "pretend to graduate men who will begin at the top or high up in the several lines of business." Almost apologetically, Harvard countered, "It does aim to teach them how to work and how to apply powers of observation, analysis, and invention to practical business problems."[80]

In fact, Draper concluded, it wasn't clear that higher education provided any intellectual or technical advantage to or in the world of business. Draper believed that "college does instill certain traits in the average individual that are a detriment to him upon starting in business" (presumably the laxity, the arrogance, and the self-regard he mentioned earlier in his essay). Draper drew these conclusions from a survey he conducted of business leaders. One replied in a way that was both circular and smacked of social Darwinism: "I think one reason college men ultimately outdistance non-college men," this businessman wrote, "is because they are a picked class, and should naturally do so, in any event. The best of the college men ought to, and I think do, inherit the best brains in the country . . . they ought to have a great advantage over any other man their age."[81] College men are the cream of the crop by virtue of becoming college men in the first place. For their success in business, what they might study or learn in college seemed to this writer entirely beside the point.

Market-Driven Schools of Business

Regardless of whether there was a genuine educational need to address and whether higher education could redeem the ethics and morals of U.S. businessmen, colleges themselves recognized that more and more of their graduates were going into business and so they might as well offer collegiate training for those careers. Indeed, William Scott at the University of Wisconsin sounded almost exasperated when he reported in a 1913 essay, "By 1900 the University found itself occupying an untenable position on the subject of training for business," because so many Wisconsin students in the law, engineering, and ag schools were going into business after they graduated.[82] The arrival of business schools on campus catered to students who intended to go into business anyway.

Take the Yale class of 1904, for example: Of 281 graduates who responded to a survey, 85 had become lawyers and 24 went into medicine. Only 9 graduates of Jonathan Edwards's alma mater that year went into the ministry, while 112, or 40 percent of the total, went into business. An almost identical number from the class of 1906 went into business, while over 50 percent of Amherst graduates from that year did the same. Things were little different in Cambridge, where more than 50 percent of Harvard's graduates in 1908 went into the private sector.[83]

When Louis Brandeis spoke at Brown University's commencement in 1912, he announced that it was high time to eliminate the distinction between "business" and the "professions" and the attendant snobbery that went with it: "Each commencement season," he told the graduates, "we are told by the college reports the number of graduates who have selected the professions as their occupations and the number of those who will enter business. The time has come for abandoning such a classification. Business should be, and to some extent already is, one of the professions." Brandeis went on, "The establishment of business schools in our universities is a manifestation of the modern conception of business," and he concluded his oration with the same soaring faith that many held that higher education could redeem American business. With higher education, "'big business' will lose its sinister meaning, and will take on new significance. . . . 'Big business' will mean professionalized business, as distinguished from the occupation of petty trafficking or mere money-making. And as the profession of business develops, the great industrial and social problems expressed in the present social unrest will one by one find solution."[84]

Telling, if a bit odd, that Brandeis should come to Providence, Rhode Island, to deliver that message. Brown did not—and does not—have a business school. But the movement to create collegiate schools of business had clearly arrived.

A Club to Join

Doctors did it. Lawyers did it. Even historians did it. They all formed professional associations in the late nineteenth century. The American Medical Association formed initially in 1847 but it formally incorporated in 1897; lawyers gathered to create the American Bar Association in 1878, and my own professional organization, the American Historical Association, began in 1884.

When he addressed the Brown graduates, Louis Brandeis defined what he saw as the three constituent elements of any profession: first, a profession is an endeavor "for which the necessary preliminary training is intellectual in character"; second, that endeavor is "pursued largely for others and not merely for one's self"; and finally, "the amount of financial return is not the accepted measure of success." Brandeis clearly sided with those during the Progressive era who believed that "professionalizing" the world of business—particularly through higher education—meant elevating it from the self-serving into something a bit more selfless. As he put it later in his address, business was "so rich in opportunity for the exercise of man's finest and most varied mental faculties and moral qualities" that "mere money-making cannot be regarded as the legitimate end."[85]

Brandeis might have added that, to be considered a profession in the early twentieth century, one needed a professional association. Virtually all the academic disciplines formed such associations at this moment—the physicists and literary scholars, the anthropologists and the chemists. And thus, in 1916 and in the midst of this associational enthusiasm, was born the American Association of Collegiate Schools of Business. Representatives from seventeen colleges and universities came to Chicago at the invitation of the deans of the business schools at Harvard, the University of Chicago, and Northwestern University to start the AACSB.[86] Those who came to Chicago adopted an organizational constitution that, along with the usual sorts of governance and procedural stipulations, articulated the AACSB's goal as "the promotion and improvement of higher business education in North America." The founding group adjourned after agreeing to meet the following year at Harvard.

On the face of it, the founding of the AACSB in 1916 would seem to signal that the process of professionalizing U.S. business proceeded apace and alongside so many other professional disciplines. Looked at a little more closely, however, the creation of the AACSB only underscored the near impossibility of turning business into a profession proper. Unlike the lawyers or doctors—or even historians—to which businessmen yearned to compare themselves, the AACSB was a professional organization of colleges and universities, not individuals. The distinction is critical.

Another aspect of professionalization that Louis Brandeis overlooked is the role of gatekeeper that professions play in conjunction with their professional organizations. Professions set standards for those who want to join them—standards of education and training, expectations of conduct and ethics. In this way, the professions are self-defining: those inside the profession essentially control who gets to be a part of the club and who doesn't. Indeed, professional associations responded in part to demands, from practitioners and from the public, for mechanisms to separate the attorney from the huckster, the doctor from the quack.

The process of wedding the professions to the university was not instant or entire. Throughout the nineteenth century, most medical schools were not attached to universities and doubtless some number of self-identified doctors had no formal training at all (not that formal training made all that much difference to patients in the nineteenth century). The same was also true for lawyers, only more so. Abraham Lincoln, after all, practiced law without having gone to college, much less a law school. But it is unarguable that as professions formalized and as they grew more powerful, they did so by aligning themselves with the transforming university. By the early twentieth century the landscape of higher education we see today had largely taken shape: universities offer graduate and professional education; colleges do not.

As a result, the path to the professions in the twentieth century was dramatically different than it had been in the nineteenth. To become a doctor, for example, requires four years of undergraduate coursework, followed by a standardized test, followed by a more-or-less standard four-year course through a university medical school. After that come residencies and fellowships—often at teaching hospitals run, in turn, as part of university medical centers—and board exams and licensures. And before they start practicing, new doctors take the Hippocratic oath. Likewise, before a lawyer can stand before a judge, she must pass a bar exam constructed by other lawyers and administered by the state, taken usually after completing three years of law school. Both doctors and lawyers are governed by laws that define malpractice, and if they violate those laws they can lose their membership in their profession. This is how professions work in partnership with universities to create and define the terms of membership and police themselves.

None of this, needless to say, applies to the world of business. Not at the front end, not at the back. To become a doctor routinely requires more than a decade of education after high school, while any high school dropout can go into business. Indeed, nearly 30 percent of the businessmen listed in the 1939 edition of *Who's Who* had not attended college at all, much less a collegiate business school.[87] The story of the self-made man has been a staple part of the American mythos since Benjamin Franklin; stories about the self-taught neurosurgeon are somewhat less common. And while doctors all carry a heavy burden of malpractice insurance as a hedge against the near inevitability of being sued, malpractice in business, at least at the higher altitudes of corporate America, often results in a lucrative severance package.[88]

So the professional body that formed as part of the larger drive to professionalize business restricted itself—read the name carefully again—to campus business schools and to the business of business education. It concerned itself only with the education of those businessmen who attended its member schools and had no role to play in developing, much less enforcing, any codes of conduct or professional credentialing or licensing for graduates of those schools. And, to reiterate, attending a business school was by no means requisite for a business career, then or now.

In his play *The Doctor's Dilemma* George Bernard Shaw has one of his characters quip that professions constitute a conspiracy against the laity, and to some extent it's hard to argue with that. By creating and enforcing norms of practice, by erecting barriers to entry, by policing rules of conduct, professions really operate to create normative cultures as much as objective standards. In this sense, professions function as updated versions of medieval guilds, deciding who can be a practitioner and who cannot, separating the amateurs from the, well, pros. And to the victor go the spoils, or the hourly rates. One can certainly argue that the reason lawyers do as well as they do is that they have effectively regulated their own competition through the trappings of professionalism.

At the same time, few of us, I suspect, would put our ailing gums in the hands of a self-taught, self-appointed periodontist. However elitist or antidemocratic professions may be, most of us would agree that they have raised the quality of work done inside each of them in ways that constitute genuine social good.[89] And we can measure those successes in the professions in ways that we can't for business. Medicine has made all sorts of demonstrable advances that allow people to live longer and better. What comparable metric could we use to measure the success of "professional" business?

But the nation's mythos is not founded on the promise that everyone can be a periodontist. It is built on the idea that everyone can achieve a measure of economic comfort and success. Business schools arrived on campus at exactly the moment when plenty of workers, intellectuals, and labor organizers and reformers questioned whether that economic openness really existed anymore. In fact, those schools were founded to serve the very corporations that were making such dreams harder and harder (often with money from those very same industrialists). So it is fair to ask whether professional business education conspired against the laity, or whether business itself did that conspiring, or whether they worked in tandem.

In its early years, the AACSB did work to create standards by which to bestow accreditation on the growing number collegiate business schools. In 1919 the group made its first attempt to establish "minimum standards to be met by all schools seeking membership to the Association"; in 1920 they tried to clarify those standards. In 1928 the association authorized "an investigation to determine whether all member schools were complying with the standards required," and in 1929 the organization reached a decision that only business schools that had been "established as a *distinct school or college* (as opposed to merely a department of a college of liberal arts) of a university where credits are accepted" should qualify.[90]

Organizational fits and starts to be sure, and surely common for any new association trying to find its footing and define its mission. But AACSB's struggle in its first decade to define even what qualified as a business school, along with the suspicion that its own members weren't complying with the rules, underscores how difficult it was, and remains, to exert the kind of control over practice that is at the heart of any profession. Business leaders and educators in the early twentieth century might have desired to have business treated as one of the other learned professions, but they had no mechanism by which to control how businessmen went about their business in the way that lawyers, doctors, and academics could. The AACSB could not manage to regulate what went on at its member schools, and even its mission to focus on collegiate schools has often seemed quixotic. By one estimate, in the 1980s only one-third of all the MBAs granted came from AACSB-member institutions.[91] Given that, the AACSB certainly couldn't exert any authority over what went on in the world of business itself.

Yet despite the basic contradiction of trying to create a profession out of something that has no barrier to entry and no standards by which to judge professional behavior, most commentators in the first decades of the twentieth century probably agreed with Frank Vanderlip of New York's National City Bank when he addressed the convocation at the State University of New York in Albany in 1905: "I believe we will in time come to recognize . . . that the road to commercial leadership will be through the doors of those colleges and universities which have developed courses especially adapted to the requirements of commercial life."[92] In fact, that time had come.

In 1926 an anonymous writer conveyed to readers of the journal *School and Society* an anxiety floating around in the world of proprietary business schools. "A Middle Western publishing company recently addressed a circular letter to the business schools of America," the author reported, "in which colleges and universities were declared to be 'the real octopus that has been swallowing up much of the business that formerly went to private business schools.'" The letter went on to declare that the "real competitor" of these schools, whose roots reached back nearly a century at that point, were "higher colleges and universities," and it fumed, "some of them are full to the bursting point. This is true North, East, South and West and has been ever since the close of the war." All this raised a real question about education, to say nothing of the business of running a business school. The letter echoed some of the arched-eyebrowed doubts about the value of higher education for a career in business that we've heard already, but it also wondered whether college ought to be the goal of every young person. "Recently, there has been a growing conviction that a university education is not the best thing for every boy and girl. There is a growing conviction that a university education is not the best thing for most boys and girls who expect to enter business." [93]

This letter from this unnamed midwestern publishing company got it right that after the First World War the "movement" to open collegiate schools of business took off. Between the end of war and the Crash, forty-six collegiate business schools opened around the country, an increase of 40 percent. [94] And it may well have been the case that some students who might have attended a Bryant & Stratton or one of the other such schools now enrolled at the local university. Those who owned and ran these proprietary schools might well have felt threatened by statements like those made by the University of South Dakota's Woodford Anderson, who wanted to "raise every first-class business school to the grade of a college," and many must have bristled when Earl Jay Glade at Brigham Young called their schools "educational excrescences." [95] These schools did not disappear, of course, and their descendants still flourish today, sometimes for better, sometimes for worse. In 1922, Leverett Lyon was also a bit dismissive of the work they did. "The private commercial school remains largely as it began," he wrote, elaborating that it was "an institution concerned with doing the immediate thing. The interests of business-college managers do not, and probably cannot ever, lie in education of a fundamental sort." [96]

But while the proprietary schools might have seen the explosion of business education on campus as a threat to their very survival, I don't think the administrators who brought business education to college campuses saw things in quite the same way. By using the high-minded language of professionalization, by insisting that higher education would enable businessmen to join the ranks of doctors and lawyers—however chimerical that goal proved to be—the new collegiate business schools didn't want to put the old proprietary ones out of business. They wanted to create a distinction and a hierarchy between the two. Extend the analogy a bit further: if businessmen trained at Wharton were like doctors or lawyers, the graduates of Peirce College would serve as the nurses and paralegals of the business world. Collegiate schools of business needed their proprietary cousins in order to draw the comparison and highlight the difference. Businesses needed them in order to stratify their workforce.

The struggle between the two was not really over enrollments. It was over status and prestige. Collegiate business schools didn't aspire to teach their students how to function in the white-collar world. They offered distinction to their graduates—the distinction between those who had a college degree and those who didn't. It was the kind of distinction crucial for marking differences of social class when mere moneymaking wasn't enough to do so. And in that fight between proprietary schools and collegiate ones, the universities have certainly prevailed.

But not precisely because they succeeded, at least not on the terms they and others laid out for them at the turn of the twentieth century. "Is business a profession?" asked a 1930 comparison of university education in England, Germany, and the United States. "In a loose way, the term 'profession' is used merely as the antithesis to 'amateur'; hence one may speak of a professional cook or a professional football player," but "is business today in itself an end fine enough, impersonal enough, intelligent enough, fastidious enough, to deserve to be called a profession?" In short, no. The author of that conclusion was Abraham Flexner, and that must have stung. Flexner was among the most important educational reformers in the country. Twenty years earlier he had written the Flexner report on medical education, which dramatically changed the way doctors were trained. As much as any other single development the Flexner report created the profession of medicine as we know it today. Flexner, therefore, knew the difference between professional education and vocational training. Fifty years after Wharton began training students to be professional businessmen, Flexner compared them to football players.[97]

Chapter 2

Teach the Children . . . What?

Business Schools and Their Curricular Confusions

Louis Brandeis missed something else about the professions when he addressed the graduating class at Brown in 1912.[1]

His three-part definition of a profession—something intellectual in character, pursued for the benefit of others, and where moneymaking was not the measure of success—neglected something far more basic. Professions, and their cousins the academic disciplines, coalesce around specific bodies of knowledge. In turn, they define what constitutes that body of knowledge and they contribute to the further production of it.[2]

It was all well and good for business to aspire to that status of a profession or for some, like Brandeis, to assert that it already was. But these statements, high-minded though they might be, remained largely abstract and hypothetical. What, specifically, did a future man of business need to know in order to be a "professional" man of business? If Brandeis was right that business was indeed an intellectual pursuit, then what was the intellectual content businessmen pursued? And more to the point, if collegiate-based schools of business were necessary to educate the professional businessmen of tomorrow, what, exactly, should those businessmen-to-be learn? Writing in the *North American Review* at the very end of the nineteenth century, James Bryce wasted no words: "Business is not an occupation like medicine or law with a definite scope, and requiring a well-understood body of knowledge." Twenty years later, the situation had not improved and the University of Missouri's Harvey Aldon Wooster put the conundrum no less bluntly: "The university school of business has had to undertake professional training for a non-professional pursuit."[3]

On any individual campus, these questions translated into the quotidian problems of course offerings, faculty hiring, and degree requirements. Taken together, those intramural debates amounted to an attempt to define a professional field and to establish, with the authority that comes with a college degree, what businessmen needed to study and how their minds ought to be trained. Writing in 1901, when collegiate business schools numbered only in the single digits, Edmund James acknowledged, "We have not, it must be admitted, worked out as yet any body of doctrine or group on studies, theoretical or practical, which will compare favorably with the system applied to law, medicine, theology or engineering."[4] As we see in this chapter, business schools struggled mightily—one could say quixotically—with the definition of that "body of doctrine" and with the question of what to teach their students.

Trying to Design a Business Education

Though the idea of a collegiate school of business was novel in the late nineteenth century, the problem of what to teach students going into business was not. In fact, the earliest proprietary schools faced the same dilemma. "It would be difficult to lay down any course of study," *Hunt's Merchant's Magazine* opined in 1846, "that would be peculiarly fitted to form a man of business." The writer believed that such students "should be brought up in the habit of reasoning closely," which sounded wise, if a bit vague. The goal was not to train "a learned man, but a man of business; not a 'full man' but a 'ready man,'" and thus, in the writer's somewhat bathetic opinion, "there is hardly anything better for him than the study of geometry."[5]

The whole rationale of collegiate business schools, as we saw in chapter 1, was to educate both full men and ready men and in so doing to distinguish themselves from the proprietary schools that already dotted the educational landscape. While the college degree would legitimate the holder as a professional, the college curriculum would legitimate the degree, and thus it had to be different and distinct from what was on offer at the Bryant & Stratton across town.

The boundaries between the two were—and perhaps are—more easily described than realized. The business school at the University of Denver offers a nice case in point. Denver's School of Commerce, now called the Daniels College of Business, marked its centennial in 2008, but that founding date—1908—is a bit squishy. In fact, something called a commercial school was established at the university in the early 1880s offering courses in "Business Arithmetic, Spelling, Business Correspondence; Commercial Law; Penmanship; Business Forms; Finance; Theoretical Book-keeping; Actual Business and Practical Book-keeping." An 1884 circular for the school noted in particular, "We teach the Spencerian System."[6]

By 1895 that operation had been closed by the university trustees and in 1908 Denver opened its School of Commerce, Accounts, and Finance. Except that the "school" had been chartered by the State of Colorado independently of the university and functioned as a proprietary unit with departmental status. Only in 1931, and one suspects only because of the financial pressures of the Great Depression, was the school absorbed fully within the university, and two years later it joined the American Association of Collegiate Schools of Business (AACSB), sealing officially its new status as a proper school of business. As Denver's experience illustrates, the line that separated a collegiate school from a proprietary one could be fuzzy, but as we have already discussed, the stakes in drawing that line were fraught.

Wharton was the first to confront the problem of what constituted a college-level education in business. Initially, Wharton's amounted to a two-year course of study taken by students after two years taking courses in the college. After entering Wharton in their junior year, students took classes in theory and practice of accounting, political economy, political science, history, finance, business law, and bookkeeping. In addition, Wharton's 1883 annual Announcement promised that "original research by the students, under the direction of the professors, is a part of the work of the School," though it did not specify research about what.[7] When it opened its doors in 1898, Berkeley's College of Commerce was structured similarly. There, "the first two years were entirely background work in languages, history, science, and so on," according to Dean Ewald Grether. After those two years, "they would now at the junior level transfer to the School of Commerce." Likewise, Woodford Anderson, from the University of South Dakota, was probably looking at the Wharton model when he sketched his ideal educational schema in 1900: "Commercial education should be the capstone of the college. In general terms, we may say that the classical education teaches how to think, to theorize; scientific education teaches how to investigate and to apply; commercial education teaches how to make and to dispose of."[8] A rational, orderly progression through college.

Twenty-five years after Wharton, Harvard opened its business school, and the two provide a useful comparison. Harvard's was a graduate school only—though it was not the first graduate business school. That distinction belongs to Dartmouth's Tuck School of Business. Among the "special fields" Harvard offered in its first course roster were "banking and finance, accounting and auditing, insurances, industrial organizations, transportation, commercial law, economic resources, and public service." Students could also take several foreign languages if they chose, but as electives, not as part of the required curriculum. (This probably irritated Edward Hurley, chairman of the Federal Trade Commission during Woodrow Wilson's administration. In an exhortation to U.S. business, Hurley fretted that Americans were losing the competition for markets around the world in part because Americans remained so linguistically parochial. "Schools of Oriental languages were established by the various governments in Berlin, Vienna, Paris and Vladivostok," he told his readers. Further, "These schools offer primarily a commercial education." He then chided, "As far as I am aware, commercial training for this promising field in the East seems to have been wholly neglected in our country.") Foreign-language electives notwithstanding, as Alfred Chandler noted, "the initial offerings of the new Harvard Business School indicate a concern from the start with the training of managers for large multiunit enterprises."[9] Wharton, therefore, created a model of undergraduate business education: specialized courses, sprinkled with a few liberal arts offerings, taken after students had already completed two years of a liberal arts program. Harvard's graduate program assumed students would enroll with a liberal arts degree already in hand and offered specialized and technical courses.

Today, of course, business schools come in three basic flavors: the undergraduate business school, the graduate business school, and the school that offers both undergraduate and graduate degrees. And here is yet another difference between business education and the medical and law schools that business schools hoped to emulate. As the training of doctors and lawyers became fully absorbed by universities, that training took place after students graduated with an undergraduate degree. No one graduates with an undergraduate major in medicine and goes off to see patients. But certainly during the first half of the twentieth century the vast majority of business degrees awarded were of the undergraduate variety—graduate degrees, particularly MBAs, grew in popularity after the war. This created something of a curricular debate that has continued since the early twentieth century: At the undergraduate level, how to balance the professional courses in things like marketing and accounting with some broader, more expansive exposure to the liberal arts? At the graduate degree level, should students be admitted who already had business degrees or should MBA programs fill themselves with liberal arts majors instead?

At either level, this tension between business and liberal arts courses continues to exist precisely because business has not succeeded in developing an intellectual domain of its own and of the sort commensurate with a profession or academic discipline. It reflects an uneasiness inside business schools that what they teach does not really constitute serious academic work at a modern university. Call it a lack of intellectual self-confidence, and it has been woven into the fabric of business schools from the very beginning. Doctors in training probably ought to read more poetry or study history, but med schools themselves have not anguished to nearly the same extent over the basics of what doctors need to learn. Nor have the engineers, as anyone with an engineering degree will attest. There is a broad consensus of what should be studied—with variations across the different kinds of engineering—and the sequence of when those courses should be taken.

The confusion over what should be taught proved no impediment to growth. Business schools began to multiply during the First World War, and they proliferated in the 1920s. Membership in the AACSB had grown to 42 by the end of the decade, and as many as 117 colleges and universities had established some form of business school on campus between 1919 and 1924, and roughly 400 were offering some business curriculum.[10] Yet as Eliot Mears at Stanford described it in 1923, "At the present time courses in commerce are offered in the majority of colleges and universities, but the scope and contents are heterogeneous and seem to have no static place. They start in almost anywhere in the undergraduate curriculum and end almost any-where."[11] Advertising, precursor to contemporary marketing, arrived in the curriculum in the 1920s as did "management," a somewhat fuzzily de-fined grab bag of ideas about how to most effectively supervise workers. That latter was embodied in Walter Dill Scott's 1923 book *Personnel Management: Principles, Practices and Point of View*. Drawing from Freudian psycho-analysis, industrial psychology, and the shop-floor efficiency techniques of Frederick Winslow Taylor, *Personnel Management* proved influential on campus and off.[12]

For their part, businesses were willing to help sort things out. In 1928, the U.S. Chamber of Commerce surveyed local chambers to find out what educational work they were doing. The chamber discovered that a number were working with collegiate business schools to, in the words of the cham-ber in Portland, Oregon, broaden "their curriculum with reference to com-mercial subjects."[13] But having a college curriculum designed by the local chamber of commerce hardly provided much gravitas.

This muddle is surely part of what prompted Wharton professors James Brossard and Frederic Dewhurst to undertake an extensive survey of busi-ness schools during the academic year 1929–30. They published their result in a large book the following year.

The book provides a thorough and useful snapshot of the state of business education at the end of the Roaring Twenties. By their estimation, roughly 23,000 college graduates were entering the private sector annually, almost a third of whom were graduates of business schools. At the same time, while college enrollments overall had increased by two and a half times between 1915 and 1926, enrollments in college business schools grew by more than six times, leading the authors to declare, presciently as things turned out, that "academic training for business is an integral part of modern educa-tional plans. The collegiate school of business is neither an isolated incident nor an experimental fad." Invoking the now-fifty-year-old analogy, Brossard and Dewhurst believed that business schools and the education they offered stood alongside other "vocational" programs at colleges and universities, like medicine, law, engineering, and social service administration.[14]

Yet despite the charts and tables that filled their study and despite the care-fully collected data about enrollments, courses offered, and degrees granted, the two Wharton professors were somewhat more vague about exactly what a business education was in 1930. They echoed the broad consensus that had emerged about business education, writing that it "should involve primary emphasis upon a broad and sound understanding of the forces and problems confronting our industrial civilization rather than upon mere technical familiarity with the superficial routine of business operations." Pause here, and note that Brossard and Dewhurst did not describe what those problems were or even how they should be studied in a business school; nor did they sketch by what method, theory, or practice that "sound understanding" should be arrived at. Later in the book, they were no more specific: "The content of the curriculum should recognize the educational necessity of a broad background of general and cultural knowledge, appreciation of the social and ethical aspects of the material studied." If one of the original purposes of a college business education was to train men for the more rarified work of upper-level management in large U.S. corporations, Brossard and Dewhurst had to acknowledge, "it is questionable how far university training can be successful in developing the capacity for leadership," though they did find that "certain aspects of executive work are definitely teachable."[15] The goals and aspirations of business education had been clear since the 1880s, but how to achieve them remained as elusive in 1930 as it had been a half century earlier.

The confusion over what to teach, naturally, created an equivalent conundrum over who should teach. Collegians might sneer at the quality of instruction given at the proprietary business schools, but if they were honest, they had to acknowledge that their faculties were not necessarily much better. L. C. Marshall, the dean of the University of Chicago's business school, pulled no punches about it all. In 1928 he undertook a study of collegiate schools of business and found that the teaching, in the main, was lousy. He put it this way: "If a visiting scholar from Mars were to make the rounds of the nearly two hundred colleges and universities which allege that they have instructing staffs in business, he would find the general situation all but incredible."[16]

But maybe none of this mattered. Brossard and Dewhurst also checked in with businessmen and employers as part of their study, and what they found must have been deflating to college leaders trying to craft their curricula to suit the needs of business. "Employers . . . are sometimes reluctant to engage the most brilliant scholars," they found, suggesting that employers in the 1920s were no more interested in whether junior executives knew their Herodotus and their Heine than employers had been in an earlier generation.

The University of Wisconsin's William Scott reported that when he talked to business leaders, some "went so far as to claim that the College of Letters and Science not only did not train for business, but actually spoiled good business material."[17]

Instead, businessmen were looking for character, not skills or knowledge, in their new hires. Businessmen were "insistent that the men they employ possess the requisite personal traits and attitudes which make for success in cooperative enterprises." Things don't seem to have changed much four years after Brossard and Dewhurst's study when a survey of five hundred businessmen found that "the trouble with the young college graduate just entering the business world is that he has an inflated sense of his ability and importance, and, consequently demands a better job than he deserves."[18]

Without being altogether cynical about it, we might infer that employers may have recruited from the new business schools precisely because they were *not* training "the most brilliant scholars." When Edmund James addressed the conference at the University of Illinois to inaugurate the new business school there in 1913, he reminisced about the students he encountered when he was at Wharton by quipping, "Some students with whom other departments were not satisfied were thrown out of them and into ours as the newest department of all, until the nickname which the Wharton School of Finance and Economy had was Botany Bay." In 1931 Brossard and Dewhurst found that the British penal colony analogy still applied. College athletes, many of whom had gravitated to business schools, "reported earning considerably above those of other graduates," and as an aside they noted, "Incidentally, athletes also had the poorest scholastic records."[19] Cynical or not, it is hard to avoid the paradox that, on the one hand, American business wanted the social prestige that came with higher education, but on the other hand, American business did not want to hire the brightest bulbs in the chandelier, at least if the wattage was measured by more rigorous collegiate standards.

Serving Which Master?

Sophisticated academics, especially in humanities departments, will tell you that there is no such thing as the disinterested pursuit of knowledge. They will explain that knowledge is simply the exercise of power. All claims to truth are merely political positions—except, apparently, that one. Whether you find that point of view persuasive or tendentious, it is hard to argue that business schools found themselves confronting that view when they tried to promote academic research as an integral part of what they did.

They did so by opening "bureaus of business research"—that was the most common term before the Second World War—which proliferated during the first decades of the twentieth century. Not every business school set up one of these bureaus. They were confined largely to those universities already regarded as prestigious and where scholarship and publication were increasingly becoming the coin of the realm. Harvard led the way, opening its bureau in 1911, just three years after its B-school itself opened its doors. Nineteen opened during the 1920s and another ten during the 1930s, according to one survey. Berkeley did not get around to opening its bureau until 1941, despite repeated pleas from the Bay Area business community.[20] Designed at one level to carry out research projects in business, they existed at another level to demonstrate that business schools had research programs like other parts of the university. Professions, and disciplines, create new knowledge through the process of research and publication, and bureaus of business research set out to show that business deserved to be treated as a serious intellectual topic and that the business school truly did belong on campus.

Fair enough. Yet the establishment of these bureaus begged certain questions: What kind of research? Sponsored by what organizations? And for the benefit of whom? After all, as one commentator noted matter-of-factly in 1921, "University schools of business were first started for the most part on the initiative of business men. . . . And this is as it should be."[21] Findley Weaver, writing in 1938, summarized the dilemma concisely: "Does the bureau take the public view or does it serve special interests?"[22] Think of it as a question of prepositions. Should universities conduct research *for* business or *about* business? Medical research, investigations of the law, and innovations in engineering all took the public view, or they were supposed to at any rate. Serving special interests violated many people's sense of the very purpose of a university.

Thus was the battle joined.

Serving special interests certainly had its defenders in between the wars. Speaking to the Illinois Chamber of Commerce on "the university's service to business," Edward Fitzpatrick told the assembled businessmen, "The university would stimulate in modern business the intellectual element and the ideal element, and thereby contribute to its efficiency, viewed even in the matter of dollars and cents." University-based research could make business better: "It would substitute for a rule of thumb, scientific principles; for experience, knowledge; for immediate gains, a comprehensive view of the business as a public service institution, serving the community as well as making profits for the owner." He pressed the point more succinctly a few moments later: "There are two specific services that the university may render to modern business. The first is the training of the type of man to meet the conditions of business in the Twentieth Century. The other is the utilization of research for the development of business."[23]

Those who saw no problem with using the university to foster the development of business sometimes made an agricultural analogy. "The agricultural interests have their farm bureaus to bring them the newest and best of scientific agriculture," A. C. Littleton of the University of Illinois pointed out at a roundtable on the subject. He continued, "The business interests have nothing to correspond to these." Lewis Haney, who taught at NYU's business school, concurred and offered a variation on the analogy: "In general," he told a group gathered in 1923, "the University Bureau of Business Research should be regarded as the University's business laboratory. . . . The slogan of the University Bureau should be 'Extending the Service of the University.'"[24]

For his part, Haney made no apologies that "in New York University most of the faculty do outside work for various industrial and commercial concerns." He nodded toward the disinterested ideal by insisting that such work "must retain its scientific integrity" and must not "lose the social point of view." But his description of NYU's bureau of business research certainly made it sound self-interested, at least from the point of view of the faculty. "The Bureau of Business Research," he told the roundtable, "may serve as a middleman in marketing the services of competent faculty members who may be called in as experts to deal with the subject in which they are qualified."[25] Haney did not specify what cut the middleman took brokering these arrangements.

However neat the analogy between agricultural extension programs and bureaus of business research, Findley Weaver was not persuaded. Farmers were individual, small-scale business operators, not enormous corporate enterprises (that would come later), and on top of that, most farmers, in Weaver's view at any rate, were backward and benighted. In contrast, "a great part of commerce and manufacturing is carried out on a large scale by highly competent specialists who are able to work out for themselves the best policies in conducting their business." In Weaver's view, it was not clear who was helping whom. As he surveyed the landscape in 1938, he found, "It is, therefore, frequently the case that those who are studying business problems from a scientific point of view go to the business man to find the answer to their questions, rather than for the business man to go to the economist or expert in business administration."[26]

Besides, what kind of research could universities do for business that was not being done already at public expense? Z. Clark Dickinson noted just that for readers of the *Economic Journal* in 1925: "My readers doubtless noticed that the functions which I have mentioned as being carried out by the university organs are also exercised by a growing number of governmental bureaux, such as those with our State departments of labour and industries, and in our federal departments of Commerce, Labour, and Agriculture, for example, or in the Federal Reserve system and Federal Trade Commission." Given that, Dickinson went on to wonder whether these research bureaus were "actually worth their keep to business supporters" and confessed, "I am a little doubtful."[27] Those doubts might have been exacerbated for anyone listening to the dinner talk given by NYU's Haney on February 19, 1931. There he confidently predicted a quick end to the economic "recession."[28]

Nonetheless, support them they did. Dickinson noted that these bureaus usually started with a push from local business interests. Northwestern's version, launched in 1918, was assisted by the National Association of Retail Clothiers, for example. The bureau at the University of Denver began at the prompting of the city's chamber of commerce. Founded in 1924, the business school of the chamber and the university created "a joint research statistical and publicity bureau" with a particular focus on "the business and economic problems confronting Denver and Colorado." The collaboration must have looked exciting, reservations like Dickinson's notwithstanding. The following year the bureau received $37,500 "to enlarge its work" from the Laura Spelman Rockefeller Foundation. Looking at it all, Dickinson concluded, "Business houses are paying enormous sums to their trade associations, accounting firms, 'management and efficiency' experts, and so on, for goods which differ from those supplied by the university bureau chiefly as to the colours with which they are painted by their salesmen."[29]

These bureaus also became another target at which satirists could take aim. Dickinson noted that their partnerships with business associations tainted them. These "stigmata" he observed, "lead some by-standers to call the movement a travesty on research." C. E. Ayers was even more indignant: "By special invitation the more intricate problems of commercial chicanery are submitted to the staff of the university department to be solved with the eager assistance of the squads of novices. All this in the name of 'extension service,' 'cooperation with related industries,' and—crowning insolence of humanitarian cant—the 'Bureau of Business Research.'"[30]

Most of the bureaus of business research that started between the wars did not survive too long into the postwar world. Some closed, others morphed into other kinds of research ventures commensurate with the changed landscape of American higher education. In Denver, the bureau of business research, which had already been changed into the Bureau of Business and Social Research, was subsumed by the university's Division of Research. University administrators wanted the new bureau to produce more publishable, academically respectable work rather than function primarily as a service to the local business community.[31]

Ohio's dry cleaners provide a useful illustration of this trajectory. Ohio State's bureau, modeled on Harvard's, had been established in 1925. Just after the war, it began to publish a statistical bulletin about the dry cleaning industry and sent it every month to Ohio's dry cleaners. In 1964, however, the research bureau's director, James Yocum, sent a letter to Charles Truxal, executive secretary of the Ohio Dry Cleaners Association with some sad news: "I've been meaning to write to you for some time to express my regret upon the termination . . . of the monthly statistical Bulletin." Yocum explained, "The termination of this Bulletin is in accordance with the new directions we are giving our Bureau of Research program—viz., to place more emphasis on research of a more fundamental nature, and to curtail 'service-type' projects unless they are at the request of and have the overwhelming support of the members of a specific industry or trade." Besides, Yocum had to acknowledge that the dry cleaners didn't really care much about the data: "The smallness of the number of firms participating was indicative of lack of interest in your industry in this kind of information. Since industry interest did not expand over the years and apparently could not be increased, I think the right thing to do was to discontinue the program." Yocum concluded with the almost self-effacing "hope that the efforts expended on behalf of the Ohio dry cleaning industry did make some small contribution over the years."[32] Maybe Z. Clark Dickinson had been right in 1925 when he wondered whether these university bureaus provided anything businesses really needed. In any event, in 1968 OSU's bureau of business research morphed into the Center for Business and Economic Research. The goal here, as in Denver, was to produce more academically respectable research and to encourage "collaborative research efforts of faculty from the College of Administrative Science, the College of Social and Behavioral Sciences, and other colleges."[33]

Still, the prepositional tension remained for the research projects carried out in collegiate business schools. Dickinson recognized the problem in 1925: Should these bureaus conduct "research *about* business" or "research *for* business"?[34] That tension remains. Statistical tables for Ohio's dry cleaners to one side, does the public really benefit from business school research or do private businesses? More to the point, especially at public universities, should public money be spent for work that business ought to pay for itself?

Professors of Tax Evasion

The struggles of those who ran business schools to figure out just what to teach their students and in what proportions had exactly no effect on the proliferation of these schools after the First World War or on their enrollments, which continued to climb across the decade of the 1920s. If Calvin Coolidge captured the ethos of the decade when he told a gathering of newspaper editors in 1925 that "the chief business of the American people is business," he might have added a corollary that in the 1920s the business of American higher education was fast becoming business education.

Simultaneously, of course, the celebration of business in the 1920s generated its own reaction in the form of satire and mockery. Sinclair Lewis, most famously, inserted a new word into the U.S. lexicon when he created the character George Babbitt in the 1922 novel of the same name. "Babbitt" has become a term to describe "a business or professional man who conforms unthinkingly to prevailing middle-class standards," and in 1930 Lewis became the first American to win a Nobel Prize in Literature. From a distance of nearly a hundred years, satirizing the business culture of the twenties seems almost too easy to do. Bruce Barton's recasting of the story of Jesus Christ as a tale of a business go-getter in his book *The Man Nobody Knows* seems genuinely farcical today, but it topped the best-seller list in 1925. Barton was a founder of modern advertising, and his fellow adman Earnest Elmo Calkins, not to be outdone by his competitor, published *Business the Civilizer* in 1928. The title more or less captures the thesis of this work, but Calkins made it explicit at the very beginning nonetheless: "Business runs the world. The world gets civilized just as fast as men learn to run things on plain business principles."[35]

So it should come as no surprise that business schools found themselves on the receiving end of Lewis-like mockery in the 1920s. Arlington Stone was particularly merciless as he savaged what he saw as the pretentions of these "seminaries" of business. They dotted the landscape north and south, east and west, Arlington wrote, and their evident deficiencies notwithstanding, these "shrines . . . seem to be making money. Indeed," he continued, "next to football teams and schools of education, they are probably the biggest money-getters in the world of the intellect. At some places, as at N.Y.U. for example, it's only the takings of the School of Commerce that enable the Chancellor to pay the university's bills."[36]

Tongue firmly in cheek, Stone observed that "the main pride of these seminaries . . . is their scientific method," and he illustrated this by quoting generously from the course catalogs of various business schools in what amounted to a petard-hoisting exercise. The University of Cincinnati's offerings, Stone told his readers, included "Advanced Traffic Management, Pistol Marksmanship, and The Handling of Explosives." He wasn't finished with Cincinnati: "The most original touch, however, appears in Packing House Operations. Divided into two sections, known as Pork Operations and Beef Operations, this new science is given by the Cincinnati professors with the help of *intelligenzia* lent by the Institute of American Meat Packers and the Association of Cincinnati Meat Packers."

And so it unsparingly went. Stone asked readers to pause over courses in "scientific laundering" and "equipping the kitchen," both available at NYU. "Boston may be on its last legs in literature and art," Stone archly wrote, "but in the science of commercial engineering it is certainly alive and kicking." Especially at Boston University. There "the B.U. business engineer is . . . given a chance to engorge the latest scientific data about Easter gifts, indelible ink, lubricating oil, tooth-powder, soap-powder, automobiles, men's furnishings, celluloid novelties, pianos, theatrical productions, perfumery, and confectionery."[37]

Poking fun at such a litany was easy, especially in H. L. Mencken's *American Mercury*, where snide was the house style. In fact, "Stone" might well have been Mencken himself. But the business schools of the 1920s fared no better at the *New Republic*, where C. E. Ayers began his more earnest essay by telling readers that business schools were, in essence, cheating their students. "Most of these," he announced, "are getting a business training by scamping their college education. The enterprise of liberal education is suffering accordingly, and all educators know it." Though he was considerably less funny than Stone, Ayers conveyed his belief that a business education did not amount to a real college education. "The logic of the school of business is a logic not of education but of business," Ayers stipulated, and what followed from it was almost inevitable: "A shift in the center of gravity of a university, still more of higher education generally, will sooner or later affect every department of learning however remote from commerce and finance." Case in point? Ayers offered the University of Pennsylvania, where in 1925 just over a thousand students had enrolled in the college, while 2500 students were getting their degrees in the Wharton School.

Beyond the intramural dynamics, Ayers saw almost philosophical issues at stake. "Humanism," he pleaded, "culture, gets its definition by contrast with commerce and industry. . . . The two are incompatible. The period of education which youth is allowed for the cultivation of its mind cannot be shared with apprenticeship for trade because the two cannot be mixed." Ayers was just warming up. Mixing the two, he went on, would corrupt the entire university enterprise: "Not only does the institution as a whole bend the knee to Mammon; he has his personal representatives upon its staff, his professors of financial manipulation, instructors in labor management, and assistant professors of tax-dodging. Under the auspices of the School of Mammonry the foremost buccaneers of the period pass in solemn procession through the academic groves bearing the palms of special lecturers."[38]

Professors of tax dodging took things too far. Probably. But satirists like Stone and critics like Ayers could go after the business schools precisely because the schools themselves remained uncertain about exactly what to teach their students and how, and they had failed to demonstrate just what their utility was. What's more, even some business school supporters had to agree, at least tacitly, with these kinds of critiques. As one writer put it about accounting, a staple at both the old proprietary schools and the newer collegiate ones, "in a half-century of experience of a society of chartered accountants, not a single fundamental economic principle has been determined."[39] That is hardly an intellectual basis on which to build an academic enterprise.

W. H. Lough did not object in principle to collegiate schools of business. Lough, who worked for the Business Training Corporation of New York and who therefore might have seen these schools as the competition, simply did not see the need for the fancy window dressing that business schools wanted to put on their education. "My first postulate," he wrote in the *Journal of Political Economy*, "is that business education should be designed to educate men for business." An "innocent enough" statement, Lough offered, but he knew it amounted to a swipe at what he saw as the puffed-up aspirations of these business schools. He recognized that "it is tantamount to saying that our university schools of business are vocational schools. If anyone dislikes the sound of the word 'vocational,' I am quite willing to substitute 'professional.'" Lough did not want to quibble over the semantics: "The essential point is that the aim of courses on instruction in business is . . . to develop work-a-day knowledge and skill."[40] Using "vocational" and "professional" interchangeably must have caused leaders at many collegiate business schools to grind their molars—the distinction between "vocational" and "professional" was precisely the raison d'être of business schools in the first place.

Lough's specific concern was how best to teach finance, and what he saw, writing in 1921, did not please him. Quoting a Professor Moulton, Lough agreed that "courses in the field of finance have, until very recently at least, just grown—without any attempt to organize the material into a coherent whole." One might say, like business schools themselves, but Lough thought he knew why this was the case. "I cannot believe that so elaborate a program is called for," he wrote about courses in finance. He continued, "It is the outgrowth, as I see it, of a conception of finance as a vaguely mysterious 'science of funds,' which can be grasped only by superior minds that are trained to grapple with large figures." Finance simply was not that complicated, Lough asserted, but those who taught it at universities had made it needlessly so. They would be "severely shocked," Lough charged on, "at the idea that forethought in providing payment for the family wash would deserve to rank as a genuine financial operation. The truth is that the essential principles of art of handling money and credit are simple and almost self-evident."[41] That hardly sounded like the description of a science or of a profession.

Harvard got into the business of business education in 1908 when its graduate school of business was founded. In the early 1920s, and under the leadership of Dean Wallace Donham, it thought it had solved the curricular problem. The B-school began to teach using case studies, just as they had been doing over at the law school for decades. Donham explained as this new system was launched, "The business school should furnish a background of facts and general principles upon which the mind trained in the solution of executive problems by the educational processes of the school may react."[42] Despite that turbid explanation, the case-study method was regarded as a brilliant innovation, and it has been adopted widely.

In fact, borrowing the case-study approach from law schools was conceptually flawed, perhaps fatally so. The principles of law are built on precedents that derive from cases. By contrast, what goes on inside one particular business organization and in one particular circumstance does not in any meaningful way dictate what goes on in all others. The Berkeley B-school dean Ewald Grether understood this completely when he said to an interviewer, "The law is never established until there's been a series of judicial decisions. ... A law is built case by case. Now, some people thought that perhaps we could use the case method in business. You could have a file of cases, a library of cases. Then you'd get a problem, you'd punch the computer, and out comes case so-and-so and the answer they gave at the time. Well, we haven't arrived there yet; I doubt if we ever will arrive there."[43] The analogy between law and business simply does not hold, because case law is cumulative, whereas business cases are taught on the assumption that inferences can be drawn from one case that apply in others. That might be true; it might well not be.

Whatever the merits of the case-study method, it did not settle the debates over what to teach in American business schools and certainly not at the undergraduate level. In truth, the case-study approach cleverly sidestepped the central intellectual question faced by any discipline or profession: is there a specific and coherent body of knowledge around which the study of business could cohere?

By the middle decades of the twentieth century the jury still seemed to be out on that matter. In 1940 Paul Cherington, a veteran of business education and former professor of marketing at Harvard, cited "a recent study of the catalog descriptions of the marketing courses given in about 50 leading American colleges," which found "a sad paucity of invention in such work."[44] By that time, thousands of academic degrees had been granted for courses of study that no one really believed had much academic integrity.

The Lapse of Ethics

The first curriculum at Berkeley's College of Commerce in 1898 included a course called "The History and Principles of Commercial Ethics."

As we discussed in chapter 1, some Progressive-era reformers, inside higher education and out, saw a collegiate education in business as an antidote to the rapacious and amoral culture of U.S. corporate capitalism, as a curative for its worst excesses. Higher education meant giving future business leaders higher ideals and a higher purpose, or so the faithful believed.

As collegiate business schools popped up and enrollments swelled, that reforming impulse focused more specifically on the role ethics could or should play in the business school curriculum. Ethics taught in college, the reasoning went, would create businessmen who would both do well and do good. Talk of turning business into a noble profession in the late nineteenth century had been vague; ethics offered a specific avenue through which to reach the goal. "Business . . . is far from being a profession," Harvey Aldon Wooster wrote from the University of Missouri in 1919, precisely "because it lacks the ethical codes of service that distinguish the professions." When Harvard's business school dedicated its new building in 1923, Owen Young told the assembled, "Today and here business formally assumes the obligations of a profession, which means responsible action as a group, devotion to its own ideals, the creation of its own codes, the capacity for its own discipline, the awards of its own honors, and the responsibility for its own service."[45]

Edward Jones saw ethics as part and parcel of the larger goal to make business an academically rigorous field. Writing in 1913, he exhorted his colleagues, "It is our duty to raise industrial activity to the plane of an intellectual pursuit, governed by a high code of professional ethics." Writing in the same year, A. B. Wolfe, who taught at Oberlin College, worried about allowing undergraduates to study business. He certainly acknowledged "the great necessity for the development of commercial education in this country," but he cautioned that "we need to guard it, in the *undergraduate years*, very carefully." If undergraduates, presumably young, impressionable, and easily seduced by the lure of moneymaking, were permitted to pursue courses in finance and marketing and real estate, then, Wolfe believed, their education "should include a carefully planned course in business ethics and commercial morality."[46] As we have seen already, those in the late nineteenth century who wanted business to be viewed as a profession and who saw collegiate business schools as the vehicle through which to achieve that status, routinely pointed to medicine, law, and the ministry as analogies. Wolfe's hypothetical course in "commercial morality" might split the difference between business and theology.

It would seem hard to argue with the idea of teaching ethics, but just after the First World War, W. H. Lough did just that. When he insisted that the purpose of business schools was to train students with that "work-a-day knowledge and skill," he juxtaposed that knowledge with ethics, writing that the job of business schools was precisely "not to cultivate cultural or ethical insight." Besides, advertiser Earnest Elmo Calkins asserted, the problem had been solved. "Even the most jaundiced observer must admit," he wrote, "that business is ethically better than it used to be." How Calkins measured that improvement he did not say, but ever the adman he went on to claim that business "is attracting the men who once gravitated to the old professions, because it now offers not only the interest appeal of the older professions, but also the higher ethical standards."[47] Calkins wrote that in 1928, a year before those higher ethical standards would contribute to the collapse of the U.S. economy.

For those on college campuses, however, the question of whether or how to teach ethics to business students remained unresolved by the end of the 1920s. Ralph Heilman, the dean of Northwestern University's business school, delivered a public lecture in 1929 in which he laid out the dilemma as he saw it. Begging to differ with the likes of Calkins and Lough, he started by saying, "In the development of collegiate business education thus far, one important factor has been largely overlooked—the necessity for developing a strong sense of social and ethical obligation in the student preparing to enter the business world." More to the point, Dean Heilman challenged the notion that "merely training young men to increase their earning capacity does not constitute adequate justification for the inclusion of business instruction in university curricula." It was not sufficient for college business schools like his "to provide the young man with better tools for business" without also "inculcat[ing] in him a strong sense of social obligation in his use of such tools." Offering that combination of useful, moneymaking skills with some sense of an ethical compass was, in Heilman's view, the obligation of a business school. He told the crowd, "The maintenance of colleges of commerce and business administration is justified only in so far as they promote an increase in our productive capacity, an equitable distribution of the products of industry, and better service by the business system to the needs of society." He drove the point home by invoking, yet again, the comparison between business and other, more established professions. "The older professional schools have long recognized the necessity for developing standards of professional ethics," he said. Acknowledging that business schools had not yet risen to this challenge, he continued, "It is clear that the ethical point of view is entitled to far greater and more specific recognition than it has been accorded heretofore."[48]

If the promise of joining ethics with business education to create a real profession remained unfulfilled in the decade after the First World War, the situation does not seem to have improved much after the Second. The University of Southern California business professor Lawrence Lockley had grown impatient with the barbs directed at business schools and pushed back: "I suspect that the charges leveled at business education—in view of the tremendous growth of the liberal-arts curriculum—are more properly indictments of college-level education as a whole." Even so, he admitted in 1951 that he and his colleagues "must teach our students to recognize and accept social responsibility." Further, "we must teach our students to accept and to follow ethical standards."[49] Two decades after Dean Heilman had said virtually the same thing, ethics and social responsibility were apparently still missing from the fabric of a business school education.

In 1958, Clark Kerr, perhaps the most influential figure in American higher education after the war, traveled to Pittsburgh to speak at the University of Pittsburgh. His topic: business schools. Thirty years after Heilman gave his lecture, Kerr found himself questioning the basic equation between ethics, professionalization, and business. "It is often said that management should become a 'profession,'" Kerr remarked. (It's worth pausing over the word "should." After all, by 1958 business education had been making the claim that it amounted to professional training for three-quarters of a century.) He went on, "If what is meant by 'profession' is what is usually meant by 'profession'—a code of ethics and entry only after a period of controlled training—then we should take a second look at the phrase."[50] Kerr was skeptical. Teaching ethics might, or might not, have been able to give business education the imprimatur of professionalism. Either way, it does not seem to have been given much of a chance.

The Great Earthquake of 1959

When Clark Kerr gave that speech about business schools, his sense was that at that moment "schools of business administration are trying, sometimes almost desperately, to find their souls." That might have struck some in the crowd as perplexing. After all, as Kerr noted, "the school of business has really come of age only since World War II," and since the end of the war student enrollments had more than doubled. And he added, perhaps with a bit of cheek, "The work is now called 'business' instead of 'commerce,' and that seems to make quite a difference. The changed terminology, though not inherent in the words themselves, seems to carry the aura of 'executive' instead of 'merchant.'"[51] In fact, at Berkeley, Kerr's home institution, that name change had taken place in 1943, shortly after Ewald Grether became dean. "The College of Commerce in its old form had outlived its usefulness," Grether recalled years later, and "my major job was to reorganize our entire structure and also to get ready for the postwar period."[52] Changing the name was the first step in that reorganization.

Business (education) was certainly booming. Business (or commerce) degrees constituted 3 percent of all undergraduate degrees awarded in 1920. By 1940 that figure had risen to 10 percent. By 1950, 17 percent, or roughly 72,000, of graduating seniors had majored in business. They attended one of the 163 business schools found on college campuses in 1950, an increase of 150 since 1910. Importantly, business schools no longer resided only at the venerable private institutions—Penn, Dartmouth, Harvard, Chicago. According to one survey, between 1914 and 1940 "almost every important public university in the United States established a school of business."[53] Business education, along with the rest of higher education, had become more democratized.

But the bigger issues remained unresolved in Kerr's estimation. Business education "is here to stay," Kerr acknowledged, "but it has not yet made peace with itself or with the rest of the academic world." Business schools still had not figured out even what to teach their students: "What subjects should be taught in economics," Kerr asked, "and what in business administration?" As Kerr saw it, business schools had "jurisdictional problems," and he explained, "If business administration has not yet settled its jurisdictional claims over subject matter, it has also not reached a consensus about its approach to its disputed subject matter. It lives in two worlds—the academic and the business."

Kerr was fully aware of the difficulties faced by these schools, and he framed it as a "hard choice." If business schools simply served the needs and interests of businesses, "it can never demonstrate high enough intellectual attainment to gain more than the second-class citizenship it now largely holds in the academic world." On the other hand, if the business school strove to be more strictly academic, "it has a problem carving out a discipline of its own which will distinguish it from economics and which will have enough inherent possibilities to permit its followers to gain intellectual stature." Described this way, Kerr did make the problem of the American business school's soul sound not merely curricular or institutional but almost existential.

In the middle of this diagnosis, Kerr offhandedly mentioned that "two of the leading foundations have joined in this urgent quest" to find the soul of the American business school.[54] That might have taken some of those gathered in Pittsburgh by surprise, but Kerr was right. In what is either an example of kismet in the foundation world or an extraordinary philanthropic redundancy, both the Carnegie Corporation and the Ford Foundation were busy studying and producing reports about the state of American business education even as Kerr gave his lecture.

Carnegie came to the idea in 1954, and late in the year the corporation, through its vice president, James Perkins, tried to recruit G. L. Bach, dean of the business school at the Carnegie Institute of Technology, to direct a survey of U.S. B-schools. There wasn't, I don't think, anything institutionally incestuous about that—the business school at the Carnegie Institute in Pittsburgh caught the eye of observers as being innovative and rigorous, and Bach had already prepared his own confidential report on business schools for the corporation. In any event, Bach turned Perkins down, and he did so somewhat sourly. "The biggest problems facing the business schools and business education," he wrote to Perkins, "are not, in my judgment, factors that will be readily divulged by any survey of the business schools, or that can be readily spelled out bluntly and openly in a general, public report." He was specific about what he saw as wrong with business education: "The problems are inadequate and poorly trained faculties, a narrow a-intellectual atmosphere in the business schools and among the student bodies, the absence of a tradition of intellectual inquiry and research, and the failure of the system to produce a substantial number of potential leaders for teaching and research in the future. While all of these facts must be obvious to any wide-eyed observer . . . none of these is supportable by the superficial evidence provided by college curricula, student enrollment data, and other such 'objective' facts."[55] As far as Bach was concerned, why bother with such a study?

Undaunted, Carnegie went ahead anyway and found its man the following year on the Swarthmore College campus: economics professor Frank Pierson. In 1956 the corporation awarded Swarthmore and Pierson a grant of $100,000 (nearly $900,000 in 2017 dollars) to undertake the survey and study of U.S. business schools. An internal Carnegie memo laid out the research objectives for the study: "1. What are the varieties of business schools? Obviously they aren't all alike, but we know little about the range. We need a taxonomic study. 2. What kinds of curricula may be identified in the various schools? How do they vary? How does the business school curriculum compare in vigor and quality to the other schools on the same campus? 3. What kinds of students are the business schools getting? Are they being used as a dumping ground on some campuses? Or as an easy degree? 4. To what extent is the business school curriculum dominated by a spurious 'practicality' . . . ignoring fundamental skills and disciplines which will permit adaptation to a broad range of situations?" When the corporation approved the award, the resolution announced, "There has never been a serious attempt to evaluate objectively the kind of education this large segment (= 15%) of the American student population is receiving."[56]

At the same moment, the Ford Foundation was embarking on its own study, and the foundation found its research talent in California, engaging the University of California economist Robert Aaron Gordon and the Stanford economist James Howell to do the work. People at Ford might have been intrinsically interested in the question of business schools during the postwar expansion of U.S. higher education but they also found the study to be an expedient project to undertake during the nation's McCarthy moment. As James Howell remembered, it was "a combination of education and business, it was politically safe. This last point had special significance, for the Foundation . . . had been the target of a variety of attacks, especially from a couple of Congressmen and the conservative press." In other words, a study of business and education "was a philanthropoid's dream." Howell also remembered that Ford had a three-part objective in working with business schools: first, to "raise the academic respectability of business education"; second, to "reorient higher education for business so that it would better serve the needs of American management"; and finally, to "achieve greater efficiency in the use of educational opportunities"[57]

Whatever prompted the foundations to take up the task of studying business education, foundation officers and the researchers they hired shared a set of assumptions going into their work. Or rather one basic assumption: U.S. business education was terrible. One member of the Carnegie staff attended an AACSB meeting of business school deans in 1957 and reported back: "The deans as a group are not an especially impressive lot." In fact, many dean chairs sat empty, the foundation official found, because "professors are reluctant to accept deanships." To move into those jobs "involves reduction of income. This is because of the loss of consulting work which results from a conscientious man becoming a dean." And lest people reassure themselves that quality had not suffered as a consequence of rapid postwar expansion, Howell disabused them. By the early 1950s, he wrote, "Wharton, the grande dame of them all, was embarrassingly mediocre. And Stanford, closely modeled on Harvard, was so isolated . . . that it didn't even realize it was on the verge of almost total obsolescence." Almost sixty years after Edmund James joked that the quality of Wharton students was so bad that the place was referred to as "Botany Bay," Gordon found that the waters had still not been cleaned up, and he said so to the AACSB. "What is striking," he told them, "is the evidence that business administration gets a much larger fraction of poor students ["poor" as in "terrible," not "economically disadvantaged"] and a smaller percentage of the best students than do the traditional professional fields."[58] Better students, in fact, might have been put off by the poor teaching. Even before the two reports of 1959, people were complaining that the faculty in business schools was subpar. "Arts and science teachers are often dedicated men," opined Duncan Norton-Taylor in 1954, "business teachers seldom are."[59]

Ford and Carnegie—Gordon, Howell, and Pierson—stumbled into each other almost from the get-go, and while officers at the two philanthropies fretted over the possible confusion, competition, and overlap their two projects might create, Gordon and Pierson seem to have crafted a perfectly cordial working relationship. In a letter Pierson wrote after a two-day meeting between the two groups at Swarthmore College in March 1957, he informed all the deans and department chairs he intended to solicit for his survey that "the Ford Foundation is conducting a similar survey but wherever possible the two studies are being dovetailed to avoid duplication. Accordingly, the results of this questionnaire will be utilized in both studies."[60] However collaborative the process of the work became, the two projects did get in each other's way when it came time to publish their results. "This business of the two studies of business education is with us again," the Carnegie vice president Perkins wrote to his Ford counterpart Tom Carroll, "I gather that Pierson and Gordon are having some difficulty getting straight the nature of the understanding about the publication of their reports."[61]

Whether they straightened things out or not, both books landed in 1959, and the thud they made upon landing was tremendous. Gordon and Howell's book came in at just under 500 pages, while Pierson's tome topped out at over 700. There are important differences between the two, but what is striking now is just how similar they are. Taken together, they amount to 1200 pages of blistering critique. Gordon and Howell: "What passes as the going standard of acceptability among business schools is embarrassingly low, and many schools of business do not meet even these low standards." Pierson: "All too many of these schools concentrate their efforts almost exclusively on average or even mediocre students; all too few call forth the best work from the best students." They agreed, too, in their assessment of the AACSB as the keeper of professional standards, or rather of its failure in that role. Gordon and Howell: "Membership in the Association provides no guarantee of excellence. It is merely a certificate of a minimal and conventional kind of respectability." Pierson, taking a slightly more historical view: "Even by 1940 only fifty-three schools belonged, twenty-eight of which were located at state universities. . . . Its standards were at no time more than minimal; the specific core requirements established in the early twenties, for example, had been dropped by World War II. . . . In general, the association lacked vigor, imagination, and any real sense of purpose during most of these years." And as if in a tag team, Gordon and Howell: "Widespread and significant reform will be difficult to achieve through the Association, which thus far has not been noteworthy for bold and vigorous action or imaginative and progressive leadership."[62]

The three authors also agreed, in broad strokes, on the remedy for this dismal state of affairs. As Pierson wrote, "The general thesis developed here is that business schools could raise the content and quality of their programs and still meet the needs of the bulk of their students." Raising standards meant, by and large, infusing business education with more study in the liberal arts. As Gordon and Howell took pains to explain, "The issue, as we see it, is not a simple choice between liberal education and business education. The issue is how to combine both, and how to insure that the business part of the combined education adequately develops the basic skills we have emphasized." In the view of all three, this was the only way to leave behind "the narrow and low-level kind of vocational training that has brought discredit on particularly the undergraduate business schools." After all, Gordon and Howell found, increasingly business leaders themselves "have come to stress the values of a liberal education and the need for 'the range of interests and the mental disciplines that education in the liberal arts or humanities is peculiarly well fitted to give.'" As things currently stood, the core of the postwar curriculum in business schools consisted of six subjects: accounting, economics, finance, management, marketing, and production. An internal memo circulated at Carnegie simplified categories even more: "The main stream of the present curriculum of collegiate schools of business comes primarily from two sources: 1) classical economics and 2) bookkeeping." That seems even less broad that the original Wharton curriculum of the 1880s suggesting that not only had the curricular confusions not been resolved but they had gotten worse. Carnegie gave a sneak preview of the study to the Carnegie Tech dean George Bach, who had turned down the corporation's offer to conduct the study himself. Bach predicted that "the Pierson book would kick up quite a storm" and that "the great majority [of business school deans] would be highly annoyed" with it. He hoped the foundation was prepared for the reactions.[63]

If all this seems overly harsh, it was not. Gordon, Howell, and Pierson were capturing in copious detail the drift of opinion about business education, inside and outside the academy, in the postwar years. *Fortune* magazine featured a story in 1954 whose title illustrated the skepticism the piece conveyed, "The Business School: Pass or Flunk?," and ran a subheader to the section on business students that read "the legion of misfits." That wasn't the snide observation of *Fortune*'s reporter, however. It was drawn from a statement by none other than the Wharton dean C. Canby Balderston, who said, "We spend most of our time with misfits and personnel problems."[64] Another writer two years later tacitly acknowledged that business education as it stood did not a profession make and urged more "zeal and rigor" in the curriculum. The only way that would happen, in his opinion, was for business education to become "more liberal." *Business Week* reported in that same year that "many are swinging to the idea that a good half of all business student courses should be in liberal arts." Even Lawrence Lockley, who thought that business education was getting a bad rap, believed that, as it improved, "we will find a closer kinship between the humanities and business education." In 1957, a committee of faculty at Wharton looked at the teaching of business after the First World War and found that it was "lacking a substantial body of theory relative to the management process, [and] management itself was often taught through description of techniques, or through the presentation of 'practical' cases. . . . [These] may have the effect of discouraging the rigorous search for basic causal relationships and theories which underlie and connect classes of problems." Given that, the committee went on, in the post–Second World War era, "it is safe to say, in this respect, that the liberal arts people have succeeded in persuading some business educators that 'too much business' in a curricular sense, is a bad thing."[65]

Liberal education was in the air in the 1950s—a faith that "liberal education provides a much-needed emphasis on the human and the humane if modern man is successfully to cope with the problems of a world increasingly unpredictable." Besides, in delivering the hard truth about business education and what was needed to improve it, the three authors were, to a certain extent, making public what leaders of business schools had been feeling queasy about for some time. "After World War II," Pierson discovered as part of his research, "many business schools were themselves evincing genuine doubts about the direction and quality of their work."[66]

However "annoyed" business schools might have been by the two books, one group of educators, at least, greeted the Carnegie and Ford reports with applause. "Those of us who operate private business schools in the shadow of the college and university business schools are happy to see once and for all the truth told about what is going on," wrote Ernest Viegel, the president of the Rochester Business Institute in Rochester, New York. He went on, "Many of us have known for a long time much of what has been reported by the two studies."[67] Given the disdain with which they had been viewed by their collegiate betters, the proprietary schools can be forgiven their fifteen minutes of schadenfreude.

The Aftershocks

"A couple of reports coming out this week," wrote *Business Week* in October 1959, "are going to knock the stuffing out of the business schools." Even before the two books hit the stores, *Business Week* summarized the conclusions of both studies for its readers. They came to the "same basic findings: Most business schools are doing a very poor job. All too often they give a sort of white-collar vocational training instead of real higher education." And it went on with the takeaways: "Academic standards are low. Business schools do not get the brighter students. . . . The undergraduate business schools . . . have become the dumping ground for inferior students who probably should not be going to college at all."[68] No punches pulled.

The magazine had been following the Carnegie and Ford projects for some months. Anticipating the recommendations that the two books would offer, *Business Week* predicted that "graduates of collegiate schools of business . . . a few years hence are likely . . . to resemble more closely the liberal arts man [because] of radical changes now taking place within the nation's B-schools." *Business Week* pointed to schools where change was already afoot. Not all readers welcomed the news. One F. C. Kirk responded angrily in the letters section—and in verse:

> We're the new B-boys, cul-
> tured, you bet,
>
> We came for Business and
> what did we get,
>
> Warmed over Arts and
> Humanities classes,
>
> We're an excellent bunch of
> hybrid asses.

The editors, not content to let this missive go unanswered, responded:

> Hybrid asses, better known
> as mules,
>
> Have always come from the
> business schools,
>
> They sweep the floors and
> shovel the snow,
>
> While the liberal arts boys
> run the show.[69]

Whatever their poetic merit, these dueling doggerels did capture the debate that Gordon, Howell, and Pierson had hoped to foster: Would adding liberal arts courses to business school curriculum produce students who understood neither business nor the liberal arts? Or would it give students the flexible skills necessary to rise in organizations where they would one day run the show?

Most business schools may have kept their stuffing in, but they were certainly chastened by the two reports. When the University of Denver celebrated the fiftieth anniversary of its business school in 1958, planners invited Robert Gordon to deliver the keynote. It must have been something of a downer for those gathered. Gordon gave the crowd a peek at his research when he told them, "A good deal of the specialization in business schools is mere window dressing designed to impress students and businessmen." He went on to stress that business students needed fewer business courses and more training in the liberal arts. Denver's dean Theodore Cutler rushed to reassure everyone "that DU had been thinking along the same lines in announcing a new curriculum for the college last week." Early in 1960 Wharton, that "embarrassingly mediocre" grande dame of business schools, announced a major overhaul of its curriculum to increase the number of liberal arts courses its students took, to take effect in the academic year 1961–62. Dean Willis Winn insisted that the changes, described by the student paper as "radical," had come from the school's curriculum committee, but the timing could hardly have been coincidental.[70]

In fact, the files of the Carnegie Corporation hold several letters from deans writing to express their gratitude for Pierson's book. "We have made some basic decisions with respect to modifying our own curriculum quite substantially," the University of Florida dean D. J. Hart wrote, continuing, "We expect to spend several months in reorienting our course content to coincide with the objectives that we are trying to reach." Likewise, the University of Minnesota dean Richard Kozelka reported, "You can rest assured that the ripples caused by the stone which Frank Pierson dropped in the pool of growing complacency will travel far."[71] Rather than being annoyed, a number of business school deans seemed to view the two studies as useful pretexts to reform their curricula.

By 1961, Carnegie declared victory. The foundation decided its work was done, and certainly Frank Pierson wanted to move on. He reported back to the corporation that "the amount of soul-searching currently going on in the business schools has far exceeded" anything he thought possible. Further, "a great many of them have accepted or are in the process of accepting the major recommendations of the Pierson and Gordon studies."[72] The project was regarded by people at Carnegie as a rousing success.

The people at Ford, however, had always had larger ambitions. In fact, sponsoring the Gordon and Howell study was only one piece of Ford's efforts to transform business education in the 1950s. By 1956, Ford was sending money to several business schools to pilot experiments in changing business education. Harvard and Carnegie Tech received the first checks from Ford, followed by Columbia, Chicago, Berkeley, MIT, and the University of California at Los Angeles. Ford had specific goals in mind, including raising the quality of students enrolled in business schools and of the faculty who taught them, increasing the teaching of "foundation disciplines" and reducing the emphasis on narrow vocational training, and encouraging an academic research program for faculty. Harvard, in fact, spent half its grant money on developing doctoral programs in the business school.

In 1960, Ford worked with the AACSB and Harvard to promote Harvard's case-study method as the gold standard in business school curriculum. Ford funded the AACSB to create the Intercollegiate Case Clearing House to collect, develop, and distribute business case studies around the country. As an internal evaluator of the grant remarked, "A conspicuous feature of new and improved programs in business education throughout the country is the increasing use being made of the case method of instruction." Thanks to the foundation, "more original cases are being written by college professors each year." By the midsixties nearly 2700 separate cases had been written by over seven hundred faculty, and the AACSB had distributed several hundred thousand of them.[73] No one at Ford, and certainly not at Harvard, asked that basic question about the efficacy of case studies in teaching foundational principles in the first place.

Even so, not everyone wanted to genuflect toward Harvard, nor were they persuaded that the case-study approach was the final answer to the question of what to teach business students. Berkeley, as we have already seen, was not impressed, and though the case-study method was discussed, it never became the way business was taught there. One student wrote gratefully to Berkeley's dean Richard Holton, saying, "I am well pleased with the school's rejection of the case study approach in favor of learning more basic and universal approaches and principles."[74] This student, however, did not mention what those principles were. The case-study method might evade the question of "basic principles," but it wasn't clear that those principles had been discovered elsewhere.

The results of Ford's campus demonstration projects turned out to have been decidedly mixed—"As primary centers . . . Chicago and Columbia were mitigated and unmitigated failures, respectively"—yet still the people at Ford talked about "revolution." A letter written in 1960 to the Ford associate director Thomas Carroll and marked "confidential" concluded that "the Foundation has been instrumental in bringing about a major revolution in the field of business education over the past five to seven years" and that "this revolution . . . is in full swing at a number of leading business schools, and is getting under way in others to varying degrees." The writer acknowledged that "there is no clear quantitative evidence available as to how much change has taken place in the great mass of the business schools," but the writer was confident that "significant parts of the revolution have begun to appear at all except one or two of the dozen leading business schools. . . . Even at many of the lesser known schools, a surprising amount of change is taking place already." The foundation had spent roughly $15 million on its business education initiatives, and the letter expressed confidence that it was "highly unlikely that any other Ford Foundation program can claim anything approaching equal impact in its field, certainly not with anything like such a small total expenditure." The letter's author was none other than the Carnegie Tech dean George Bach, so perhaps not surprisingly he also wrote, "The full revolution is most completely established at Carnegie Tech."[75]

As Bach assessed Ford's programs in this letter he also pleaded that they continue. By 1960 Ford too was preparing to declare victory and walk away from the field. Bach wrote to encourage Ford to continue its involvement, and while he was not above flattery, telling Thomas Carroll, "I think it is beyond doubt that Foundation action has been by far the single most powerful force in bringing about these changes," the flattery did not persuade. Ford wrapped up its business education projects in 1961.

Too bad too, in James Howell's estimation. Looking back on Ford's work—and his own—from the vantage of 1966 he acknowledged that, "measured against its own objectives, the Foundation effort was successful," but he found the revolution to be "incomplete." The foundation's support "faltered at a crucial time, a time when the good guys had the bad guys on the run." The people at Ford searched for other pastures, and Howell now found that, "where before there had been individuals in the Foundation who were visible externally as supporters of the revolution, there were now suddenly none."[76]

Even as Ford and Carnegie exited the scene, the AACSB stirred to life. In 1960, stung by the criticisms in both books, the AACSB sponsored no fewer than seven conferences around the country—from State College to Palo Alto, from Stillwater to Minneapolis—to discuss the reports and respond to them. (Ford provided the money to put on these conferences.) *Views on Business Education* grew out of those meetings and also appeared in 1960. Maurice Lee opened the volume with an upbeat, chirpy assessment of business schools. "Business schools are on the move," he wrote. "They are one of the dynamic forces in American higher education today." The criticisms leveled by the two studies, he insisted, had already been addressed and the problems resolved. Now business schools were incorporating disciplines like math, psychology, and sociology. Business schools did not sit on campuses like a slow-witted, embarrassingly uncouth uncle at Thanksgiving. Instead, "Today the business school is in the mainstream of the intellectual life of the university." Indeed, to hear Lee tell it, business schools "are becoming the leaders in the drive to build a stronger liberal arts background under the professional curriculum."[77]

Not everyone's glasses were so rosy. Fred Foy also contributed an essay to the AACSB's 1960 volume, and he sounded closer to Gordon, Howell, and Pierson. He acknowledged right away, "I agree with the authors of the two reports that well under half the total undergraduate curriculum needs to be devoted to technical business courses. We need only a modest amount of detailed specialization." In fact, he wrote, "I'm not even sure that [students] need a special course in each of the functional areas of business."[78]

In this, Foy sounded an awful lot like William Benton, who contributed "The Failure of Business Schools" to the *Saturday Evening Post* the following year, and what makes that worth noting is that both were high-profile businessmen. Foy was chairman of the Koppers Company and Benton was half the ad agency Benton & Bowles, among whose claims to fame is the invention of the soap opera. Benton was considerably more direct with his readers than Foy had been with his. "The blunt truth is that these programs," he began, "too often are a waste—of time, money and the priceless opportunity to prepare for successful careers." Benton joined the chorus of those bemoaning the quality of the students in these schools. "The evidence is overwhelming," he insisted, "that business courses in many cases are catchalls for inferior students who cannot or will not try to make the grade in more rigorous programs." And he made the quite dramatic suggestion, which even Gordon, Howell, and Pierson could not bring themselves to say out loud: "I'd like to see the complete elimination of undergraduate business schools and courses." In fact, the University of Chicago had done just that, phasing out its undergraduate business program in the 1940s in favor of the Harvard model, which produced only MBAs and no undergraduate degrees.[79]

Benton wrote in the wake of the Carnegie and Ford books, but the authority he invoked to say things came not from the academic world but from the world of business itself. In fact, Benton opined, "virtually all top business leaders agree a solid background in the liberal arts is the best preparation to cope with the barrage of new ideas constantly clamoring for an executive's consideration." John McCaffrey agreed, and he sat as the president of International Harvester Corporation. "The world of the specialist," McCaffrey complained, "is a narrow one and it tends to produce narrow human beings." Narrow human beings, he went on, make narrow decisions because "the specialist usually does not see over-all effects on the business and so he tends to judge good and evil, right and wrong, by the sole standard of his own specialty." Benton offered, by contrast, that "the traditional liberal arts course is as practical as a cash register for a businessman. Indeed, even four years of Latin are more useful than a once-over-lightly course in production or merchandising." Actually, said Benton, businesses certainly did not need two big studies critiquing business education, because they had known all this for years. "Employers seeking young executives reached the same melancholy conclusion long before the two weighty reports were published last summer. Businessmen have been complaining about the scarcity of efficient junior executives since the end of World War II." And then Benton went in for the kill: "Surely something must be wrong with business colleges if the 500,000 men and women they have graduated in the last decade cannot meet the demand for promising personnel."[80]

Business figures may have rushed in to join the hallelujah chorus of those who agreed with the findings made by the three economists about the need for more liberal arts education, but *Fortune* magazine writer Robert

Sheehan wasn't letting them off so easily. The sorry state of business education was not solely the fault of the B-schools, Sheehan wrote, because "during the years that collegiate business education was growing at such a tremendous rate and piling up the practices that are now so greatly deplored, businessmen stood by" and did or said little. Nor, he added, "are they responsible for the revolution in business education that is now stirring." Businessmen might have endorsed the idea that the liberal arts would "cultivate the requisite 'bigness' of mind," but they were talking the talk, not walking the walk.[81]

Still, in keeping with the optimistic and expansive zeitgeist of the era, commentators felt that in the wake of the Ford and Carnegie studies, and with the models established by Ford's demonstration grants, business education was changing for the better across the 1960s. That was the conclusion of a 1964 study by the Committee for Economic Development and reported on by *Fortune* magazine. Maybe not revolution, but the report found "some mighty stimulating things going on in some echelons of higher education for business" in 1964. And in 1969, ten years after the two studies, the AACSB revised the criteria for accreditation to require that 75 percent of courses offered at business schools be taught by full-time faculty, a considerable improvement over past practices.[82]

Writing in 1968, Temple University professor of insurance Charles Hall also wanted to pronounce the revolution a success, though he did so somewhat defensively. After the two studies, Hall wrote, business schools decided "to aim at the education of middle and top management." As a consequence, "the trade school approach has largely disappeared from the scene." Taking aim at those who thought business education needed more liberal arts, Hall countered, "We can, in fact, possibly lay claim to being the real center of a 'liberal' education, in its true historical meaning, on the modern university campus." For those whose eyebrows might have arched, Hall went on to explain, "Can anyone truthfully maintain that a man is free in any meaningful sense without some degree of economic independence and self-sufficiency? . . . And what is the source of economic independence in a modern society? For most of our population, at least, the clear cut answer is Business."[83]

Milton Friedman might have cheered statements like that, but Hall did not offer much by way of evidence that business schools had changed fundamentally and along the lines sketched at the end of the 1950s. Instead, his concerns circled back to those expressed three-quarters of a century earlier about the professional respectability of business altogether. "It's about time we started to hold our head high," an aggrieved-sounding Hall exhorted, "and proclaim our strengths and accomplishments." Business schools, he went on, "ought to shed our inferiority complex," thus acknowledging that they still had one. He then pointed an accusing finger across campus and demanded, "It's time that our academic colleagues recognize us as equals, with just as noble objectives as their own, with just as rigorous and demanding disciplines and, perhaps, with a great deal more relevance in the modern world."[84]

More often than not, revolutions generate counterrevolutions. In the 1920s, business leaders complained about the "college boys" and their useless college knowledge. By the 1950s, virtually all business leaders, at least according to advertising executive Benton, thought that the nation's business schools were churning out little better than glorified vo-tech graduates. By the end of the 1960s the pendulum of complaint had swung again. Malcolm Baldrige, the chairman of Scovill Manufacturing, griped in 1973 that "too many people from B-schools are over-educated and under-experienced." Plenty of "top managers" agreed with him, according to *Business Week* magazine, including Ross Perot, who thought that these grads "tend to have a God's Chosen People complex. . . . They are taught, and I disagree, that the definition of the problem is everything. That's the fun part, but solving the problem is more important."[85] Baldrige would go on to serve as Ronald Reagan's secretary of commerce, and Ross Perot made a quirky and quixotic run for the presidency in 1992.

The Chosen People Perot referred to were those who held MBA degrees. By the early 1970s the crisis of quality and intellectual integrity had settled on the MBA, the growth of which was astonishing in that decade. As *Business Week* tallied it, there had been a 140 percent growth in MBAs granted between 1970 and 1978. This surely accompanied what the magazine called "the worrisome boom in second-rate B-schools" across the decade, which translated, in their estimation, to new MBA programs "springing up at the rate of about 35 a year." Almost inevitably, many of these offered "short, painless—and some say worthless—degrees."[86] And no wonder that MBAs were proving a disappointment. "Most of the MBAs," *Business Week* found in 1970, "majored either in business administration or engineering as undergraduates." Even after the revolution of the 1960s, the magazine went on, "recent studies show that many leading B-schools and top executives take an equally dim view of undergraduate business education."[87]

Once again, the AACSB seems to have failed in its role as the minder of professional standards. "Part of the problem may well be the lack of clout carried by the AACSB," *Business Week* concluded, because "only about 25 percent of the B-schools in the country have bothered to attain accreditation."[88] In 1975, the AACSB did its own report on the state of business education, and the tone was somewhat sad. Dredging up the comparisons that had helped create business schools in the first place, the report noted, "While medicine, law, engineering and other professional fields of higher education are continuously reviewing their development and assessing their futures, management education has received comparatively little attention." Not for the first time, the report went on, business schools were failing to keep up with the changing world outside their walls. Courses that dealt with the public and nonprofit sectors remained "elective course options" at most places, despite the growing importance of those areas. As a result, "because schools of business in general have continued to emphasize their private sector functional and core courses, they are increasingly challenged today both from within and without the University." Almost dolefully the report concluded, "There is reason to believe that we are poorly training managers today for the past and clearly not well at all for the future."[89] Twenty years after Ford and Carnegie launched the revolution in business education, the landscape looked remarkably unchanged.

In their struggles to figure out what, exactly, to teach students of business that would both prepare them for the work they would do and that would allow business to rise to the level of a profession, business schools deserve some sympathy. Serving two masters—the academic world and the private sector—has proved near impossible, in large part because the two worlds have never decided just what each wants from the other. Clark Kerr noted the irony in his 1958 lecture in Pittsburgh as the "liberal arts" revolution was swelling at business schools: "It is common to say that business administration students should have a liberal arts background, but the people who say it the most, according to several studies of the matter, did not have such a background themselves and do not hire students with such a background."[90]

When the Ford and Carnegie reports came out, *Business Week* sounded genuinely perplexed when it wrote, "Nobody knows what is the right education for business."[91] That was after more than a half century of trying to figure the question out; a half century later the question remains. Not that it seems to have mattered much. Between 1965 and 1972 the number of BAs granted by U.S. colleges grew by just over 50 percent; the number of MAs by almost 49 percent. Business degrees, however, grew by over 67 percent and graduate degrees in business by 65 percent.[92] There may have been a broad uneasiness about what *Business Week* in 1965 called "the paradox of the curriculum" and about the quality and coherence of the education students got in a business school, but that did not stop the students from coming.[93]

In January 1984 James Baugham traveled to Scottsdale, Arizona, to deliver a keynote speech at the Business–Higher Education forum being held there. Baugham knew of what he spoke. He had taught at Harvard's B-school and had also been an executive at General Electric. "What I'd like to look at this morning," he began, "is an anomaly. We have a massive boom in the quantity of business education in the United States, and at the same time, we seem to have pervasive dissatisfaction with the quality of the results." This unhappiness went in both directions, Baugham continued, saying, "We have dissatisfaction from employers who don't see this playing through to increased competitiveness, and we have dissatisfaction with many business majors . . . whose careers don't seem to pan out the way they were forecast while they were in the university." Business schools, though Baugham didn't say this directly, did not even seem to grasp the basic principle of supply and demand. He told the panel, "In quantitative terms, American business schools are producing far more graduates than American business can employ in meaningful entry-level work."[94]

The goal of making business into a profession had turned into a search for a pot of gold at the end of a collegiate rainbow. Collegiate business schools had no problem agreeing on a set of subjects to teach—accounting, finance, marketing, banking, and so on—but most of those had been borrowed from the proprietary schools and elaborated on. Teaching them differently, somehow, or theoretically rather than practically, hadn't worked either. Teaching those subjects through a series of potted case studies only sidestepped the issue. To be sure, there has been change in what gets taught at business schools. Since management became a staple topic it has been joined by a salmagundi of others like real estate, supply-chain management, and things attached to the word "data." Many schools promise now to teach "entrepreneurship" and "leadership," though there is scant evidence that these things can be taught in any meaningful way. At the same time, history and political economy (about which more in chapter 3), part of Wharton's original offerings, are now virtually extinct. Change certainly, but hardly progress toward creating the kind of education business schools have yearned for. Baugham gave his talk one hundred years after the Wharton School opened its doors. Thirty years after that, and business schools seem no closer to figuring out just what to teach students in order to turn them into business professionals.

Chapter 3

Dismal Science versus Applied Economics

The Unhappy Relationship between Business Schools and Economics Departments

Whatever the balance between courses in the liberal arts and those that provided essentially vocational or technical training, plenty of commentators at the turn of the twentieth century insisted that the new business curriculum needed to be "scientific." That was entirely of a piece with an age where everything aspired to the authority of science—from scientifically managed labor on the shop floor to scientifically organized merchandise in department stores.

Here was another reason that business ought to be taught in the new, dynamic colleges and universities, rather than in the more old-fashioned proprietary schools. Only there could "the scientific study of commerce" be developed and then taught to a new generation. "Business practice has become a science," proclaimed the catalog of the business school at Syracuse University in the 1920s, as if by asserting the claim it became true, and Syracuse's counterparts at the University of Nebraska agreed. Their catalog hit the now-familiar notes: "Business is now . . . as much a learned profession as theology, law, medicine, engineering, agriculture and other difficult and complicated arts, and demands from those who would rise from the ranks a thorough, scientific . . . training." The fetish of science also explains why so many of these schools offered degrees with "science" in their names in the first half of the twentieth century: bachelor of commercial science, bachelor of science in commerce, and doctor of commercial science to name three variations on the theme. Except at the University of Cincinnati, where business school graduates received a commercial engineer degree. For the puzzled, UC offered this explanation: "The work in commercial subjects is accompanied by a considerable amount of instruction in the sciences upon which engineering is based, and the relation between the two is emphasized."[1]

Yet even while collegiate schools of business were awarding bachelors of commercial science degrees, some believed that the larger problem with business education was that business itself had not gotten with the scientific program. "Business has eagerly appropriated the results of science," charged Willard Hotchkiss, founding dean of the University of Minnesota's business school, "without itself becoming scientific." Several years later, William Kennedy, who taught at a business school, agreed and cautioned that "business is not yet a sufficiently exact science so that it can be taught without danger to college undergraduates." In fact, Kennedy suggested, what was being taught in "the so-called business courses" was just the opposite, because students "are not learning, as in science, a body of principles underlying the whole field." The hedge against the danger, at least in Hotchkiss's view, was to teach the scientific method, what he called "the first article in the creed by which business training must be guided." Hammering the point further, he continued, "The first great element of training which the university can give to future business men is a mastery of scientific method."[2]

Or more aptly, the social scientific method. The social sciences—sociology, psychology, political science, and economics—took shape in the late nineteenth century with delusions of scientific grandeur. Convinced that social relations were also governed by the same first principles as chemistry or physics, social scientists worked to figure out the laws of the human mind, of the past, and of the market. Those who believed that business should be a subject of academic study, therefore, wanted to find those scientific principles that governed business: laws of commerce, axioms of trade, theorems of marketing.

That aspiration brought the new business schools into obvious proximity with the academic discipline of economics. After all, in the minds of plenty of ordinary people, the two are basically the same thing. Notice how many Americans think the nation's economy ought to be run like an individual business (though one wonders which) and think therefore that government ought to be run by businessmen (though one wonders who). Notice as well how many economists try to remind us that making a profit and managing an entire economy have little in common.

More importantly, whatever else their curricular differences might be, virtually everyone associated with the new business schools agreed that business students ought to be taught economics. Economics, first and foremost, would put the starch of "science" into business education. That consensus, however, only raised other questions. One set related to institutional real estate: where would those economists have their offices? Would they be housed in departments within business schools or alongside other departments associated with the liberal arts—like history or classics? The other set related to intellectual proximity. Just what was the disciplinary relationship between economics and the other subjects taught in business schools? When Ohio State studied the question in the early 1930s, the committee concluded firmly that the Department of Economics sat "as the scientific core of the College of Commerce and Administration" but fretted that "the basic character of economics had not been recognized sufficiently in the professional work of the College." In fact, the committee could not even figure out when in a student's course of study in the College of Commerce he or she ought to take those courses.[3]

If it wasn't obvious where economics belonged in the business school curriculum, where did economics belong on campus altogether? Did economists share more in common—methodologically, theoretically, even temperamentally—with historians or with accountants? These questions created considerable confusion and tension on campus. Figuring out just where economics belonged proved to have no obvious solution.

From Political Economy to Economics

Before U.S. colleges offered courses in economics, students studied "political economy." In 1875, two years after it opened, Ohio State University listed a course titled "Political Economy and Civil Polity" as one of ten courses on its roster.[4] Political economy as a subject has its origins in the eighteenth century as the study of the economic activity of nation-states, and as the title of OSU's course suggests, well into the nineteenth century the subject combined the study of economics with politics, ethics, and moral philosophy. Some of the greatest thinkers of the eighteenth and nineteenth centuries worked in the field of political economy: Adam Smith, David Ricardo, Karl Marx, John Stuart Mill.

Economics, as related to but distinct from political economy, began to emerge in the second half of the nineteenth century. More specifically, in the United States it began to develop after the Civil War and, more specifically still, only after a younger generation of scholars went to Germany to study. They came back prepared to rebel against courses like Political Economy and Civil Polity and against those who taught them. That rebellion was part of the larger war against the old higher education that transformed universities in the last quarter of the nineteenth century that we discussed briefly before.

Richard Ely was one of those young rebels. Ely attended Columbia, class of 1876, and had studied political economy there. His teacher also taught English literature and philosophy, and he assigned students the textbook *Political Economy for Beginners* written by one Mrs. Fawcett. Looking back, Ely wondered whether "more harm than good was accomplished" in this course. He recalled, "We really gained no useful knowledge, and perhaps were left with an insufficient appreciation of our own ignorance."[5] Things at Harvard weren't much different, where political economy was treated as an adjunct to moral philosophy and "an extraordinary number of instructors in the subject were trained for the ministry."[6]

So off Ely went to Germany. He had plenty of company on that intellectual journey. J. B. Clark, Henry Walcott Farnam, E. J. James, Simon Patten, Edwin R. A. Seligman, and many other founders of U.S. economics made the pilgrimage to German universities. As Ely described it, they discovered to their delight that in Germany political economy "was a large and inspiring subject," and they came back to the United States "with a two-fold message—a scientific method and a practical message." Their sojourn in Germany helped them see that the warmed-over political economy they had learned as undergraduates was, "generally speaking, rather barren." It helped them see too that the "endless harangues" over paper money, free trade and protectionism "savor[ed] more of political partisanship than of scientific inquiry." They returned to the United States in a "pugnacious" mood, "prepared to fight any such conceptions as not belonging to the realm of science."[7]

Ely recounted all of this in a speech marking the twenty-fifth anniversary of the American Economic Association, which he helped found in 1885. The AEA would be the vehicle through which Ely and the rest would carry out the two-part German mandate: scientific economics applied practically to solve social problems. The AEA would coalesce a new discipline of economics distinct from the old political economy. In so doing, the AEA was of a piece with the larger process of intellectual professionalization and was one among many disciplines that formed a professional body in the late nineteenth and early twentieth centuries. Five years later, in 1890, Alfred Marshall published his textbook *Principles of Economics*, generally regarded as the first of its kind. After that, few students were going to read Mrs. Fawcett any more.

But note the timing of all this. While no academic discipline was more influenced by German methods and ideas than economics, when those American converts returned to proselytize they did so just as business schools started to appear on campuses. The AEA was started in 1885; the Wharton School in 1881. In other words, American economics as an academic discipline grew up within, alongside, or otherwise entangled with American business schools. The relationship between economics and business education at Northwestern was cozy enough that it was hard to know where one started and the other began. Willard Hotchkiss declared that the School of Commerce there was "essentially an off-shoot of the economics work in the university."[8] That was certainly not the case in Germany or the rest of Europe, where economics developed on its own and business schools didn't arrive until after the Second World War.

So the question: Where to put the new, scientific economists? Several answers presented themselves at the turn of the twentieth century. In many institutions, economists and indeed whole economics departments found themselves housed administratively inside the business schools. At the University of Pennsylvania, the Wharton School came first, and thus economics, along with sociology and political science, was part of the Wharton School, an arrangement that lasted until the mid-1970s. That model was repeated elsewhere. At Berkeley, the economics department was founded in 1902, four years after its College of Commerce.

At Harvard, by contrast, the economics department predated the B-school; in fact, the business school spent the first five years of its life housed in the division of History, Government, and Economics before becoming its own independent unit.[9] Economics came before business at Miami University in Oxford, Ohio, too. The economics department was established in 1909; the business school in 1927. The business school swallowed up the economics department, though the chair of the economics department became the first head of the business school. And at Miami the economics department remains in the business school to this day. Meanwhile, in his midcentury survey of fifteen historically black colleges and universities, Joseph Pierce discovered that "six institutions list their offerings in economics in departments that are separate from the departments of business." And therefore nine of these HBCUs taught economics and business together. "One solution," Pierce offered, "would be to retain a close structural tie-up between economics and business administration." But then he quickly reversed by quoting "a critic of an existing arrangement where economics and business subjects are taught in the same department" who complained, "The . . . Department of Economics and Business Administration is an amorphous hybrid. It is something 'betwixt and between,' neither one thing nor the other." [10]

The arrangement of campus office space and administrative reporting lines—which departments go where and who belongs with whom on the organizational chart—always reflect, however imperfectly, certain assumptions about the intellectual nature and purpose of disciplines. That there was no consensus about just how business and economics should relate to each other institutionally—the "betwixt and between" problem—therefore revealed a basic intellectual confusion about the relationship between the two.

Economics, the Conscience of Business?

When Richard Ely (and the other young economists who returned from Germany with fire in their eyes in the 1870s and 1880s) complained about the "conceptions of orthodoxy" that stifled economic thinking, he was referring to the laissez-faire, free-trade doctrines associated with so-called classical economics. When those young economists gathered in 1885 to found the AEA, they issued a "Statement of Principles." From the vantage point of today's economic orthodoxies, the statement sounds bold and bracing, and from the outset it positioned the AEA in opposition to the advocates of laissez-faire, which the young economists dismissed as so much "speculation": "We regard the state as an agency whose positive assistance is one of the indispensable conditions of human progress," read principle number 1. And from number 3: "We hold that the conflict of labor and capital has brought into prominence a vast number of social problems, whose solution requires the united efforts, each in its own sphere, of the church, of the state, and of science."[11]

The "speculation" of laissez-faire doctrines may have been the presiding ethos of the Gilded Age, but it was not a faith held unanimously. Among the dissenters were businessmen in Philadelphia and a small group of thinkers in that city allied with them—sometimes dubbed the Philadelphia School—who believed that government should exercise a muscular role in economic affairs, primarily by imposing protectionist tariffs to promote U.S. industry. In some ways, their ideas traced back to Alexander Hamilton almost genealogically. Henry Carey, perhaps the most prominent member of that Philadelphia group, was the son of Mathew Carey, the great champion of Hamilton and his protectionist tariff. Another member of that Philadelphia School was none other than Joseph Wharton. So when students studied economics at the school he founded, they studied Philadelphia School economics, at least initially. In fact, Joseph Wharton insisted that protectionism be taught at the school bearing his name and reserved the right to rescind his gift if it was not.[12]

In 1883, Wharton hired Edmund Janes James as its first professor of economics. James was among that new generation who had returned from Germany, in his case the University of Halle, with a new doctorate (1877) and filled with new ideas. He quickly became director of Wharton as well. Two years after he started at Wharton, James was elected vice president of the new AEA; two years after that, 1887, he hired a fellow Halle alumnus and founding member of the AEA to join the Wharton faculty, Simon Patten.

James and Patten shared a belief in a role for government more expansive than imposing stiff tariffs. They believed government had a responsibility to help solve the social problems created by the new industrial economy. James, for example, helped found the American Academy of Political Social Science in 1889 with the goal of bringing social science research to a wider public audience. James decamped for Chicago in 1896, and Patten took over his position as head of the Wharton School. From his perch in Philadelphia Patten become one of the leading economists of the Progressive era. The real job for academic economists, he told the AEA in his presidential address in 1908, is to mobilize public opinion for reform. He ordered his fellow "revolutionists" to take their place "on the firing line of civilization."[13]

A historical approach, in fact, sat at the heart of the scientific posture of German economics, and its U.S. acolytes took that to heart. History, so the Germans reasoned, could be deployed to critique prevailing economic ideas and their underlying assumptions about human nature and morality. Shedding the abstract for the empirical, Patten wrote, "It is not what Mill, Carlyle, Spencer or Marx thought would take place but what has actually happened that should interest us." In addition to shedding the doctrinaire posturing of the earlier political economy, Patten also lifted the gloom that permeated classical economics. Gone, in his view, was a world of scarcity and suffering, replaced by one where economic growth could create prosperity and happiness. In his 1896 book *The Theory of Social Forces* Patten argued that "pain economies" were evolving into "pleasure economies."[14]

That a progressive thinker like Patten should be running the Wharton School in the early years of the twentieth century says a great deal about how the school conceived of itself and about what it thought a collegiate business school ought to be. And students responded. In 1892 Wharton had an undergraduate enrollment of 59; by 1912 that figure had grown more than tenfold, to 625.[15] Patten also attracted similarly innovative and energetic faculty talent. At the very end of the nineteenth century Wharton hired W. E. B. DuBois as an "assistant in sociology" and with that albeit temporary appointment Dubois produced the pioneering sociological study *The Philadelphia Negro* (1899).[16] Scott Nearing also came to Wharton, where he fell under Patten's spell, earned a BA and then a PhD in economics in 1909, and began teaching economics and sociology at Wharton.

Patten was a progressive reformer committed to the precepts of the Social Gospel movement—he published *The Social Basis of Religion*, for example, in 1914[17]—but his student and protégé Nearing was even more committed to putting economics to work solving the pressing social problems of the age. Between his BA and his PhD, Nearing served as the secretary for the Pennsylvania Child Labor Committee. And as a scholar he was astonishingly prolific. During his time as a member of the Wharton faculty, Nearing published no fewer than eight monographs on economic questions, ranging from an examination of family wage earning to a study of coal as an example of a resource monopoly.

He inherited from Patten a sunny view of the economy and of the possibilities of economics to make the world a better place. In his 1913 book *Social Sanity,* he described the "new economics" as parting "company with the ominous pictures of an overpopulated, starving world, prostrate before the throne of 'competition,' 'psychic value,' 'individual initiative,' 'private property,' or some other pseudo-god." Instead, he went on, "the day has dawned when economists must explain that welfare must be put before wealth; that the iron law of wages may be shattered by a minimum wage law; . . . and a host of other economic maladjustments will disappear before an educated, legislating public opinion; and that combination and cooperation may be employed to silence forever the savage demands of unrestricted competition."[18] The economist as crusader. It all left the mathematician Simon Newcomb a little bemused. He quipped that the AEA functioned as "a sort of church, requiring for admission a renunciation of ancient errors and an adhesion to the supposed new creed."[19]

Nor was Nearing alone at Wharton. In fact, he was among a cohort of faculty dubbed the Wharton Eight, who, in Nearing's words, believed that they "should make a contribution not only to our students and the University but also to the society at large." As far away as it may seem today, in the early years of the twentieth century the Wharton School was an epicenter of progressive—occasionally radical—thinking about economic and social problems. Nearing taught the single largest class at Penn, with an enrollment of over four hundred students.[20]

All this would be counted a fine career by any academic, but Nearing's achievement at Wharton stands as all the more astonishing because his stay there was so brief. Nearing's political activities rankled a number of Penn's trustees, and in 1915 fourteen of them voted to fire him. As Penn's provost Edgar Fahs Smith put it at the time, "I do not believe in muzzling any member of the faculty, but I do believe, however, that no man may go too far."[21] That might well have been a statement of principle, though how going too far should be measured and by whom Smith did not make entirely clear. One trustee, however, was refreshingly candid in describing why he had voted to sack Nearing: "He advocated the ruthless redistribution of property."[22]

Nearing had been among those who founded the American Association of University Professors just the year before in response to the threat of restrictions at Penn and elsewhere on what professors could teach and say in public. (In fact, Provost Smith's statement about how far faculty could go came in reply to the founding of the AAUP.) Nearing's firing became a cause célèbre for academic freedom and for the organization. Wharton faculty expressed "deep concern" about Nearing's fate to the Wharton dean Roswell

McCrea; one of them proclaimed, "Scott Nearing has become the Dred Scott of the teaching profession. . . . His experience has become a case, his treatment a precedent that menaces the teaching profession."[23] Despite the national outcry, Nearing still lost his job.

One hundred years later, the Nearing case stands as an example of the proverbial victory won despite the battle lost. His dismissal by Penn's trustees helped shape the nature of tenure and academic freedom at American universities. For our purposes here, however, Scott Nearing's departure from Wharton serves as another piece of symbolism. Those whom we met in chapter 3 who believed that American business schools could professionalize, uplift, and make U.S. business practice ethical had faculty like Scott Nearing in mind. They believed that progressive economics taught at business schools could be put to work in American society through a transformation of American business.

Though the Progressive movement waned after the First World War, a combination of dissipated energy, perhaps, and a virulent conservative backlash, it left an enduring legacy, from women's suffrage to child labor laws of the sort Nearing had fought for. As collegiate business schools began to proliferate in the 1920s, however, they did so without much of the Progressive impulse that had defined Wharton in the previous decade. Nearing's teacher Simon Patten left Wharton two years after he did, forced into early retirement by Penn's trustees who did not approve of Patten's outspoken criticism of the First World War. One chronicler of Wharton's history described Patten's departure in a way that applied more broadly to business schools after the First World War: "The school lost its intellectual, a man who lived for ideas. Thereafter it had to make do with professionals, men who lived off ideas."[24] As economics and business struggled to coexist on campus in the years following the First World War, the synergy between the two that Progressives had imagined could be possible faded away. Simon Patten died in 1922, and Scott Nearing never taught in a business school again.

Turf Battles

Regardless of the institutional configuration, plenty of economists and some business figures too bristled at this close academic association between business and economics. The Stanford economist Eliot Mears, writing in 1923, found the "the introduction of courses in business" to be "the most startling development during the twentieth century in American higher education." Startled, perhaps, but Mears was also perturbed because of what he felt was the encroachment of those business courses on the discipline of economics. Trying to describe difference between the two, he continued sharply, "Economics is no more inclusive of commerce than is mathematics of engineering. . . . The subjects are distinct."[25]

Shortly after the Northwestern dean Hotchkiss described the close association between economics and the School of Commerce, the Northwestern economist Earl Dean Howard produced what amounted to a twenty-eight-point rebuttal from which he proceeded to reject the analogy between pure sciences and applied sciences. "Theoretical economics, as taught from the textbooks and even as modified in the past generation," Howard stipulated, "is not the basic science of business as physics is of engineering and chemistry of medicine." The goals were fundamentally different: economics was an attempt to understand production and distribution, while business was concerned only with acquisition, "not social service," as Howard put it, "but private profit." And mastering economic precepts was not even necessary to achieve those private profits. "No engineer would dream of ignoring the laws of physics," Howard wrote, "yet business men do not make much use of concepts, laws and principles of economics in their calculations." And he added the swipe, "Most successful business administrators have never read a book on economics."[26]

Howard took specific aim at business schools when, in point number 6, he charged, "Even in schools of commerce the instruction in practical business subjects does not build up naturally on theoretical economics, but really throws it overboard for the empirical rules and concepts of the unscientific business man." He elaborated on that point: "Lack of a science of business has left business practice without adequate scientific guidance; the same errors are made over and over again and improvement comes but slowly by empirical methods." That word again: without "scientific" guidance businesses groped in the dark, following rules "unsystematized and traditional." Insofar as there was a science at work here, "the science of business is the science of profit-making."[27]

There was something almost of hurt feelings and disciplinary sour grapes in Howard's complaints. "The theoretical economist is not sought eagerly by practical men of business," he noted, "but when the psychologist seems to offer a science the principles of which may be applied to advertising, management of men, and sales, he receives a warm welcome." Nonetheless, Howard wasn't necessarily in favor of a closer union between business and economics, and in insisting on the distinction, Howard made the case that business ought only to pursue profit and leave the larger issues to others. "The objection will at once arise," he anticipated, "that this ideal of business efficiency is not socially desirable. This is true," he conceded, "but science does not concern itself with the application of the principles which it formulates." He went on to assert, "Whether it is expedient for a business man to ignore all considerations and ideals other than pure business efficiency [is a question that] belongs to the political economist and sociologist." He reiterated this point in the form of a hypothetical question: "How far may I, or shall I, or can I, depart from the strict policy of business efficiency in dealing with men? Besides being a business man I am also a citizen, a Christian, a man of human sympathies; a policy of cold-blooded, conscienceless administration forces me to violate my duties, sentiments, and ideals." This was an important question, Howard acknowledged, but not one for any science of business. Instead, he believed, "this is a problem for ethics and religion."[28]

About a decade after Howard nailed his twenty-eight theses to the door of the academy, Roswell McCrea, now at Columbia University's school of business, published another musing on the "place of economics in the curriculum of a school of business" in the very same journal. He felt that in teaching economic theory to business students "our educational scheme has put the cart before the horse." Business schools "have attempted to build up a body of sweeping abstractions in the minds of students . . . related neither to current economic nor business life." Business schools would have to find a solution to this problem, McCrea worried, "unless we are satisfied to divorce our offering from partnership with social studies." The cost of that divorce, as McCrea saw it, was an "educational scheme [serving] merely as preparation for those private acquisitive employments which form the main body of interest and activity on the part of business men."[29]

Exactly. That was the point, or at least it should be, of a business education in the view of W. H. Lough, the man who ran a business training company in New York. We heard his complaints about the way finance was being taught in the new business schools in chapter 2. He offered his own prescription for how to do it right: "My notion of the right approach to our subject," he wrote, "is to start by studying the local laundry or shoe store instead of the United States Steel Corporation." Warming to his topic, Lough critiqued the academic approach to business more broadly. These business schools, he asserted, had been started largely by businessmen "or educators who were familiar and sympathetic with business practice." Writing in 1921, Lough believed things had gone bad: "Unhappily for business education, there were previously in existence organized departments which were also busy with the study of business; I refer of course to departments of economics." Lough thought that economics hung like an albatross around the neck of business education. He minced no words about it either. "I should say that a school or department which enrolls students on the implied promise to prepare them for business pursuits," he wrote, "and then offers them chiefly elaborations of economic theorizing is—quite innocently—selling gold bricks." The answer was straightforward, in Lough's view. "The sooner we all cut loose from an enervating dependence on political economy and begin to build a new structure on a firmer foundation the better for everyone."[30] Lough did not get his history altogether right—as we have already discussed, in some places economics departments grew up within the business schools. His remarks to the readers of the *Journal of Political Economy*, however, suggest that those in the world of business education were no happier being tethered to economics than the economists were.

Whether or not Howard's twenty-eight-point broadside on "economics and the science of business" was persuasive, it certainly underscored a fundamental intellectual—and therefore pedagogical—confusion at American business schools. Surely business was connected to the economy? And thus, surely business students should study economics as part of their professional training? But for some economists at any rate, the two weren't necessarily connected at all, except in an incidental sort of way. More to the point, did businesses really want or need to hire workers with this sort of intellectual training? Just after the First World War, Edward Mott Wooley canvassed some business leaders about what they wanted from college graduates. "To what extent should the old-fashioned four-year 'cultural' course apply to business training?" he asked. He learned that "the rapid development of modern business during the last few decades apparently has rendered the old idea of culture narrow." In fact, as he talked with businessmen, he reported, "I have discovered many situations apparently indicating that the chief need of the average collegiate business school is more research into the actual management problems of business men, and less of abstract economics and philosophy, based on broad theories only."[31] Maybe running a business and theorizing an economy had little to do with one another after all.

Teaching a rarified discipline like economics, however, helped distinguish a collegiate business school from the proprietary ones. McCrea believed that business schools were "treading the ground between a trade school and a professional school" and that the "effective, permeating influence of economics in a school of business is the *sine qua non* of a 'professional' school of business."[32] In other words, would there be any real distinction between colleges and trade schools if business students didn't study econ? After all, that distinction was the sine qua non for creating collegiate schools of business in the first place.

Writing in 1926, Roswell McCrea made a prediction about the unhappy marriage between the discipline of economics and collegiate schools of business, perhaps drawn from his experience serving as Wharton's dean just before the U.S. entry into the First World War. Though he agreed with Willard Hotchkiss that "as a matter of recent history it may be observed that our schools of business are proliferations of departments of economics," he went on to add, "All in all, I suspect it will not be long in many of our universities before there will be a sharp line of division between faculties of business and faculties of economics." In institutions where that division wasn't drawn, "the result [will be] the old story of the lion and lamb, with the economics department playing the part of the lamb."[33] In the interwar years, neither the business schools nor the economics departments seemed particularly happy to be joined at the institutional hip.

In December 1927, amid this confusion and debate, the American Association of Collegiate Schools of Business (AACSB) and the AEA came together at a roundtable aimed at brokering some sort of détente or at least sorting out who was doing what and how. The discussion included several economists from both inside and outside business schools. William Kiekhofer, who taught economics at the University of Wisconsin, hewed to the familiar analogy about the relationship between economics and business, "What biology is to medicine and what physics is to engineering," he told the group, "economics is to commerce." And therefore, economists deserved their own departments outside the business school. The University of Illinois's E. L. Bogart tried to massage the differences by noting that "it is not always easy to distinguish between social economics and private economics, between courses given to make better citizens and those to make more efficient workers." George Dowrie, from the University of Minnesota, however, wondered whether these kinds of distinctions were easy to see and if they really mattered. "I dare say," he offered, "that the relationship between the work in economics and that in business administration in most institutions has been the product of a local situation rather than the result of a careful formulation of educational policy."[34] The roundtable, titled "The Relationship between Departments of Economics and Collegiate Schools of Business," ended without consensus about what that relationship should be.

It was a nonconclusion echoed in the same year in a book by L. C. Marshall, who "noted in passing that the matter of the appropriate relationship between a school of business and a department of economics is one of the outstanding problems connected with the development of collegiate education for business." He sounded almost bemused when he continued, "What is the content of the word 'appropriate'? No one knows, and considerable differences of opinion have been expressed."[35] Almost fifty years after the Wharton School had been founded, Marshall's was a startling admission. No one in 1928 doubted that medical students needed some background in biology or engineers some exposure to physics. Business schools, however, still did not have a solution to that "outstanding problem" of where economics belonged in a business education.

The tone of the AACSB-AEA roundtable was cordial, and everyone acknowledged happily that whatever the organizational relationship between business schools and departments of economics might be, both would enjoy fruitful and mutually beneficial interactions. "There is, of course, no antagonism," E. L. Bogart insisted, "in the methods or purposes of the department of economics and the college of commerce," and one can imagine everyone else in the room nodding their heads in affable agreement. Yet even amid this spirit of cooperation, a few comments must have caused the economists to feel, frankly, antagonized. Bogart, from his vantage at the University of Illinois College of Commerce, believed that "the department of economics, like those of mathematics or modern languages, is and should be a service department, ready to offer any economics course which is required by any college on the campus."[36] Maybe the economists didn't take that as personally as they might have since Bogart also managed to demean the French faculty as well.

The nature of the "service" economics should provide to business schools might have rankled even more. Rather than making a compelling intellectual or even functional case that business students ought to study economics, Bogart revealed, once again, the status anxiety that lay at the heart of business schools from the very beginning. "Which one of us," he asked the roundtable, "has not heard the slurring remarks that truly cultural courses are not to be found in the college of commerce any more than they are in engineering or agriculture?" Without economics, Bogart went on, "the college of commerce seems to some of the students to offer only dry husks without much cultural value."[37] The choice of words here is interesting. As we have discussed, many of those shaping business schools believed that the new and developing field of economics would give their studies the scientific rigor business currently lacked. Bogart's use of the word "cultural" suggests that, in addition to rigor, economics could give the study of business more social cachet. Economics as a kind of finishing school course for business students: surely that did not make the economists happy.

No one who participated in that roundtable knew what was coming less than two years later. Not the economic crisis of the Great Depression or the political response to it either. In 1930 Congress passed and Herbert Hoover signed the Smoot-Hawley Tariff Act as an attempt to bolster the flailing U.S. economy. The bill became law in part because certain influential business leaders supported it (though a number, including Henry Ford, did not) and despite a petition objecting to the tariff signed by over a thousand members of the AEA. Despite how close they might have been on campus, business and economics were never so far apart as they seemed at that moment. The Smoot-Hawley tariff, and the disastrous consequences that flowed from it as the Depression went from bad to worse, serve as a measure of just how differently businessmen and economists saw the world.

That disconnect, according to Herbert Towle, had campus roots. Writing in *Scribner's* in 1936, Towle assured readers that businessmen weren't wicked, necessarily, just not very well educated. "Most economists saw clearly what was going on," he wrote, "but their voices were lost in the general hurrah." Then he asked, "Now, suppose that business men at large had seen what the few saw in 1928 and '29. How many would have persisted in over-borrowing, over-lending, and over-investing?"[38] The question was largely rhetorical. Businessmen could have been saved from their follies if only they had known what the economists knew. (Actually, Towle gave economists more credit than they deserved. They may have had a better grasp of the economic situation in the 1930s than the businessmen did, but that grasp was still pretty tenuous.)

Towle spread blame in both directions. Economics, he pronounced, "has been taught—even in the better universities—by men of high ability but without the practical business experience that would show how best to apply its rules." At the same time, business schools remained the campus "catch-all into which to steer students who were unable to succeed in other courses." Therefore, Towle offered, "what is needed is combined knowledge of economic principles and of business practice," because "hitherto the two have run almost in separate channels." That all seemed straightforward enough, but clearly Towle did not realize just how hard that combination had proved to create. In the middle of the Depression decade, the question Towle put to higher education had an urgency: "What will the colleges do about it?"[39] Of course, by 1936 colleges had been asking that question for several decades.

Trickle-Down Economics

After the Second World War the AACSB decided the time had come to revisit and revise its membership standards. Whether or not he saw the great postwar expansion of higher education and of business education in particular coming, Berkeley business school dean Ewald Grether, who became president of AACSB in 1948, led the effort to update the standards. The new standards were issued in 1949, and economics retained its first-among-equals status in the curriculum that any business school needed to offer in order to join the club.

By 1949, as Grether saw it, the core of business education remained accounting, business law, and economics. Marketing and finance were now also expectations, but as Grether noted, finance had really started as an outgrowth of economics "in relation to money and banking and public finance."[40] Indeed, the 1949 standards can be read as an attempt to give more heft to the subjects other than economics taught in business schools. For example, the AACSB now required that "there shall be at least five faculty members, *exclusive* of those in general economics, of professional rank . . . giving instruction in business administration." Likewise, standard number 3 stipulated that 40 percent of coursework for a BA degree "must be taken in subjects other than business and economics provided that economic principles and economic history may be counted in either the business or non-business groups." [41]

However sensible that all seemed in 1949, the standards avoided an important question: what kind of economics should be taught at business schools? Which "economic principles?" And by avoiding that question, by treating economics almost generically, the AACSB ignored the developments that had taken place in the discipline since the First World War.

To wit, the terms "microeconomics" and "macroeconomics." These both first appeared in scholarly publications during the Second World War and remain a basic and broad division within the field and certainly within the course offerings in economics departments. In 1949, however, the AACSB did not indicate which of these mattered most to an education in business, presumably leaving that choice up to each campus. Recall that in his speech at the University of Pittsburgh in 1958, Clark Kerr noted that business schools had still not figured out "what subjects should be taught in economics." [42] And when Carnegie and Ford issued their studies of U.S. business education, AACSB did not require that students take any advanced courses in economics as part of their business curriculum. [43]

This vagueness wasn't entirely an oversight by Dean Grether and the AACSB. In fact, U.S. economics during the interwar period was in a state of flux, if you like, or confusion, if you prefer. The U.S. reaction against classical dogma coalesced into something often called institutionalism. A varied school of economic thought, it retained an aspiration to serious science and empirical investigation brought over in the 1870s from Germany, and as the label suggests, institutionalists shared an understanding that economic institutions played a critical role in shaping economic outcomes. The way to alleviate the social problems created by the economic system, therefore, was to exert some control over those institutions or to build new ones altogether.

Even at its height, institutionalism, with its implicit commitment to some variety of social justice, was never the only game in town. Laissez-faire economic ideas had not vanished entirely, and they would certainly come roaring back in the larger culture during the 1920s. The AEA dropped its more crusading language to make space for economists who held other points of view. And even the institutionalists differed from one another in method and approach. Then the 1930s saw the arrival of Keynesianism and planning economics in the United States. To make matters even more complicated for the keepers of AACSB's standards, even as those 1949 guidelines were adopted, the pendulum of economic thought was swinging back. What once was old became new again, and the pseudogods that Nearing and others thought they had toppled were climbing back onto their thrones.

Put crudely—and perhaps a bit unfairly—the laissez-faire doctrines of classical economics came back as neoclassicism. Out went state interventions and attention to institutions, replaced with Platonic, perfectly functioning unregulated markets and individual economic actors behaving perfectly rationally. Gone was any sense that economics should concern itself with social or collective welfare, not when individuals were free to compete unrestrained and untrammeled in those markets. The Social Gospel waned, while the Prosperity Gospel rose.

For the victors, the triumph of neoclassical economics in the postwar years represents nothing less than better ideas outcompeting bad ones in the disciplinary marketplace. It isn't that simple, needless to say. Several elements combined to replace the institutionalism of the interwar years with the neoclassicism of the postwar decades. Not the least of these was the war itself. Economists who contributed to the war effort laid the groundwork for continued interactions between the field and what Dwight Eisenhower would later call the military-industrial complex. Neoclassicism's focus on calculating the optimal means to achieve a specific end, rather than a focus on competing or conflicting goals, dovetailed nicely with the Pentagon's needs. Not coincidentally, from the mid-1950s through the 1980s, nearly 50 percent of all the funding the National Science Foundation directed toward the social sciences went to economists.[44]

The Cold War that followed on the heels of 1945 also played a role in promoting neoclassical economics. In the new political environment, anything that smacked of left-wing thought might well be seen as suspiciously Soviet, including versions of Keynesianism. Even before the Second World War ended, the editors of the *American Economic Review* stopped publishing articles or even book reviews that dealt with socialist or Marxist economic analysis.[45] The story of émigré European economists like Friedrich von Hayek bringing Mittel-Europan neoclassicism to the West has been well told. The story of U.S. economists who had their careers derailed as a consequence of McCarthyism and the environment it created has not.

Finally, neoclassicists turned away from the sorts of social surveys favored by some of the institutionalists and toward more mathematics. Increasingly complex, abstruse math at that. The mathematical turn taken by economists satisfied what we might call the field's physics envy. The scientific dreams dreamt by economists hadn't died after all. The syllogism for the economists worked like this: Real scientists use complicated equations. Economists (now) use complicated equations. Therefore, economists are real scientists too. Math, though, was not only an end unto itself. By speaking increasingly in the language of math, economists positioned themselves as speakers of objective economic truth. What followed from that was an assertion that the conclusions they came to must also be entirely disinterested. This shift became increasingly dominant, and woe to those economics departments that did not jump on the mathematics bandwagon. An assessment of the economics department at Ohio State in the early 1980s found that "the reason for the marked deterioration in the Department's national standing by 1964 was that it had not kept abreast of the main developments in economics that had taken place after the war and had not incorporated these developments—centering on quantitative analysis of economic activity and the mathematization of economic theory—into policies for faculty recruitment and curriculum development." Other economics departments in the postwar period "simply passed by Ohio State."[46]

Much like their Gilded Age, laissez-faire predecessors, therefore, the new economists of the postwar era created a set of natural laws about the economy, not dressed up in the pseudoscience of social Darwinism this time but in differential equations and lots of graphs.[47] For their part, the institutionalists had made no attempt to hide their political agendas. The neoclassicists who followed them, on the other hand, pretended that they had no politics at all. After all, complex equations have no ideology. By extension, the public policies that flowed from their work, a flow that began in earnest in the 1970s, were packaged as similarly free of ideology. That, of course, was and remains utter nonsense. One newspaper had smirked as far back as 1889 that "this science of political economy . . . is subject to change at the polls on elections day by the will of the people," and that was no less true in 1989.[48] Yet few of these economists acknowledged that scientific "objectivity" might be less straightforward and more problematic than they insisted it was—even as physicists and other scientists were becoming more aware of the contingent nature of their own work.[49] What the neoclassicists sold, then, amounted to morality tales masquerading as mathematics.[50]

All of which is to say that after the war, it was not clear exactly what "economics" meant for business schools, even as they insisted that their students take this many or that many hours of it to complete their degrees. In fact, the intellectual (and curricular) traffic seems to have flowed in only one direction. The economics that business students studied trickled down from the economics on offer from the institution's economics department, regardless of what that economics might be or how it might change over time. By contrast, none of the ideas generated in the accounting department or by the marketing faculty made much impact on the economists, nor were business schools seen as sources of new economic thinking.[51]

This ferment within economics, and the drift toward increasingly abstract theory, did not sit well with the National Association of Manufacturers. A 1962 pamphlet titled "Center Stage for Economic Education" called the new economics "antiseptic," and it fretted about the dangers of too much free-thinking on the nation's students: "In the formative years of a young citizen's life, the antiseptic approach can produce in economics—as it already has in philosophy and other fields—only intellectual chaos and economic agnosticism." The association wanted a return to the true faith, and the way to get there was to teach "the firm" [the company or corporation], rather than the higher math. "It is with and through the firm that most people will have access to and participate in the economic system and its fruits," the manufacturers' pamphlet reminded the nation. After that gentle chiding, the pamphlet went after the economists, charging them with behaving irresponsibly, or worse, unpatriotically: "Whether the profession is prepared to offer the public what it needs to build a virile force for a free society in a world threatened by clean-shaven barbarians with a fanatic devotion to an ancient collectivism can only be answered in the heated dialogue now beginning. . . . One hopes that we economists will tear ourselves away from the sterile model-building and mathematical tinkertoys which fill the reviews, long enough to develop some genuine feeling of responsibility for the preservation of our traditional individual freedom as well as our too often derogated but still munificent and still uncentralized horn of plenty."[52]

Thus, as economics became increasingly mathematical, the math expectations in business school requirements both rose and changed. In one of those conferences sponsored by the AACSB in the wake of the Ford and Carnegie studies, Samuel Goldberg greeted the new emphasis on math with some enthusiasm, though he linked the "importance of mathematical techniques" to the "accelerating ability by means of electronic computing systems to make such techniques usable in the day-to-day operation of a complex business enterprise" as much as he did to math-dependent economics. By 1966, the AACSB found that "the preferred course at present is a one-year course covering some review of algebra; a basic treatment of sets, matrices, and probability; and an introduction to differential and integral calculus."[53] That might well have addressed the complaints of the two 1959 reports on the sponginess of business school requirements by adding academic rigor, but it was not at all clear that mastering calculus really prepared students for careers in business.

Breaking Up Is Hard to Do

As much as any single person could, Viva Belle Boothe embodied the tensions between the new economics and the imperatives of the business school in the postwar years.

After majoring in English, wishing she had been born in the Middle Ages, Boothe was hired to work at Ohio State University's Bureau of Business Research in 1928. In 1941 she became the bureau's director, the first woman to hold the post and perhaps the only woman anywhere to head a business school's research bureau. Though she had earned a doctorate in economics and sociology from Wharton, as director she made her phobia of economic theory as plain as you would expect from a woman who grew up in a small town in east Texas. "What we need," she told an interviewer in 1960, "is a revolution in the teaching of economics based on fact and not theory." In fact, her antagonism toward academic economics was so great that she stopped teaching altogether in 1935 because economics textbooks were a "lot of bunk." So instead she worked to produce research—factual research, that is—and published it in the bureau's various bulletins, pleased along the way to have "smashed many of the so-called theories that were, in some cases, nothing more than whimsical ideas dreamed up years earlier."[54] For Boothe, economics had lost its way, and it wasn't worth the bother of trying to lead it back home. And for those who lamented the state of OSU's economics department in the 1980s, Boothe represented all the things that the department had missed.

In the 1950s, when the Ford Foundation began funding its initiatives to revolutionize U.S. business education, it gave grants to Berkeley, UCLA, and MIT in addition to the other schools mentioned in chapter 2. These three, in Ford's reckoning, were "the economists' schools," and as such, "they viewed business administration more or less as applied economics."[55] That was not meant as a compliment to the business schools at those three universities. As the postwar decades rolled on, more and more economics departments bristled that they were still somehow functioning as service units for their schools of "applied economics." That was certainly the case at the University of Denver. There the dean of the business school, where the economics department resided, acknowledged that as late as the mid-1950s "the department was looked upon largely as a service department in that each [business] student was required to take 15 hours in economics." While one-quarter of Denver students majored in business, hardly any—1.3 percent of the whole undergraduate population—majored in econ.[56]

Roughly fifty years after the AACSB-AEA roundtable of 1927, fifty years after Marshall scratched his head, Roswell McCrea's prediction of divorce had proved largely right and W. H. Lough's wish for it largely fulfilled. Economics had separated from business schools in many of the places where the two had been joined.

As early as 1935, Berkeley's President Sproul created a committee to study the economics department and its relationship with the school of commerce. The committee recommended "a sharp demarcation be made between the academic Department of Economics and the College of Commerce." In 1955, Berkeley's business school began offering its own doctoral degree, but the school insisted "that this would not be at the expense of Economics."[57] In his 1966 study of undergraduate education, Daniel Bell discovered that "the economics department is beginning a two-track system, offering an intensive specialized sequence for those seeking to become economists (and recommending the study of calculus) and a concentration for students interested in learning about economics or business."[58] The two were clearly drifting apart.

A survey conducted in 1980 of nearly 550 economics departments found that that 350 were located in the liberal arts college—almost two-thirds—while 155, or 28 percent, were housed in the business school.[59] When the University of Denver examined the issue in 1985 it found that only 4 of its peer institutions still housed economics inside their business schools.[60] The

Wharton School at Penn remained the home not just of economics but of several of the university's social science departments as well, and Penn's reputation in those fields was quite high. But by the late 1960s the social scientists in West Philadelphia had grown restless. Divorce proceedings began with the circulation of a 1969 report by a university committee and referred to as the Mott Report. Among several of the other irreconcilable differences, the report broached the idea that the university create a new division of social sciences and locate that division in the College of Arts and Sciences. Wharton and the economics department went their separate ways in 1975.

The same thing happened at the University of Denver a few years later and with considerable bitterness. There the economics department had been a part of the business school until 1977, when administratively it was moved to the College of Arts and Sciences. That decision seems only to have made some faculty unhappy. Vice-chancellor Irving Weiner assured the economists in 1981 that, "for the University of Denver to continue making progress toward becoming the kind of institution we would like it to be, it is very important for our College of Arts and Sciences to have a strong, discipline-oriented Department of Economics," but nonetheless in that same year the department was effectively split in two—some economists returned to the business school while others stayed in Arts and Sciences.

Pandemonium and a decade of crises ensued. In a 1988 memo to Provost Roy Wood, William Burford explained, "Since the 1981 split a two-track system has been instituted for BA and BSBA degrees with enormous confusion for students as to what course will be offered and what counts toward their degree requirements. And since the 1981 split graduate education in economics has become virtually extinct." At about the same time, another angry economics faculty member wrote to the provost explaining that "the 'problem' of Economics at DU arises from the chaos and doubt surrounding the teaching of economics here over the last few years." As a consequence of this chaos, "one entire Economics Department, of very high quality, was completely eliminated between 1985 and 1987." The way forward, at least in the eyes of this faculty member, was clear: "*The only way for DU to have an economics curriculum of high quality NOW is to guarantee the continued existence of this Department.* If this Department is eliminated, or if it is incorporated in the Business College, the present faculty will leave, the teaching of Economics as a social science will cease to be a part of the DU curriculum, and the quality of such economics courses as remain will decline." And in case there was any doubt about who was at fault, the faculty member pointed the accusing finger: "It is hard to avoid the conclusion that the chief cause of disruption has been the actions of the Business College, made in bad faith, and with a persistent refusal to acknowledge the aims of liberal education at DU."[61]

No doubt the time of troubles at Denver resulted from local history and the personal animosities that are found everywhere in the groves of academe. But as administrators tried to strip those away, the issue they found was the old one: Was economics a theoretical discipline or an applied one? By 1986, when political science professor James Caporaso weighed in on the matter, economics had firmly established itself as the former. "The growth of modern economic knowledge did not occur within the organizational framework of professional schools," Caporaso wrote in a memo, and business schools "depend on traditional disciplines for the production of fundamental knowledge."[62]

At exactly the same moment, a review committee at Berkeley found that its economics department was in a vertiginous decline. It was slipping in the national rankings, and it didn't have enough faculty to meet student demand. But the report also suggested that at Berkeley the economics department was still haunted by the ghosts of applied economics. At least two other units on campus offered economics—the business school and the Department of Agricultural and Resource Economics—and that created a fair bit of overlap, duplication, and for students, confusion. "Given the strength of applied economics outside the Department of Economics," the report suggested, the department itself could "be more focused on the core of economics."[63] Whatever might constitute that "core," it meant the opposite of "applied." The abstract rather than the concrete; the theoretical rather than the practical; the economic system rather than the individual firm. Those latter belonged at the School of Business Administration, not in the Department of Economics itself. Though it had been fifty years since another Berkeley committee recommended a "sharp demarcation" between economics and business on the Berkeley campus, the lines separating them remained frustratingly fuzzy.

Like families in Tolstoy's *Anna Karenina*, all universities are dysfunctional, each in their own way, so the separation of an economics department from a business school surely had its own internal dynamics and logics at every university where it took place. Still, there were larger questions at stake about the nature of economics as a field and about what ought to take place in business schools.

For their part, business schools needed economics from the very beginning as a way of establishing their intellectual legitimacy and their claim to science in a scientific age. In response to the Mott Report at Penn, Wharton finance professor Douglas Vickers wrote to the dean in a way that revealed that continuing intellectual insecurity: "As you know, the notion is too easily current in the School that the Finance Department should become a department of financial management primarily engaged in business management studies. This comes, of course, from a shallow understanding of the scope, content, and academic character of finance as a discipline. . . . Our work is essentially applied economics of a high order." Vickers went on to offer that, should the economics department leave Wharton for the College of Arts and Sciences, the Finance Department ought to go with it.[64]

The economists needed the separation, however, precisely to establish the intellectual independence of their own research. They no longer wanted to be seen as a service unit for business schools, and they wanted to establish a disciplinary unity. The 1985 report at the University of Denver was insistent on this point: "The suggestion that there are two different *kinds* of economics for each population is not confirmed by the structure of economics curricula in universities across the country. . . . To the extent that differences between *economists* employed in research positions and those employed in the corporate sector exist, these differences are the consequence of differences in professional responsibilities. The training of both groups of economists at the undergraduate and the graduate level is exactly the same."[65]

Getting out from underneath the shadow of the business schools was the only way economics could establish its own intellectual autonomy and authority. Ironically, economists staked their claim to that authority on the continued power of science. Never mind that as often as not different data yield different answers, even when economists use the same methods. In the last quarter of the twentieth century, with their increasing reliance on baroque mathematics and obscurantist equations, economists doubled down on the idea that they should be considered scientists like the chemists and astronomers. No coincidence that in 1969, the same moment when the separation between many economics departments and business schools took place, the Royal Swedish Academy of Sciences awarded its first Nobel Prize in Economic *Sciences*. By that time, no one inside a business school or out was still talking about a "science of business," but economics still clung to the illusion.

Let's turn my interpretation in this chapter around 180 degrees and in two ways. I have argued that while business schools have always required that their students take economics courses, the content of those courses has always come from economics departments, even as economic fashions have come and gone and regardless of whether certain economics courses really had much to do with the subject of business. In addition, I have suggested that business schools have generated few ideas that have had any substantial impact on the discipline of economics. Indeed, we have seen that economics as a field came to believe that it would flourish only if it was no longer associated with what went on the business schools.

What if, however, it is the economists who have little to say to those in the business schools or, indeed, to the rest of us? What if the neoclassical economists who so dominated the economic discourse in the second half of the twentieth century had become increasingly disconnected to anything actually going on in reality?

At one of the annual conferences on economic issues hosted by Middlebury College in 1988 and funded by the Institute of Economic and Monetary Affairs, Robert Clower asked exactly these questions. Or rather, he answered them, and without pulling any punches. "Much of economics is so far removed from anything that resembles the real world that it's often difficult for economists to take their own subject seriously" was Clower's opening salvo to the group. He said, "Publishers have sometimes asked why we economists don't write as if we were intellectually engaged; why don't we produce books about the marvels of our science?" The answer, he went on, "is simple. Economics doesn't have much to marvel at. Once you've got beyond some elementary arguments, it's as though most of economics dealt with footnotes to material that has already been spelled out a hundred years ago."[66]

Clower was no crank. At the time he made those statements he held an endowed professorship in economic theory at the University of South Carolina. He knew of what he spoke. Nor was he alone. David Colander, himself an endowed professor of economics at Middlebury College, followed Clower on the program. Calling the latter's criticism of the field "biting," Colander then offered, "In my view, Clower's critique of the profession is correct."[67] In the subsequent years, a number of apostate economists have said much the same thing.

Over the course of the twentieth century, many economists looked down their disciplinary noses at their colleagues in the business schools as peddling mere applied economics rather than the pure stuff. The 2007 financial meltdown left many of those economists, especially those who had prostrated themselves on the altar of unregulated markets—Alan Greenspan preeminently among them—dazed and confused.[68] Given that, it is probably fair to ask, therefore, which was the emperor, and who was standing on campus naked?

Chapter 4

It's a White Man's World

Women and African Americans in Business Schools

When *Fortune* magazine released its Fortune 500 list of the nation's largest corporations early in June 2016, it found that only twenty-one of those companies were headed by a woman. A stunningly small 4.2 percent. And that number was down from the previous year when there were a whopping twenty-four female CEOs at the helm of the nation's biggest firms.

But those numbers look large indeed when compared to the number of African American CEOs in the Fortune 500. The magazine also reported in 2016 that there had been only fifteen African Americans in the corner office—ever. At the start of 2015, to take one data point, there were a grand total of five African American CEOs on that *Fortune* list. Thus, there were nearly five times as many women as African American CEOs in the middle of the second decade of the twenty-first century.

Fortune 500 CEOs represent real power in the corporate world, but the list also serves a symbolic function—top of the top, biggest of the big. For that reason it could also be easy to dismiss—a scant five hundred companies out of the thousands that exist in this country. Yet further down the corporate pecking order things aren't much different. According the Bureau of Labor Statistics there are roughly 16.2 million management jobs in the country. African Americans hold 6.7 percent of those.[1]

Those numbers have not gone unnoticed, nor have they gone unremarked. Explanations abound. The first most obvious of these is that the isms—sexism and racism—still predominate in the business world. Those attitudes play out in all sorts of ways, large and small, obvious and subtle, but all with the same result: women and African Americans continue to find corporate America a largely inhospitable place, a club largely closed to them. Many observers have wondered about just how committed corporations really are to diversity, about the genuineness of hiring policies intended to diversify the workplace, and about the difference between real career opportunities and mere tokenism. All justified concerns I have no doubt, and to varying degrees in different places. Then there are the policy issues for women in particular. Our nation's inadequate childcare options, parsimonious leave benefits, and more mean that when one parent's career must take a back seat to family demands, that parent is usually mom. And mom's career opportunities suffer accordingly.

There has been less discussion, however, about the role business schools have and have not played in training women and people of color for the business world. As we explore in this chapter, business schools, certainly across much of the twentieth century, cared little and mostly did less to attract those kinds of students. By and large, the world inside collegiate business schools mirrored the world of private enterprise: almost entirely white, almost exclusively male.

Building the Boys' Club

As we have discussed already, businessmen wanted the social status and respect that came from being a professional and working in what was seen as a profession. While business leaders and their advocates inside higher education drew an analogy with medicine and law repeatedly at the turn of the twentieth century, what they did not say—because it hardly needed saying—was that those professions were the domain of men. Turning business into a proper profession through higher education would help ensure that business, like law and medicine, would be a boys' club too.

And so it has been, though in the late nineteenth century that outcome did not seem inevitable.

When the Frenchman Eugène Léautey did his remarkable survey of commercial education in 1886, it wasn't only the sheer number of such schools that impressed him about the United States. In addition, he devoted a section of his study to the fact that American business schools taught women as well as men. Except at Nelson's Ladies Business College in Cincinnati, where, as he pointed out bemusedly, "co-education is not one of the distinguishing features" of the school. But he added quickly that "this system is endorsed by the most profound educators in the land, and is strictly in consonance with the laws of nature and the judgement of reason."[2] Whatever that might mean.

Coeducation set American business schools apart from their European counterparts, and Cincinnati is as a good a place to visit as any. When the International Business College Association met in that city in 1873, the subject of coeducation came up. R. C. Spencer, of the business school that bore the family name, told the association that "the fact that woman has become sufficiently free to earn wages for herself, own property, carry on trade, and transact business as principal as well as agent, has created a necessity for offering her a chance to obtain a business education."

Lest that sound a bit too close to a statement of mid-nineteenth century feminism, Spencer went on to explain that if "women propose to fill such positions, they must prepare themselves to do the work as well or better than men, and at lower prices." In fact, Spencer was impatient with "female agitators of women's rights" because they did not "comprehend and practically apply this universal and simple law of trade"—that law apparently being that women must always work better and cheaper than men. That failure of understanding, Spencer concluded, "shows woman's need of such education as business colleges can give her."[3]

Whatever R. C. Spencer's own brand of feminist politics, his address in Cincinnati demonstrates that the resurgence of feminist activism in the post–Civil War era rippled to the proprietary business schools. When James Garfield addressed the graduates of Bryant & Stratton in Washington, D.C., in 1881, he told the group, "The career opened in Business Colleges . . . for young women, is a most important and noteworthy feature of these institutions." Garfield anticipated what Eugène Léautey would report just a few years later, and he echoed what General R. D. Mussey had said at the commencement of the Washington Business College in 1873. "I received another lesson tonight," Mussey told the graduates, "namely, that we are recognizing the mutuality of help which men and women can give, and that it is not disgrace to be a business woman."[4] I can't be positive that this is the earliest use of the phrase "business woman" in a U.S. publication, but it surely must be among the very first.

In fact, Mussey's celebration of businesswomen on the dais at the Washington Business College was not as guileless as it might have appeared. Mussey had demonstrated his commitment to racial equality during the Civil War when he energetically recruited African Americans into the Union Army. After the war, he married Ellen Spencer; she, in turn, joined her husband in his law practice. She even took it over after his death in 1892, though this required a special dispensation and a special bar exam, which she passed in 1893. Having been unable to attend law school herself, Ellen Mussey helped establish the Washington College of Law, the first law school for women in the country. And her maiden name is not coincidental: she was the daughter of Spencerian College founder Platt Rogers Spencer and the sister of Robert C. Spencer. At least at the Spencerian Colleges, the connection between business schools and women's rights in the late nineteenth century ran in the family.

A circular for the Spencerian Business College's Milwaukee outpost put the matter boldly: "We favor business education for women because we regard her as the equal of man, with the same natural right to self support. We believe in it because her entrance into business life carries with it a refining and healthful influence." Whether wishful thinking or a genuine report of conditions, the circular went on to claim, "Much of the prejudice which has existed among business men, against the employment of women in office and counting room has given way, and in its place has come a disposition to recognize their ability and worth." Further, Spencerian's Milwaukee administrators believed, "It is beginning to be understood that young women are in many cases preferable to young men, owing to their quickness of perception and motion, their uniform freedom from bad habits and consequent reliability."[5]

These references to the role of women in late nineteenth-century business in the United States and the role of business education in getting them there are tantalizing hints rather than conclusive evidence, and I don't want to make the point too emphatically. Business surely remained male dominated no matter how many women graduated from Bryant & Stratton or a Spencerian College. After all, it was the age of robber barons, not robber baronesses. At the same time, however, we shouldn't discount entirely that these proprietary schools did create opportunities for women in the world of business that might not have been available to them otherwise. Back in Milwaukee, for example, Mary Busalacchi was the daughter of Sicilian immigrants who would not let her leave the city to attend college. She enrolled in the Spencerian College instead, graduated early in the 1920s, and then landed a job as bursar at Marquette University.[6]

A woman like Mary Busalacchi, even if her parents had let her leave town, was not liable to get a business education anywhere other than a proprietary school. The Tuck School at Dartmouth and Harvard's B-school sat on campuses that were all-male to start with. But even on campuses that admitted women, business schools remained largely male enclaves. The Wharton School was founded in the same year that James Garfield extolled the virtues of women's education for business. Women began enrolling in Penn classes in the 1870s, and they started to earn degrees there in the following decade. But when the Wharton School was founded in 1881 it was decidedly not open to women. Coeducation is written in the founding articles of incorporation at the University of Chicago, a promise to "provide, impart, and furnish opportunities for all departments of higher education to persons of both sexes on equal terms," but Chicago's College of Commerce did not award a doctorate in business to a woman until 1929. In fact, Ursula Batchelder Stone was the first woman in the country to be awarded a graduate degree from any collegiate business school. At Berkeley, co-ed from the start, the business school granted 5500 undergraduate degrees between its opening in 1898 and 1942. Of those, 13.5 percent went to women.[7] Those few women who did wind up in collegiate business schools before the Second World War stand as the proverbial exceptions proving the rule.

At places that were already co-ed and where the baggage of a certain kind of social status did not weigh as heavily, women may have been a bit better represented in business schools. Additionally, the U.S. entry into the First World War—and more specifically the disappearance of young men from campus and from the workforce into the army—may have given women a brief opening in business schools. That seems to have been the case in Denver. A University of Denver circular from 1918 reported, "There never was a time in our history when so many women were seeking to enter into business life and when so many inviting doors of opportunity were open. . . . The demand for high-class trained women is out of all proportion to the meager supply." In response to that meager supply, "an increasing number of young women enter the school every year." According to this announcement, "The number of women taking the work in Commerce has increased five or six fold during the past year." The circular assured prospective female students that higher education would be worth the trouble because, at least in Denver during the First World War, "there is an over-supply of girls and women able to take up non-skilled and merely clerical work" but that "but the new demand is for women of higher training." "Women managers, accountants, buyers and organizers," it trumpeted, "whose native executive ability has been developed by the hard discipline of a standard university course are everywhere in demand." Women could prepare themselves at the University of Denver for these kinds of jobs "rather than for typewriting, bookkeeping or school teaching." And as an additional enticement, the university promised new female students that "their special problems will be looked after by a Faculty adviser especially fitted to assist young women in matters of business, and also on personal and social questions."[8]

Still, I think it is fair to conclude that for the most part women who wanted a collegiate business education had few options. When Ellen Spencer helped start the Washington College of Law for aspiring female lawyers, it joined the New England Female Medical College in Boston and the Women's Medical College of Pennsylvania in Philadelphia, places where women could train as doctors. Both of those schools had been founded before the Civil War, and while the New England Female Medical College merged with Boston University a few years after the Civil War, Women's Medical College of Pennsylvania remained all-female until 1970. By contrast, no one opened a collegiate-level school of business specifically for women. Nor did women's colleges themselves open business schools on their campuses. None of the prestigious Seven Sisters colleges—Bryn Mawr, Barnard, Vassar, Smith, Mount Holyoke, Radcliffe, and Wellesley—started business education when the movement for collegiate business education took off in the early twentieth century.

This is not to suggest that women who wanted to be doctors or lawyers somehow had broader vistas. Medicine, as it professionalized in the late nineteenth century, did so as a male occupation. A group of female doctors formed the American Medical Women's Association in 1915 in response to the indifference and hostility they faced in the American Medical Association. At least there were enough of them to start such a group.

My point is that the proprietary world of business education seems to have been far more coeducational than either medical or law schools, and that as collegiate business schools positioned themselves against the proprietary schools as places with more intellectual prestige and social status, they implicitly helped create a gendered hierarchy as well. In a 1911 circular, the Peirce School of Business in Philadelphia still promoted business education for women, but not quite in the same way that Mussey and Garfield had. "Of the avenues of employment open to young women," the advert read, "there is none more desirable than that of amanuensis, and its higher development, the private secretary."[9] Collegiate business schools promised training for men to join the upper ranks of business; proprietary school students would provide the clerical staff, and many of that staff would be women. From businesswoman to amanuensis in the space of a generation.

And there the matter generally rested for decades; at Wharton, for more than half a century. Only in 1952 did Wharton faculty permit women to sit in on some classes. Their presence was not, apparently, too upsetting to the boys, because in the fall of the following year the Wharton faculty voted to admit women formally to the program, though not on an entirely unrestricted basis. As the student newspaper the *Daily Pennsylvanian* reported, "No definite quota has been assigned to restrict the number of women admitted to the Wharton School other than that which applies generally to women students of the whole University." Fifteen young women enrolled in the Wharton School in the fall semester of 1954.[10]

Wharton got the jump on Harvard by at least a few years. In 1956 Harvard announced a partnership between itself and Radcliffe, Harvard's sister school, to funnel women into the business school. In considering this idea, the B-school dean Stanley Teele "was hard put to answer logically the question of why the Business School continues to refuse to admit women applicants for graduate degrees." One concern the dean raised was "whether the number of men that could be trained by the Harvard Business School should be further limited by admitting women when it was believed that a woman's business life would be limited to approximately five years, while the average man might remain active in business for approximately forty years."[11] An answer, of a sort, to explain Harvard's reluctance.

Women weren't entirely excluded from business school curriculum in the mid-twentieth century even if they didn't occupy many of the classroom seats. In 1937, New York University students voted Shirley Densen, a student in the commerce school, as "the most exquisite co-ed," and Duncan Norton-Taylor wryly noted in 1954 that a business major at Boston University could chose "free electives" that included courses clarifying "the psychology and philosophy of women, using practical material to help those in supervisory positions to a more practical understanding of the female employee."[12] The mind boggles at what might have been taught in those courses.

Meanwhile, some of those proprietary business colleges morphed into secretarial schools catering more and more to women. "Our expanding economy urgently needs more, better trained secretarial, executive secretarial and junior business management personnel," S. M. Vinocour announced in 1957, and proprietary schools were the answer. Vinocour referred to the National Association and Council of Business Schools, an umbrella organization formed in 1949 to improve and monitor nearly 450 member business schools. The association was meant to demonstrate that this new generation of independent business schools had standards and were reputable educational institutions.[13]

Gone were "the days of the old 'third-floor, dusty walk-up' concept," Vinocour reassured readers; instead, "the independent business college is attractive, well-staffed and thoroughly professional in its approach." More and more women "over 35 are quitting the home to take jobs in stores, offices and industry," and proprietary schools could train them for these opportunities. After all, as Vinocour pointed out, "Hundreds of thousands of young women will be disappointed because collegiate doors will be closed in their [women's] faces—because there simply won't be the facilities, staff or money available for the adequate expansion of the publicly supported colleges. The independent business school, on the other hand, is prepared now to meet the education wave of the future."[14] Proprietary schools remained more welcoming of women in the mid-twentieth century just as they had been in the late nineteenth.

The Color of Business Is White

If women made only occasional appearances at business schools across much of the twentieth century, attendance by African Americans might well have been even rarer, though it is hard to know for sure. Eugène Léautey did not make any racial observations in his 1886 study. This might have reflected a certain color blindness in his data or, more likely, that there were no racial observations to make. Then there was the question of institutional geography. Léautey's survey revealed far more business schools in northern states than in southern ones. This surely reflected the regional disparity in educational investment more broadly and in differing regional economies. Southern states did not fund education of any kind to the same extent that northern states did, nor did the South's economy industrialize to the same extent as it did in the North. For example, at the time of Léautey's work, Minnesota and Mississippi had almost identical populations. But Léautey counted eight business schools in Minnesota and only three in Mississippi. Indeed, Léautey found only two in North Carolina despite the fact that three hundred thousand more people lived there than in the Gopher State. Until the First World War the overwhelming majority of African Americans still lived in the states of the Confederacy, and it seems unlikely that too many African Americans would have found the handful of southern business colleges all that welcoming in the segregated late nineteenth century.

Of the two schools Léautey listed under the state of Georgia, however, one is particularly intriguing: the Business College of Clark University. Clark was opened in 1869 by Methodists to educate freedmen after the Civil War, and it did so in Atlanta, the heart of the old Confederacy. In 1877 it became a university, and by the 1880s it boasted a business college along with its other schools. The Reverend C. J. Brown served as its principal.

In all my research for this project I have not seen Clark University's Business College listed as among the first collegiate business schools. Indeed, had I not been scrutinizing Léautey's tabulation carefully I would not have known about it at all. Clark University's business school stands as just one more episode of African American history not so much written out of our history as never written into it in the first place.

The course of study at the business school in Atlanta did not differ too substantially from that at Wharton. Students took business writing and business correspondence, bookkeeping, and commercial law along with a dose of liberal arts including astronomy, geology, and the "history of civilization." Reverend Brown himself taught "commercial law, bookkeeping and penmanship." And the college offered internships, though that is certainly not what they called the experience: "During the Senior year," the Circular of Information read, "the student is placed in charge of a complete set of books which are kept in connection with our store. Here he deals in real merchandise and is thus required to record *actual* transactions as the sales of books, pens, pencils, etc."[15] In this sense, Clark's school resembled the hybrid created at the University of Denver—a school that taught the same subjects at Bryant & Stratton but that issued a bachelor of commercial science. But another reason why Clark's business school may have vanished from the historical record is that it seems itself to have vanished. I have found no indication that the Business College survived beyond the turn of the twentieth century, though the university itself certainly did and exists to this day, having merged with Atlanta University in the late twentieth century.

For African Americans in the South, black colleges and universities were effectively the only opportunity they had at a higher education, and thus, at the risk of stating the obvious, as collegiate schools of business opened on the campuses of white-only institutions, black students were ipso facto barred from attending. None of the students who entered the University of Mississippi's school of business administration when it opened in 1917 were black; nor were there any black students attending when the school received its accreditation from the American Association of Collegiate Schools of Business thirty years later. And so it went across the South.

In 1938, V. V. Oak, a professor at Ohio's Wilberforce College, the first college in the nation to be owned and run by African Americans, wrote, "There is no other place but the Negro college where adequate and practical background for business can be secured," and business courses were surely taught at what we now call the historically black colleges and universities.[16] The 1945 course catalog at Southern University in Baton Rouge lists a course in elementary accounting in which "customary business forms and papers will be emphasized . . . with a special stress being placed on Negro business." Yet separate schools or colleges of business seemed to have arrived late at the HBCUs. The business school at Texas Southern in Houston was founded in 1955 and stands as the first business school at an HBCU to receive AACSB accreditation, and that came only in 1968, even as Jim Crow segregation in higher education drew to a close.

Just before the United States entered the Second World War, the U.S. Office of Education published *National Survey of the Higher Education of Negroes*. It is a remarkably extensive piece of work and an invaluable record of midcentury black America. In addition to demographic, geographic, and financial information, the survey included a tally of the kinds of academic programs available to black students. It found that while "twenty-one fields of specialization in commerce are available" in black colleges across the South, a whole slew of business fields were not. These included much of what would have been standard issue at majority-white schools—everything from "accounting, advertising, banking and finance, business statistics" to "insurance, management, marketing, real estate," and more.[17]

Just after the war, Atlanta University professor Joseph Pierce expanded on the survey to examine the opportunities for business education in more detail. Pierce noted that in a 1925 survey, even as collegiate business schools had begun to sprout like mushrooms across the landscape of higher education, only six of the HBCUs offered a business curriculum that led to a degree. That survey found that, in fifteen colleges, three offered business in the last two years of the undergraduate course and the remaining twelve offered it as a four-year program. None had opened a graduate school of business, though Pierce's own Atlanta University offered a master of arts in economics and business.[18]

Though Pierce wrote twenty years after that 1925 study, he felt it was still fair to conclude that not much had changed and that "little attention is being paid to the preparation of Negro college students for business activity." As he looked at the course offerings at those fifteen schools, however, Pierce had some more specific complaints. "The lack of opportunity for Negroes to engage in businesses which concern themselves with transportation and foreign trade," he wrote, "is reflected in the fact that these courses have scant attention in the curricula of Negro institutions." Likewise, "the fact that manufacturing has played a minor role in Negro business is probably related to the lack of courses in Negro educational institutions in this important area of business endeavor." There were doubtless other reasons why black Americans did not participate in the higher echelons of the manufacturing economy, but Pierce identified an intriguing question: Did the business education offered at HBCUs in the middle decades of the twentieth century reflect or reinforce the racial segregations in the larger economy? Certainly Pierce's survey of black-owned businesses in twelve (unidentified) cities paints a stark picture of that segregation. Pierce counted six hundred beauty shops, for example, and only seven "loan and investment companies." He found exactly one accounting firm. He was right about African Americans and manufacturing. Of the nearly four thousand black-owned businesses he tallied, only nineteen were manufacturing companies.[19]

Pierce had no doubt that black colleges had an important role in developing future black business leaders and in creating "an inclusive philosophy of business, which when put to work will have as its goal the unqualified participation and integration of Negro business into the general American economy." Pierce hopefully reported that Atlanta University had just established a graduate school of business with ambitions of granting MBA degrees. He did acknowledge, however, that few schools could actually answer the question "What should be the aims of vocational business education in Negro colleges and universities?" On the basis of his survey, he admitted, "in some instances the departments of business in Negro colleges and universities appear to have but vague notions of the ends they are striving to achieve." Back at Wilberforce, V. V. Oak was a bit more pointed in the pages of the NAACP's *Crisis* magazine. In the twenty years between 1917 and when he wrote in 1937, Oak noted, "more than five hundred students have received bachelor's degrees from the business departments of various Negro colleges." And yet, he went on, "some of our leaders and successful business men are complaining that most of these graduates are inadequately furnished with business knowledge." Further, the students were no good. "The wholesale admission of large numbers of ill-trained and improperly qualified students [is] partly responsible for the poor showing of our business graduates," Oak noted. And to compound that problem, these mediocre students "instead of acquiring sound knowledge in business principles" end up "owning an inflated head which is carrying a vocabulary of high-sounding financial words and phrases without proper understanding of their significance."[20]

Oak categorized business education at the HBCUs finally as "aimless." Yet as we have already seen, that charge had been and continued to be leveled against business education as a whole. So too were his complaints about the quality of the students. In that sense, business education at HBCUs differed from that at majoritarian institutions only in degree, perhaps, rather than in kind. As black colleges and universities began to grant more and more business degrees, they had not done any better job than their white counterparts at figuring out what the purpose of business education was or how to achieve it. But they had certainly done no worse. The "inflated heads" of business school grads came in white and black.

As African Americans moved from South to North during and after the First World War, new educational opportunities were, theoretically, available to them. But much like women in business schools in the middle decades of the twentieth century, black students were, in the main, very few and very far between. Arthur Turnbull became the first African American to receive a doctorate from the University of Chicago's business school in 1926, beating Ursula Batchelder Stone to that distinction by three years; Lionel Wallace became the school's first African American to receive an MBA in 1942. Even so, in 1966 a grand total of fifty black students were enrolled in MBA programs at AACSB-accredited schools nationwide.[21] Five zero.

Not surprisingly, things began to change at just about that moment. Or rather, the question of black students in business schools became an issue people began to discuss finally in the 1960s. In 1964, the University of Chicago's dean George P. Shultz—who would go on from Chicago to a distinguished career in several Republican presidential administrations—began the Careers for Negroes in Management at the Graduate School of Business. Part internship program, part financial aid program, the Careers project partnered with several local and national corporations that helped fund it and, in turn, provided job placements for participants. Shultz was convinced that "there is substantial evidence of the growing desire of business organizations to employ capable Negroes in management positions" and that opportunities for African Americans in management "far exceed" the number trained for them. Looking back on why he started the Careers project, Shultz remembers that "prior to the program, we had received no applications from [African Americans]." Shultz wanted his program to bridge the desire he believed existed in the private sector and the perception of African Americans that the corporate world was simply not open to them.[22]

Business Schools in the Age of Black Capitalism

Campaigning for president in 1968, Richard Nixon began to champion the idea of black capitalism. In short, Nixon wanted to pivot the role of the federal government in advancing the civil rights agenda away from expanding political gains and social welfare programs and toward promoting black-owned small businesses. As a political strategy, black capitalism had much to recommend it. It allowed Nixon to promote a civil rights cause that fit comfortably within a conservative economic framework. And since those business projects would germinate primarily in the black sections of U.S. cities, it demonstrated Nixon's commitment to do something about the urban crisis that had erupted over and over again in violence during the long hot summers of the 1960s. At the same time, it allowed Nixon to adopt, or co-opt, the language of certain black activists who called for black economic independence or even separatism. After all, wasn't it Malcolm X who said in his *Autobiography*, "The American black man should be focusing his every effort toward building his *own* businesses." Nixon couldn't agree more. Black capitalism seemed the antidote to black power, and Nixon would be only too willing to help administer it.[23]

The tensions between economic integration and economic segregation long predated the fraught 1960s. Robert Kinzer, a graduate student in business at NYU, wrote his thesis on the topic just after the war. Published as a book in 1950 with coauthor Edward Sagarin, *The Negro in American Business* laid out the dilemma at the very beginning: "The Negro entering business or preparing himself in business education is faced with a problem of choosing the most advantageous road to follow. . . . On the one hand, he finds the separate economy, consisting of businesses owned and operated by Negroes exclusively, making or selling products to the Negro market alone." On the other hand, the authors counterposed "an integrated economy where products and services are sold in the general market. . . . This is a way of business not only difficult to achieve, but which may actually be in conflict with certain present economic interests."[24] If white liberals had hoped to integrate the economy, along with all the other institutions in American life, during the civil rights era, Nixon wanted to promote the separate economy. One writer for *Harvard Business Review*, critiquing the way Nixon's community development proposals were structured, complained that black capitalism would only perpetuate ghetto isolation and racial separatism. It amounted to "separate but equal" economic development.[25]

Whatever his motivations, and whatever his level of commitment to promoting black capitalism, Nixon was not alone in the late 1960s in his enthusiasm for a greater African American presence in U.S. business. Plenty of observers saw that the natural path for African Americans into business was through business schools. "Prior to 1960," Charles Fields told readers of *MBA* magazine, "industry systematically excluded the majority of black professionals from even entry-level lower management or sales promotion." That was all starting to change. "The number of black MBA graduates increased drastically in 1967 and 1968," Fields continued, "and greater numbers of graduates are expected in 1969 and 1970." As Penn State economist Bernard Booms put it, the black MBA could be the alternative to black capitalism because it would enable black graduates to move into the corporate mainstream.[26]

Others, like Lincoln Harrison, saw business schools at historically black institutions as key to achieving greater black participation in business in the age of black capitalism. If HBCUs struggled with their purpose as the rest of higher education moved toward integration, Harrison retorted, "I submit that even at a time when some persons are expressing doubt about the worthwhileness of any educational program at predominantly Negro colleges and universities, the black business school has an indispensable role to play in the network of programs seeking to elevate the economic status of minorities through greater participation in business and industry." The reason for this, as Harrison saw it, was that the black college remained a fixture of the black community not just symbolically but quite literally. Black business schools were "in a unique position to make significant contributions to the activation of the concept of black capitalism." A black business school "[is often] located in the heart of a black community, primarily has a black student body, and has a long history of service to the black business interests."[27] Whether or not U.S. business would achieve racial integration, the nexus of black colleges and black businesses presented opportunities for black economic advancement too good to ignore in the early 1970s.

Nonetheless, the rest of higher education was also waking up to the issue of black business education at that moment. Chicago's George Shultz moved to Washington to become Richard Nixon's first secretary of labor (where, among other things, he implemented the Philadelphia Plan, requiring the city's lily-white and deeply racist construction unions to admit a quota of black workers), but his Careers program had an influence beyond Hyde Park. Across the country business schools began to ask themselves why they had few black students and wondered what they could to do to change that.

They got some help from two foundations. In 1966 the Ford Foundation, not surprisingly, funded a group of five business schools as the Consortium for Graduate Study in Business for Minorities and, in a duplication reminiscent of the two foundation studies of business education in the 1950s, the Alfred P. Sloan Foundation put money toward the creation of the Council for Opportunity in Graduate Management Education in 1969. Sloan's council consisted of nine graduate schools of business, and they included the heavy hitters: Berkeley, Carnegie-Mellon, Cornell, Tuck, Harvard, MIT (it was named the Sloan School after all), Wharton, and Stanford. The project was based at Columbia University, and it started with a million-dollar grant.

The Ford consortium sprang from the mind and the good intentions of Sterling Schoen. In 1964 he found himself teaching management in the business school at Washington University in St. Louis. Moved by the ethos of the era, and perhaps by discussions he may have had with George Shultz at the University of Chicago where Schoen had a fellowship in 1962, he began looking into his own corner of the academic world and discovered virtually no African Americans there. He also looked into the management staff and board members at large corporations and found even fewer. And so he began to hatch a plan to increase the number of African Americans in business schools. Two years later, nearly fifty people from fifteen universities gathered in St. Louis and the consortium was officially launched. Ford stepped in with its grant at the end of that year.[28]

People inside the Sloan Foundation had been engaged in discussions about how best to increase minority representation in the professions, which, as they pointed out, hinged on access to graduate education. In turn, as Sloan noted, African Americans were "represented in very small numbers in the graduate schools of major universities." "With only a few exceptions, [an African American] has no graduate institutions of his own to which he can turn." In 1969 Sloan decided to change this in the fields of medicine and management. After all, who could argue with the idea that an MBA represented an important avenue for upward mobility for African Americans. An MBA "is tangible 'proof' of an applicant's business knowledge," and people with them earned salaries "$2000–$3000 higher than those paid to BA's" according to *MBA* magazine, despite "very little other evidence as to the applicant's ability."[29]

Recognizing that "the problems of engaging larger numbers of Negro students in graduate management education are manifold," the Sloan Foundation wanted its member institutions to examine what it saw as four key challenges: how best to recruit students to graduate programs; how to identify undergraduates "who will be likely to enjoy success in a managerial career"; how to reconfigure the curriculum to meet "the special needs, the special difficulties and the special career objectives of Negro students"; and finally, how to provide the necessary financial aid given that black students require "greater financial assistance than the average white student." Sloan's directors envisioned that they would fund the council for five years, and that by 1975 "it is expected that each management school will be able to continue activities of this kind" on its own.[30]

Quickly Sloan's council added a tenth school—the University of Chicago—and moved its base of operation to Harvard, while Ford's consortium added a sixth school to its group. And though the exact details of the interfoundation interactions are a bit murky, by the early 1970s Sloan was providing grant money to both projects.

If the problem graduate business schools faced was that precious few black students enrolled, then designing new ways to identify and recruit such students, as Sloan's participating schools proposed to do, would seem the obvious answer. But as a number of observers pointed out, the schools themselves might not have been the primary reason black students stayed away. The reason, instead, might have been in the U.S. private sector. By the late 1960s the expansion of the managerial economy had been under way for roughly a century, and for that entire century black Americans had been excluded from it. That discrimination created its own set of expectations about how corporate America might now respond to blacks knocking on its door even if they were holding MBAs. As Raphael Nevins and Andrew Merryman described it in their survey of the question, "When graduate business schools attempt to recruit blacks, especially at predominantly Negro colleges, they often face difficulties persuading students that business will be a viable career for them. . . . Business, it was felt, was no place for the Negro, for when it came to equality, business did not mean business." Likewise, when William Panschar wrote about the first group of students in the consortium, he noted that "the bright, young Negro college graduate did not turn to business for career or educational purposes. He felt that business did not offer him an opportunity at the managerial level." And even while the managerial ranks continued to swell and thus "whites [did] not see the program as a challenge to employment," in 1970, probably with good reason, the economist Bernard Booms cautioned that "some whites might consider black management a threat to self-esteem."[31] Business schools could work harder and more creatively to recruit black students, but that did not necessarily change the corporate world into which those students would go when they graduated. Whether "major corporations are successful in attracting and retaining these future executives," Charles Fields admonished, "depends upon acceptance by industry of an action-oriented program for blacks across the board."[32]

Further, some of those bright young African American students who did enroll in business schools in the late 1960s and early 1970s developed what we might call an educational double consciousness about what they were doing. However much business schools preached—or agonized—about the importance of social responsibility in the private sector, the education on of- fer remained primarily designed to serve the needs of a business world where the profit motive still reigned supreme. But when Nevins and Merry- man surveyed black MBA students they found that making a whole lot of money was not necessarily the reason they enrolled. "Black MBA's," they re- ported, "seem to be motivated by the desire to make a difference someday in the condition of black people in the United States. Well over half of those responding to the survey want to go back to the ghetto to improve life there." Charles Fields, an African American who worked for a corporate recruit- ing firm, found much the same thing. "Individual success," Fields wrote, "is considered as only a concomitant of the greater achievement by blacks as a group."[33]

Indeed, Penn State's Bernard Booms wondered whether increasing the number of black students in elite MBA programs, and in turn placing them in corporate jobs, would not have the perverse effect of draining African America of some of its best business talent. "If the black community's best college-trained political leaders or potential political leaders are drawn into leading establishment corporations," Booms worried, "only for the benefit of themselves and the existing power structure, the move to power and free- dom for blacks could be effectively blunted." Booms might have checked in with Andre Lee, who conducted a survey of students at Harvard, Colum- bia, and Cornell examining the question of "relevance" as it was viewed by black and white students. Lee reported his findings, such as they were, in the *AACSB Bulletin* in 1973. He sounded almost distressed to discover that "this segment [black students] of the population has brought with it an alien culture, a political, if not radical, stream of thought, and a basket of economic and societal complaints which heretofore have largely been ignored."[34] Pre- sumably the world of business schools was not quite ready for alien cultures, radical perspectives, and students who desired to make a difference rather than a handsome salary.

For its part, Sloan declared victory in 1975. "Management education for minorities has been stimulated greatly by the activities of two consortia," the foundation's annual reported announced in 1974, and thus "terminal grants" were made to both to be paid out during 1974, 1975, 1976. More than five hundred students were enrolled in the sixteen MBA programs, more than double the number at those schools in 1969 when the program began, and in total "more than 600 students have benefited from [Council for Opportunity in Graduate Management Education] fellowships since 1970." Corporations too had increased their contributions to the initiative tenfold, from $28,000 in 1971–72 to over $300,000 in academic year 1973–74. Sloan's five-year investment in the project totaled over $3.25 million. Sloan acknowledged that "the need for [Council for Opportunity in Graduate Management Education] and similar programs will continue," but the foundation believed that what it had seeded could now grow on its own.[35] And fair enough too. After all, when corporate recruiter William Panschar, who had been at the consortium's founding meeting, wrote enthusiastically about the project in 1969 he stated optimistically, "The long-run goal of the consortium is to go out of business. . . . Ultimately, we hope to talk to as many young Negroes, proportionally, as we do whites in the course of our regular M. B. A. recruiting efforts."[36]

There are undoubtedly sixteen different answers to the question of whether this program really had rooted deeply enough that individual campuses would pay for it on their own once the foundation money dried up. Earl Cheit had been a professor at Berkeley's business school when it was a member of the Sloan Foundation's council. He took over as dean in 1976, the year after Sloan wrapped up its involvement in the program. Yet when he looked back on his career at Berkeley, he seemed oddly detached from the whole question of black students at the business school. "The business school, at the MBA level, did a reasonably good job," he told an interviewer. "We've always had a black MBA association, and indeed at one time the national black MBA association gave an award to the school, but we never publicized it because we felt there was so much more that ought to be done." That sounded a bit like the kind of boilerplate that administrators offer when they want to sound interested but aren't quite, especially given that Cheit offered no specifics about just what ought to be done. In fact, he appeared almost baffled about the whole matter. "In the case of the MBA program, to me it was always a mystery why the market didn't work better. A black MBA coming out of Berkeley commands a wonderful array of job opportunities, and you would think that would attract more people." He concluded somewhat complacently, "People who do research and write about MBA programs have long been interested in the question of why MBA programs haven't attracted more black students. There's a variety of answers, but the reality is not a very large number apply."[37] Recall that one of the central purposes of the Sloan project was to identify and recruit black students more effectively. At Berkeley, apparently, they did not figure out how to do that. Findings from one survey in the early 1990s indicate that black enrollment at Berkeley's business school peaked at 7 percent of the class in 1989. It had dropped to 3 percent by 1992.[38] Perhaps markets don't always work the way business schools teach that they do.

By the end of the twentieth century, black enrollments in MBA programs remained frustratingly small. Black students made up 8 percent of the undergraduate population at Yale in 1995, for example, but only 2.3 percent of the students at Yale's School of Organization and Management. Harvard College routinely disclosed racial data about its students, but the B-school refused to do the same. Still, there is some evidence that African American students at the nation's elite business schools were having a better time of things. A 1997 survey of African American students generated responses that were, in the main, quite positive. "Black business students," concluded the author, "are finding the racial climate at their school to be acceptable if not cordial." As one student from MIT's Sloan School wrote, "Sloan has been very good to me. The environment is very favorable for people of color." The sample size was small and the methodology not necessarily thorough, but the *Journal of Blacks in Higher Education* reported the results as "very good news."[39]

Those elite schools, however, produced just a tiny fraction of the MBAs churned out by business schools by the end of the century. How black students fared at places other than MIT and Wharton is harder to know. The problem, as AACSB director Charles Hickman put it in 1993, is not with the Harvards and the Stanfords. "They will get their share," he said in an address on the subject, "just by buying them." The real problem, he went on, "is with schools like Memphis State."[40] By the turn of the twenty-first century, a number of HBCUs had followed Atlanta University's lead and opened their own MBA programs, eighty-five, in fact, by 2003. They were certainly producing African American MBAs, but the careers of their students seemed to demonstrate only that not all MBAs were created equal. Not a single one of those programs landed on any of the top-fifty lists that began circulating in the 1970s. As a consequence, MBAs from those HBCUs made less coming out of school than those coming from one of the top fifty, and often considerably less. For instance, a graduate of a top-fifty school in one southern city could expect an initial job offer nearly $30,000 more than an MBA graduate from an HBCU in that same city.[41] The differential might well be attributable to African American MBAs moving into jobs in the government and nonprofit sectors at higher rates, whether because of career choice or the lingering sense that corporate America remains inhospitable. Those jobs have always paid less than corporate jobs at the same managerial level. And in a cycle that, even if not vicious, is at least ironic, high starting salaries are part of what vaults a school into the list of top fifty in the first place: as long as MBAs from HBCUs earn less, their schools will never make those lists; as long as those schools aren't on those lists, their graduates will make less.

Keeping the "Men" in Businessmen

Black business schools differed from their white counterparts in the middle of the twentieth century in an important way. Women constituted a majority of the students enrolled and, during the 1944–45 school year, a substantial 85 percent majority, though that number surely reflected the absence of men who were in the military. Even so, women consistently outnumbered men at black business schools because, according to Joseph Pierce, of "the differences in kinds of occupations available to graduates." Women, Pierce explained, "typically take technical business education and enter office positions, but men usually prepare themselves for positions of greater responsibility." The fact of the matter was that "the openings are more numerous in the lower levels of business."[42]

Twenty years later, however, Charles Field, the corporate recruiter, surveyed eighty-six black MBAs who had received their degree between 1950 and 1968. Five of those eighty-six were women. When Washington University professor Sterling Schoen created the Consortium for Graduate Study in Business for Minorities in 1966 (it would later change its name to the Consortium for Graduate Study in Management) the goal was to recruit black men into the ranks of MBA students. Black women were only included in the program after 1970.[43] As business schools made a push to redress the racial imbalance in their classrooms by recruiting more black students, there seems to have been an implicit understanding that those black students, just like their white counterparts, would be men.

Even where enrollment information is available, it is hard to know exactly what kind of education those few women in business schools pursued and what happened to them after they graduated—especially at undergraduate programs. The business school at Miami University, where I happen to teach, opened in 1927, part of the explosion of collegiate business schools that took place during the 1920s. At Miami, a co-ed, public university, women shared the campus with men if not in entirely equal numbers then in substantial ones. In academic year 1962–63, for example, Miami's total enrollment came to 8284 students. This was split almost evenly: 4382 men, or 53 percent, and 3902 women, or 47 percent. Of those 8284, 1551 were enrolled at the business school, nearly 19 percent of all students at Miami that year. But only 205 of those 1551 were women. In other words, almost a third of men at Miami that year majored in business, while only 5.3 percent of women did.

But even those figures, small as they are, might be deceptively large. In 1929, just two years after the business school itself opened, Miami added a Department of Secretarial Studies within it. The department remained at the business school until 1970, and it will surprise no one to learn that a majority of women at Miami's business school gravitated there. An enormous majority, in fact. Looking back on the occasion of the school's fiftieth anniversary in 1987, Dean Raymond Glos counted the business school having granted 11,627 bachelor of science degrees in business, about 10 percent of them to women. Between 1929 and 1970, 617 students had graduated with a BS in secretarial studies, nine of whom were men. Thus 98.5 percent of the secretarial school graduates had been women.[44]

Miami's record of educating women in business looks much like Berkeley's. Between 1898, when the school of business opened there, and 1942, when the United States entered the war, Berkeley handed out roughly 5500 bachelor's degrees in business, 13.5 percent of them to women. At the graduate level, 432 students earned an MBA at Berkeley between 1961 and 1963, and about 20 of them, or 5 percent, were women. The Berkeley dean Ewald Grether remembered, "In fact, if you go back to the beginnings of the College of Commerce, you'll find that business people thought of women as secretaries. Some of the schools of business or colleges of commerce had secretarial programs for the women, you see. They didn't think of women doing the other things."[45]

By 1955, forty women's colleges around the country offered some sorts of business courses but none had opened a separate business school. And the numbers remained entirely underwhelming. Of those forty, three-quarters awarded only a handful of degrees in business; business degrees from those women's colleges accounted for only 1 percent of all business degrees. Men received 90 percent of all degrees in business despite women, even in the middle of the 1950s, accounting for roughly one-third of college degrees in all fields.[46] However equitable coeducation had become after the Second World War, business schools remained a male domain.

"Now that has all changed. Thank God," said Berkeley's Dean Grether to an interviewer in 1993, and to some degree it has. Still, it is probably also fair to say that the question of why women were not on the roster of business school classes and how to fix that situation did not receive the same kind of urgent attention that the question of how to get African Americans into business schools did. Nixon, after all, did not propose any version of female capitalism in the early 1970s.

Those few women who did brave the attitudes at business schools in the late 1960s and early 1970s faced casual and ubiquitous sexism from male students and faculty that is at once both appalling and entirely predictable. In 1971, Chicago's First National Bank began a training program to groom women to move into the higher ranks of its banking operations. As part of the program the women enrolled in an MBA program. Their classmates and their teachers, however, assumed they were pursuing an MRS degree rather than a business one. And to compound the insult, even the married women found themselves being hounded. "I need a bigger ring!" Barbara Kirshner joked, because the men surrounding her "seem to think you are there to pick up a guy, even the professors who know you're married." Pam Green reported that the faculty seemed flummoxed by the very presence of women in their classes. "All the professors have trouble coping with women," she sighed, "especially black women. They will ignore you."[47]

Employers, however, did have to contend with new federal law, and as *Business Week* pointed out in 1974, "faced with an Equal Opportunity Employment Act that requires them to hire more women managers, corporations have discovered that there are not nearly enough of them to go around."[48] Where, then, to find them?

In June 1973 the Mellon Foundation received a proposal from Pace University in New York to fund the Management Career Program for Women. Its purpose, as articulated in the application, "is to remove barriers and to open opportunities for selected women who may aspire to achieve managerial positions in business." Pace recognized that the culture of corporate America had created a cycle of diminished expectations for women. "Too few of these potentially capable young women," the proposal declared, "will achieve this objective because they have accepted the verdict that few opportunities exist for women in management," which was undoubtedly true enough. But the proposal went on to define the problem in terms that resonate with the feminism of the early 1970s: "Without admitting it, even possibly without realizing it, so great is the weight of society's restraints, that these promising young women lose hope and accept defeat even before they start."[49]

After some back and forth between Mellon and Pace during the summer of 1973, the university submitted a revised version of the proposal in which the political motivation for the program was made even more explicit. "The fact is," Pace told the foundation, "women are eager to enter fields from which they have been barred by outworn and indefensible customs and traditions." Therefore, the grant application continued, "to capitalize on the opportunities before it, society must provide quality business education for young women of talent and drive and must at the same time help remove the psychological obstacles which have diverted them from the business-managerial field."[50] For the Management Career Program for Women, the personal was educational.

At their December meeting in 1973, Mellon's trustees smiled on Pace's application and authorized $270,000 to be spread over four years. For its part, Pace promised to use the money to enroll women into both the undergraduate and MBA programs by creating a separate set of classes for them and to advertise the program around the country. The university received 120 applicants for its first class of 27 students starting in the fall of 1974.

Claire List served as the program officer for the grant at Mellon, and after the first semester she reported that "the program is going very well," though she noted that the corporate internship program that the grant helped establish was meeting some of the perfectly predictable resistance from potential sponsors. "Younger women, they say, will 'leave the company,'" List heard. Women will "'move when their husbands move' [and] have children.'" At Pace, the project was overseen by Sandra Ekberg-Jordan, who confirmed for Mellon that the first year had gone quite well. "A number of administrators at undergraduate colleges and universities around the country have written for information about the Program and a few have paid visits to Pace," she told people at Mellon. And she addressed specifically the efficacy of single-sex classes for the women business students: "The concept of special education for women for business is attracting interest and will probably continue to do so at least until women constitute a much larger proportion of most MBA programs." She also told Mellon that the program was already making a dramatic difference in enrollment at Pace. "At this time," she wrote at the end of 1975, "16.9% of our MBA students at the New York campus are women. . . . About five years ago women represented less than 5% of the MBA students." Perhaps most importantly, all twenty-seven women who started the program in 1974 had returned to finish it, and 30 percent of Pace's MBA students were women by 1977.[51]

At about the same moment that people at Pace began to plan for their Management Career Program for Women, Simmons College, a small women's college in Boston, launched the first MBA program specifically for women. Started in 1973, the program was run by Margaret Hennig and Anne Jardim, both of whom had doctorates from Harvard's B-school. Trained in the case-study method, Hennig and Jardim wanted to bring it to Simmons and tailor it for women. They hit on the idea of creating "Simmons cases," and a few years later they approached the Ford Foundation to help fund their ambitions.

In their request to Ford, Hennig and Jardim explained, "The Simmons program is based on the case method of instruction, as at Harvard and other leading graduate schools of business administration." They went on to explain the larger rationale for the program by reminding Ford that a woman tended "to enter an organization with aspirations that differ significantly from a man's aspirations. She tends to concentrate on the acquisition of competence in whatever may be her current job and to leave career advancement largely to take care of itself. The informal system of relationships . . . does not work for her as it does for a man. . . . The great majority of men, in contrast, view their initial job as a first step along a career-path." The Simmons cases would help address this issue, even if *Business Week* sniffed that the Simmons cases stressed the "soft" side of business education—behavior and sociology—at the expense of the "hard" side, like math and marketing.[52]

Rather than fund the MBA program, however, Hennig and Jardim proposed a summer training session to teach faculty from other institutions how to teach the Simmons cases. For its part, Ford's program officers saw a nice fit. "Our involvement," noted a Ford official, "combines our interest in women's studies with our long-standing efforts in the field of management education. Summer case programs are familiar territory to us as we have previously funded similar programs in a variety of other contexts," though it seems to be the case that Ford viewed this summer seminar more as part of their broader women's initiatives rather than as a continuation of their work with business education from the 1950s and early 1960s.[53]

In the early 1980s, the Ford Foundation tried to combine the two issues of representation we have been discussing in this chapter by funding a program of "case research on career decisions of minority women in management." Ford awarded almost $200,000 to the National Council of Negro Women (NCNW) in collaboration with the Women's Center for Education and Career Advancement to carry out the study, which consisted largely of interviews. The results did not, however, rank as a success. Ford program officer Alison Bernstein wrote in an internal memo in 1987, "By 1984 the ties between NCNW and the Women's Center were virtually broken, and the project fell somewhat between the cracks." She went on to piece together the course of events after that: "Eventually, Merable Reagon at the New York Center took responsibility for the project and produced the 200-page casebook 'Black Women Talk about Themselves and Their Lives.' After a futile search for a publisher, NCNW wound up publishing it. I believe that the material in the book can be of modest use to minority and non-minority women who are facing difficult career choices. At this stage, however, it is unclear whether the organizational problems of NCNW prevent it from utilizing the casebook and disseminating it widely."[54]

The programs at Pace and at Simmons doubtless mattered a great deal to those who participated in them, and the casebook "Black Women Talk about Themselves and Their Lives" might well have been useful to those who read it, despite the disappointment felt at Ford over the trajectory of that particular initiative. One Pace participant wrote to the foundation after the first year of the program in a way that made it sound part academic enterprise and part consciousness-raising group. "I'd like to emphasize something I consider to be a particular advantage of this Program," the student declared, "the *all-women nature of it*." Being surrounded by other women "was definitely a shared experience—a supportive atmosphere which helped me resolve any conflicts or anxieties I had." Quite unlike what this writer might have experienced in a predominately male environment, she "met other women who not only understood my high aspirations, but who shared and supported my managerial ambitions. This was crucial in those first few months—and it continues to be meaningful for me." The foundation itself concluded after that first year that the students "appear more confident and now have clear goals in mind as to where they want to go."[55] A few years later, Pace graduate Nancy Levien Goodman's letter to the Mellon Foundation surely summed up the feelings of many when she wrote in 1978, "I really cannot tell you all the ways in which I benefited as an individual from the program. But I left a different person than I was when I had entered. In the summer of 1974, I wasn't qualified to be a secretary because I didn't take shorthand, but by the beginning of 1975, Vice President of Citicorp (I was placed there on my internship) wanted to know what *I* thought of a particular project."[56]

At the same time, I think it is also fair to say that the question of how to recruit more women into business schools did not generate the same urgency or command the same degree of institutional attention that the problem of how to attract more African Americans did in the 1960s and 1970s. As far as I can tell, no one attempted to launch a female version of the Council for Opportunity in Graduate Management Education, nor did the most high-profile university business schools band together in any sort of consortium to advance women in business education.

Still, those programs directed at African Americans fit into a larger story of racial uplift and advancement that has long had currency in African America. I suspect that several of the letters received at the Mellon Foundation, by contrast, came as something of a surprise. Several of the applicants to Pace's program in the summer of 1974 were older women. They were rejected and they wrote to Mellon charging age discrimination and venting their pent-up bitterness. "What about the [liberal arts] woman graduate 10 years over who had family obligations in the past and now wishes to work in the business world?" asked Carol Hasto in a letter to the foundation that captured the essence of their complaints. "In other words," she went on, "a recent L.A. [liberal arts graduate] woman has her whole work career ahead of her so let the rest of the women 'drown'! Let me remind you that those 'others' in the business world are the ones that *really* had it and have it rough!"[57] At least in the area of business education in the 1970s, sisterhood proved to be complicated.

The White Boys of Delta Sig

Every high school guidance counselor says it. So does every college admissions officer and campus tour guide. A college education consists of so much more than what goes on inside the classroom. It includes all kinds of other activities and the other students you meet and with whom you interact. And as you begin to look to life after college, the social and professional networks you have built during those bright college years matter a great deal. And nowhere were those connections more central than in business schools.

And so it was that in 1907 four freshman at New York University's School of Commerce—Harold Jacobs, Alexander Makay, Alfred Moysello, and Henry Tienken—came together to found Delta Sigma Pi, a fraternity specifically for business majors.

Now the largest such organization, the growth of Delta Sig tracks almost exactly the growth of collegiate business schools altogether. It was "organized to foster the study of business in universities," according to the preamble to Delta Sig's constitution in the mid-twentieth century; "to encourage scholarship, social activity and the association of students for their mutual advancement by research and practice; to promote closer affiliation between the commercial world and students of commerce and to further a higher standard of commercial ethics and culture and the civic and commercial welfare of the community." Today, the organization boasts nearly three hundred campus chapters, more than fifty alumni chapters, and a total membership just north of a quarter of a million.[58]

In the vaguely ecumenical spirit of the Progressive age, and reflecting no doubt the ethnic diversity of New York City in 1907, the four founding members of Delta Sigma Pi were two Protestants, one Jew, and a Catholic. Something happened inside the organization, however, during the period of growth in collegiate business schools after the First World War. By 1930, the group's constitution now restricted membership to men "of the Christian faith" and "of the Caucasian race." The acronym WASP had not yet been coined, but that was essentially the species Delta Sigma admitted. And so the matter remained for roughly two decades. After the Second World War, however, that racial and religious discrimination became a thorn in the organization's side.

Delta Sigma's governing body meets every two years to review and set policy in its Grand Chapter Congress. At the 1949 gathering in Baltimore, several chapters reported being pressured to remove those discriminatory clauses by university administrators. Consequently, a few members brought a motion to the floor to eliminate them. That proposal was voted down because, "it was obvious that a large percentage of the members wanted to maintain unity within the many chapters and alumni clubs." "Unity" here apparently meant a unified policy to discriminate.

The issue, naturally, did not go away. In Dallas, two years later, another motion to remove the membership exclusions hit the convention floor. The discussion began after "Grand President Walter Sehm reviewed the agitation emanating from a certain few campuses in recent years endeavoring to force Greek Letter organizations to remove all selective requirements of membership." Spirited debate ensued, according the meeting minutes, which lasted several hours. When a vote was finally called, the motion was defeated by a margin of 40–42. After that defeat, proponents of a more inclusive fraternity put another motion forward to remove only the Christian requirement for membership. That passed 41–39. Not exclusively Christian now, but still all-white.

In fact, as I read the record, these votes were not necessarily binding on the organization. Delta Sigma's executive body appears to have removed "Christian" and "Caucasian" from the national constitution by 1951 anyway, doubtless aware that such language looked increasingly awkward. But Delta Sig also found a clever way to split the difference. In 1949, members were reminded that each local chapter had considerable local latitude to do what it wanted, especially during the initiation rituals—whatever those might have been. Grand President Sehm echoed this in 1951 when he addressed that congress about the exclusionary language: "Your Grand Council has discussed the matter on numerous occasions, completely and thoroughly, and now recommends that the selective membership requirements of DSP be removed." But he went on to say, in what seems to have been a sop to chapters at southern universities, "Your attention is invited to the inherent right of any chapter to establish such additional membership requirements as it may wish."[59] The national organization would not insist on racial and religious discrimination, but individual chapters could exclude as they wished, and doubtless many did.

Fast forward to December 1966. It took fifteen years after the racist language was scrubbed from Delta Sigma's constitution before an African American was finally initiated into the organization. It happened at Florida Atlantic University in Boca Raton, Florida, and that in itself might explain why a black student was finally able to join Delta Sig. Florida Atlantic had opened just five years earlier, part of the expansion of higher education during the postwar salad days and the explosive population growth in Florida.

Thus, its Delta Sigma chapter was also brand new and therefore did not have racial discrimination woven into its fabric—in its local membership requirements, in its secret ritual activities or in the more ineffable habits of its culture. And in a fitting gesture, Harold Jacobs, the Jewish member of the original four brothers, went there for the ceremony. He wrote, "After 59 years of effort, the ideals of the founders for a fraternity made up of members, regardless of race, creed or color has come to pass."[60]

Jacobs, an elderly man in 1966, can be forgiven if "59 years of effort" amounts to a rose-colored overstatement. In 1966 it still wasn't clear just how welcome African Americans were to the fraternity. Exhibit A: the man the organization chose as "Deltasig of the Year" for that very same year, Adolph Rupp.

Rupp had been initiated into the fraternity in 1922 at the University of Kansas, where he majored in economics at the school of business there. Even casual basketball fans will know that Rupp did not pursue a career in business after he left Lawrence. Instead, he went to coach basketball at the University of Kentucky, where he built the most successful program of his era and in so doing helped turn college basketball into a national spectator sport. The arena where the Kentucky Wildcats play still bears Rupp's name. More serious basketball scholars also know about Rupp's history of racist vitriol. Vowing at one point that the Wildcats would never have a black player, Rupp did not finally integrate his basketball team until 1970. The year 1966 will also ring a bell for historians of basketball. That was the year Kentucky's all-white squad faced Texas Western's all-black team in the NCAA tournament final. Losing at the half, Rupp screamed vile racial epithets to his team in the locker room, according to legendary sports writer Frank Deford, who also reported that Kentucky's players seemed embarrassed by their coach's racist tirade. In any event, the screaming did no good—Kentucky lost the game 72–65.

In the middle of the civil rights revolution, the symbolism of that game was lost on no one. Another bastion of the lily-white South falling to the inevitable tide of racial progress. So was Delta Sigma's choice to honor Rupp, of all people, in 1966 of all years purely coincidental or more deliberate? At the very least, it demonstrated that the fraternity remained tone-deaf to matters of race six decades after it had been started. Rupp received his Deltasig of the Year award in November 1966. The following month at Kentucky's yearend sports banquet a local sportswriter stood up and said that Kentucky could at least be proud of having the best white basketball team in the country. Rupp said nothing in reply. Nor did anyone else.[61]

No Girls Allowed

Though it probably goes without saying, I'll say anyway that the exclusionary membership requirements that found their way into Delta Sigma Pi's constitution by 1930 also stipulated that only men need apply. That isn't really all that unusual, since college fraternities by their very definition are boys' clubs. But since Delta Sig offered itself as a fraternity for business students, its requirement that pledges be male both reflected and reinforced the absence of women from America's collegiate business schools.

Women—wives, actually—became a part of Delta Sig in 1949 when several of them decided to form what amounted to a ladies' auxiliary. They did so at the same convention in Baltimore where the issue of excluding blacks and Jews from the club first surfaced. They may have had time to meet after the session on September 8, adjourned exactly at 5 p.m. so "that the delegates could be punctual in boarding the buses that left the Lord Baltimore Hotel to transport them to the Crab Feast and Stag Party." In any event, the wives who had accompanied their husbands to Baltimore decided to call themselves "the Royal Order of the Pink Poodles." Appropriately enough, the Baltimore chapter of the Pink Poodles was designated "Kennel #1."[62]

But kennels full of pink poodles could do only so much to forestall the problem of sex discrimination within Delta Sigma Pi, and by the early 1970s—nearly twenty-five years after the organization confronted the racial and religious issue—it had arrived.

Once again the impetus came from local chapters, not from the national leadership. Reports from the hinterlands suggested that local chapters risked being closed by their host universities because of the organization's refusal to admit women. So when the group met in Portsmouth, New Hampshire, for its 1973 congress, it tackled the issue head-on. Delegates considered the following resolution: "Whereas, there are and will be certain of our chapters confronted with the issue of sex discrimination; and Whereas it is imperative that each of us maintain the spirit of unity and singleness of purpose inherent in the Ritual of Delta Sigma Pi, . . . [it is] Resolved, that the Board of Directors of Delta Sigma Pi is hereby requested to establish a continuing committee in its meeting on August 31, 1973, to solicit funds and professional assistance from all available sources in order to provide legal counsel for the purpose of initiating and defending all legal actions to resolve the problem of sex discrimination at the individual chapter and national levels." One year after Congress added Title IX to the nation's education law, with its promise to balance some of the gender inequity on the nation's campuses, Delta Sig considered creating a legal defense fund to keep its chapter doors closed to women. The motion passed easily.

The environment at the Tan-Tar-A Golf and Tennis Resort in Lake of the Ozarks, Missouri, where Delta Sigma met for its 1975 congress proved no more congenial for addressing the issue of women in the club. The issue itself, needless to say, had not gone away. Delegates from the University of New Mexico arrived at the meeting having had their chapter closed by university officials. They offered, in an almost desperate tone, a motion to remove sex discrimination from the language of the constitution: "This resolution concerns a matter of vital importance to this Fraternity, namely that of its very existence. We of Gamma Iota Chapter, formerly located at the University of New Mexico in Albuquerque, feel the time has come to settle, once and for all, the question of discrimination on the basis of sex." That motion went down 67–27.

Clearly, though membership brought the issue up, membership could not solve the problem. After that 1975 vote, the national council met and decided to get rid of the language. The news was reported in 1977 when the organization met in Toronto and Grand President William Tatum delivered these reassuring words: "On our 68th Anniversary, November 7, 1975, your National Executive Committee, as directed by the Grand Chapter, invoked the Emergency Powers, unanimously voting to delete the word 'male' from our Constitution, thus admitting women to our ranks for the first time. I think each of us were apprehensive at first, but upon the admission of females, I have witnessed the greatest air of competitiveness that could ever be built by any professional management team. In less than one year, the criticizing, competing fraternities and sororities followed in our footsteps taking the identical measures. Delta Sigma Pi is the leader of the Pro Fraternities and will continue to be. Many of our chapters have initiated some 'Top Flight Girls' as evidenced by their participation at the recent Regional Conferences and attendance here."[63] When "top flight girls" began arriving into the ranks of the Delta Sigma Pi in the late 1970s, the Pink Poodles had become anachronistic. The kennels were closed in 1995.

There was more at stake than fraternity regalia, secret rituals, or even stag parties and crab feasts in the foot-dragging with which Delta Sig approached the admission of black students, women, and even Jews. For members, the fraternity has served as a first introduction into the social world of business, as an opportunity to build a network, locally and nationally, of contacts and friendships, and to benefit from the tens of thousands of alumni already in the business world. Those few women and African Americans who did attend business schools across three-quarters of the twentieth century were shut out of all that.

Indeed, the way Delta Sig's H. G. Wright described the work of Delta Sigma Pi on individual campuses made the group sound as if it was some sort of pin-striped fifth column: "It is a pleasure to note the increase in the number of Delta Sigma Pi deans in our Schools of Business Administration," he told the 1947 congress, "throughout the country, we now have about 35 such deans." He went on with a recruiting pitch, saying, "I would like to urge that chapters pay particular attention to the initiation of outstanding faculty members early in their college life, many of these outstanding faculty will become Deans in later years and if their interest in Delta Sigma Pi was inaugurated and has been sustained over a period of many years, they will be far more beneficial to the fraternity than if they were not initiated until after they became Dean." Thus could Delta Sigma Pi take over the nation's business schools, and their vision of conquest was all-white and all-male.

I started this chapter with a few statistics. They seem to suggest that whatever else has changed in our society after the civil rights revolution of the 1950s and 1960s, and after second-wave feminism crested in the 1970s, little has changed in the nation's executive suites. It is patently unfair to blame that entirely on collegiate business schools. At the end of the day, it is corporations that do the hiring, not business schools, and those statistics most immediately reflect corporate America's continued reluctance to let women and nonwhite people join their club.

And yet business schools have not been as aggressive or successful in diversifying their classrooms as the other professions like law and medicine, comparison with which they have aspired to since Wharton opened in 1881.

Even when universities were working hard to diversify themselves from one end of campus to the other, business schools either couldn't or wouldn't keep up. Remote as it seems today, in 1971 Ohio State University set up a campus-wide affirmative action initiative and asked different units to establish affirmative action goals. In 1974 the business school confessed that "a look at current figures would indicate that the College has not made overall sufficient progress toward its five-year goals." Three years later, the university's Commission on Women and Minorities singled out the business school for its continued slow progress, prompting an angry and defensive response from Associate Dean Robert Georges. "As Affirmative Action Officer in the College of Administrative Science," he fired off in a memo, "I am amazed at the content of the Report of the Commission on Women and Minorities. . . . While what we have accomplished is short of what we would like to achieve . . . it is substantially more than the purely negative assessment contained in your report."[64] Sometimes the glass is half-empty and sometimes it is half-full, but the fact that OSU's Commission pointed at the business school suggests that it was not making as much progress as other parts of campus.

Forty years later, according to statistics kept by the American Bar Association, enrollments in the nation's law schools are nearly even among men and women, and indeed, as I write this in 2018, the American Bar Association predicts that women will shortly outnumber men in law school. They already did at eighty-five law schools by 2015. (Even here, the Fortune 500 fails to keep up. According to the ABA, women constitute only 25 percent of the lawyers working corporate counsel offices, only 20 percent in the Fortune 1000.)[65]

The numbers are roughly the same at medical schools, though they lag behind law schools by 1 or 2 percentage points. As medical students make their way through their education, the men and women continue to sort by area of specialty: more women go into pediatrics, for example, than go into orthopedic surgery. And women at both medical and law schools continue to be underrepresented in the ranks of those schools' faculty to be sure.

By contrast, female enrollment in MBA programs reached 40 percent only by 2015. And only at the top twelve MBA programs. The count at an additional twenty-four schools brought that percentage down to the midthirties. That figure, as it happens, is just a tick higher than the percentage of women enrolled in Berkeley's MBA program in 1977.[66] The growth of women enrolling in those MBA programs over the five-year period 2011–2015 averaged

1 percent per year. As Virginia Ware Myers, the executive director of the National Association of Women MBAs, told *Fortune* magazine, "I think we're definitely looking at something that could be better."[67] Better indeed, especially considering that women have been outpacing men in earning degrees of all kinds for several years now.

Tracking African American enrollments can be more complicated than it was fifty years ago because what was once seen simply as a problem of black and white now includes Asian, Hispanic, mixed-race, and other racial categories. For example, nearly 10 percent of the 88,000-plus students in medical school during academic year 2016–17 identified themselves as mixed race or did not identify themselves at all. Often, now, students in studies are grouped as "minorities" or "students of color." In 2013, nearly 30 percent of law school students fell into that category, though the enrollment patterns seem to reverse those at business schools. Top law schools continue to enroll far fewer students of color, while lower-tier schools enroll more.[68] Medical schools also continue to struggle with attracting certain minority students. African Americans constituted 6.5 percent of medical school students in 2016, though Asian students made up almost 21 percent of the 88,300 students studying medicine.[69]

Here too, MBA programs have not kept pace. By 2015, enrollment in MBA programs by underrepresented minorities had reached only 11.7 percent.[70] Those data were compiled by the Consortium for Graduate Study in Management, now a fully independent 501(c)(3) nonprofit. Far from having gone out of business as its founders optimistically hoped in the late 1960s, it celebrated its fiftieth anniversary in 2016. The consortium was joined by the Forte Foundation, an organization that partners with universities and companies to launch women into business careers. And while the consortium was founded in 1966, Forte did not get started until 2001, a reminder that women seem always to have come second even to those concerned about diversifying the private sector.

Part of the challenge of doing just that traces back to the faltering attempts to make business a profession in the first place. Law schools and medical schools work with national organizations—the American Bar Association and the American Medical Association—in ways that can be mutually reinforcing. They at least provide centralized places for practitioners to talk about these things. And as we have seen already, there is nothing analogous in U.S. business. Thus, there is no way to raise the concern about minority and female representation in the private sector at a national, profession-wide level the way there is for the legal and medical professions.

Collegiate business schools can't solve that problem on their own, nor should they be expected to. But at the same time, as this chapter demonstrates, they certainly have not been leaders in trying to diversify the ranks of the nation's businesses, and certainly not to the extent that the other professional schools they have always aspired to match have. Far from being the change agents they claim to produce, they have mostly helped perpetuate the status quo.

Chapter 5

Good in a Crisis?

How Business Schools Responded to Economic Downturns—or Didn't

"If Robespierre were to ascend from hell and seek out today's guillotine fodder, he might start with a list of those with three incriminating initials beside their names: MBA. The Masters of Business Administration, that swollen class of jargon-spewing, value-destroying financiers and consultants, have done more than any other group of people to create the economic misery we find ourselves in."

So wrote Philip Delves Broughton in the pages of the *Sunday Times* of London early in 2009 as the Great Recession was still bottoming out. Broughton wrote with panache but also with a certain authority. "I write as the holder of an MBA from Harvard Business School—once regarded as a golden ticket to riches, but these days more like the scarlet letters of shame," Broughton confessed to readers of the *Times*. And he wasn't finished with his fellow alums: "We MBAs are haunted by the thought that the tag really stands for Mediocre But Arrogant, Mighty Big Attitude, Me Before Anyone and Management By Accident. For today's purposes, perhaps it should be Masters of the Business Apocalypse."[1]

Honest people can disagree with Broughton over the extent to which the "Masters of Disaster have their fingerprints all over the recent financial fiasco" and by extension just how much responsibility business schools have for the global economic collapse early in the twenty-first century, though Broughton's Hall of Shame is impressive indeed.[2] Stan O'Neal and John Thain, both heads of Merrill Lynch; Andy Hornby, head of the British bank HBOS; Christopher Cox, the asleep-at-the-wheel chairman of the Securities and Exchange Commission under President George W. Bush; and of course Bush himself all got MBAs from Harvard. Indeed, Bush campaigned in 2000 that he would be the nation's first MBA president. That certainly didn't turn out too well.

Whether or not Broughton's Robespierre ought to execute MBA holders for their crimes against the economy and putting aside his tone—funny in that particularly British way—he does raise an interesting set of questions: How has what has gone on inside business schools shaped the world outside them? How have business schools responded to the crises of business during the twentieth century? Despite their promise to educate students for the "real" world, do business schools really provide an education that matters to the world of business beyond the entrée it provides and the social status it confers?

There are too many variables in those questions to be able to answer them definitively. Nonetheless, given how much space, both literal and metaphoric, business schools have occupied on campus and for so long, these questions seem worth asking. So in this chapter we look at what happened at business schools during several moments of economic (and national) crisis to see how they responded, or didn't, to examine what, if anything, changed as a result.

In some sense, this chapter traces the history of dogs not barking. When Broughton complained in 2009 that "business schools have shown a remarkable ability to miss the economic catastrophes unfolding before their eyes," he reached back only as far as the 1980s. In fact, business schools seem to have been remarkably untroubled by any of the economic crises the nation has endured since business schools opened for business. Whether in the 1930s, in the 1970s, or at the beginning of the twenty-first century, there has been a collective shrugging of the shoulders inside most B-schools. That nonresponse helps us understand that many at business schools and the business leaders with whom they interacted defined "crisis" in a different way than most of the rest of us. For them, the crisis was one of public relations—how to make business look better when it had lost the confidence of so many Americans—not one of what business had done to lose that trust.

Weathering the Great Depression by Ignoring It

Campuses might have offered something of a respite from the ravages of the Great Depression, but they certainly were not immune to it. "On college campuses from Columbia to California this Fall," the *New York Times* reported in 1931, "a new student strides. He has shed his coonskin coat and rolled up his shirtsleeves and given up his Fall house-parties and his automobile. . . . The wolf, in other words, is showing his snarling visage even at the college's cloistered door."[3]

As I have noted already that the growth of collegiate business schools reflected the growth of higher education more broadly, even if it has often outpaced that growth. Across the country colleges and universities faced severe revenue declines in these years—whether at private institutions whose endowments tanked after 1929 or at public ones where state legislatures cut back on their subsidies. Faculty hiring essentially ceased, and those faculty who had jobs saw their salaries frozen or cut. Maintenance on the physical plant virtually stopped and capital expenditures dropped by a whopping 85 percent between academic years 1929–30 and 1933–34. Enrollments declined by 8 percent over that same period, a figure amounting to about 80,000 students. And as Malcolm Willey asked almost plaintively, "What becomes of 80,000 students returned to a world of unemployment."[4] No surprise, then, that when the Great Depression arrived on campus, business schools felt the effects of it too.

Most obviously, new business schools stopped opening. Construction all across campus virtually ceased—at least until federal money arrived in the second half of the decade—and business schools were not exempted. After popping up prodigiously in the 1920s, very few new collegiate business schools opened in the 1930s. Along with that, enrollments declined, especially in the early years of the Great Depression. Administrators at the College of Commerce at Ohio State University found that "enrollment in the College of Commerce and Administration is proving to be a dependable business barometer." In 1932 those numbers had gone down "with business headed toward the low point of the depression," falling below those of the previous year. Reaching for better news in 1933, the college announced, "This year it is taking the lead in gains." Whatever the cheery news from Columbus, Ohio, however, figures from seventy business schools around the country revealed that by 1935 enrollments had dropped by roughly 25 percent.[5]

The Great Depression stimulated a lively and wide-ranging debate in the field of economics, as might well be expected, and arguably it set the stage for economics to play an even larger role in public policy after the Second World War.[6] Doubtless, the Depression was a topic of conversation at business schools everywhere too. The School of Commerce at Washington and Lee University in Lexington, Virginia, for example, held two conferences that brought speakers to campus to opine about the economic turmoil, once in 1931 and again in 1934. That latter event featured Washington and Lee alumnus Edward O'Neal, who returned to campus as president of the Farm Bureau Association and who talked about the National Recovery Administration.[7]

But the intellectual ferment the Depression caused in economics departments seems to have largely skipped over the business schools. Businessmen in the San Francisco Bay Area begged Berkeley's business school to establish a bureau of business research throughout the 1930s, but the school didn't get around to doing so until 1941, well past the point where it might have done those businesses any good navigating the Depression and the New Deal. What is striking, though, whether in Lexington or in Berkeley, is the somewhat lackadaisical tone, the lack of urgency with which the business schools responded to the Great Depression. In 1937 a joint committee of the American Association of Collegiate Schools of Business (AACSB) and the American Council on Education released "Suggestions for a Study of Business Education at the College Level." Those suggestions made no mention of the Depression.[8]

For its part the Roosevelt administration does not seem to have had much interest in business school faculty and expertise. None of the advisors FDR brought to Washington from academe was a faculty member in a business school. Lawyers and economists in abundance, but no marketing or retailing professors. Rexford Tugwell came closest—he had had some graduate training at Wharton, tellingly under the economists Simon Patten and Scott Nearing.

While the economists wrestled to fix The Economy, viewed as a complex, integrated system, many Americans, members of the clergy in particular, saw the Great Depression as a failure of business or, more specifically, of businessmen. Pulitzer Prize–winning author James Truslow Adams displayed this sentiment in the Sunday *New York Times Magazine* in 1937, writing, "It appears to me that the big business men, the 'captains of industry' as they were called a few decades ago, have reached a definite crisis with reference to their permanence as part of our modern social machinery." Adams implored businessmen to change with the tenor of the time and recognize their social responsibility to foster not only private profit but public good as well. This was no moral or humanitarian plea but a pragmatic one: "I believe that a change is coming not only over the people but also over the business men. They have been forced, to some extent at least, to recognize new conditions. In previous hard times they expected the less fortunate to tighten their belts and starve if need be. They have found that men will no longer starve quietly."[9]

As Adams summarized it, the essential economic problem "is one of wider distribution of business profits" so that "the masses" could purchase their way to the good life and "lowered cost of business products." As Adams saw it, the problem was a matter of basic survival. "If economic progress cannot be made by business leaders along the lines suggested," he warned, "then the people, although they cannot solve the problem, will almost certainly try to do so by discarding the business man and causing the government more and more to take over private enterprise." Adams certainly did not want that to happen, so he tried to rally businessmen by concluding, "If the business men are to become leaders . . . they must regain the confidence which they have largely lost while the people were moving forward and they themselves were not." Fairly or unfairly, businessmen now stood disgraced in the eyes of many Americans.[10]

By extension, the degree to which U.S. business had let the United States down also meant that business schools had failed to train the executives prepared to lead the country out of the economic wilderness. Adams did not mention collegiate business schools, and in fairness only a tiny percentage of business leaders in the 1930s held a collegiate business degree. But as Adams complained about a failure of leadership among businessmen, as he critiqued their unwillingness to change and adapt, business schools stood as the unindicted coconspirators in his essay. After all, hadn't collegiate business schools been promising since 1881 to train men who could lead in times of crisis, professionals who could fix problems the way doctors cured the sick? Where were those leaders now, and what did business schools offer by way of solutions to the problem?

Some inside business schools did not disagree. Wharton's dean, Joseph Willits, acknowledged to the 1936 meeting of the AACSB that in the 1920s business schools pumped out graduates "with a social philosophy concentrated on the goal of 'a million before I'm thirty,'" and he sounded a note of contrition, telling his fellow deans, "All of us have been guilty in greater or lesser degree of fostering this attitude." Unless business schools changed to become part of the solution rather than remain part of the problem, the whole enterprise of business education would be viewed as "of questionable value either to the student or to society."[11]

In his role as president of the AACSB, the University of Buffalo business school dean C. S. Marsh approached the Carnegie Corporation with an idea. Writing to its president Frederick Keppel in 1932 as the Depression was still getting worse, Marsh suggested that the corporation fund a study of the state of American business education. In September Marsh sent in a formal application laying out the rationale for such a study. He acknowledged that at this moment of economic collapse the business sector had let the nation down. "The entire course of events in post-war business," Marsh wrote, "has revealed dramatically the lack of adequate business leadership." He went on to insist on the need for business education, because "economic and business planning cannot be made effective in serving social purposes unless those persons who occupy positions of responsibility and control, are adequately trained." But he also shouldered some of the blame on behalf of the AACSB: "The members of this Association are conscious of the fact that the collegiate school of business has not as yet assumed the position it should occupy as a social agency for the development of the type of business leadership needed in modern industrial life."[12]

Marsh believed that the rapid growth of business schools after the First World War "explains why collegiate schools of business have not as yet assumed a definite place in the educational structure or formulated a program based upon definitive objectives." The proliferation of business schools in the 1920s meant that there was little consistency in what students learned: "Curriculum organization at present is in part a matter of tradition, in part of accident, in part of vocational opportunity, and, in part, of analysis of business functions. Schools vary widely in their curriculum organization." Nor was there much by way of quality control in those classrooms. "Collegiate schools of business necessarily began with a teaching personnel which lacked adequate training in the technical problems of business education," Marsh admitted. "Their staffs had to be recruited from economists who had some special practical interests and from business men who could be utilized as lecturers. . . . Practically no school of business gives serious attention to the training of people to teach business subjects at the collegiate level." These complaints all sound familiar.[13]

More specifically, Marsh wanted to figure out how to solve the problem of training "professional" businessmen (who presumably would act with more professional responsibility and accountability than those who had caused the Great Depression) when business itself was not really a profession. As he explained the conundrum, "Since the graduates of collegiate schools of business do not go on to other professional schools as the graduates of liberal art divisions often do, and since there is no clearly marked path of professional procedure as is the case for the graduates of law and medicine, and since business opportunities are so varied that little is known of the lines through which advancement takes place, the problem of guidance and placement is particularly difficult."[14] In a sense, Marsh hoped Carnegie could help figure out how to do what business schools themselves had been unable to.

Marsh's proposal anticipated by twenty years what Carnegie and Ford would do in the mid-1950s. But the Carnegie Corporation was no more immune from the financial collapse than any other organization in 1932, and Keppel decided he could not afford to fund this project. So the AACSB muddled on through the decade without Carnegie money. Chief among the organization's concerns was maintaining the standards it had worked to establish for collegiate business schools in the 1920s. The AACSB's Committee on the Study of Business Education wrote to member schools in 1932 urging them, "Even though you find it necessary to reduce budgets because of present economic conditions, do not reduce quality and standards of instruction." The memo suggested that schools "telescope courses and decrease the number of offerings" as a way of preserving those standards.[15]

That might or might not have been a helpful suggestion to business schools struggling with budget cuts and the loss of faculty during the 1930s, but it also elided the basic question How was educational quality at business schools measured in the first place? As the Marquette University business school dean John Pyle told the AACSB meeting in 1938, "While all agree that there should be both qualitative and quantitative standards, there seem to be difference of opinion as to the emphasis that should be placed on each." Though Pyle did not use the term, he went on to describe a bean-counting mentality that afflicted the AACSB: "Some members of the Association want, for example, definite or precise minimum salaries and maximum hours of teaching established; a minimum number of full professors; a maximum number of students per instructor; and so many books in the library, machines and so on, per student. This point of view appears rather mechanical to me. While our objective is to secure quality instruction by such quantitative standards, we are likely to become so involved in our figures that we will lose sight of the original objective."[16]

When the Harvard professor Clyde Ruggles addressed the AACSB meeting in 1933 he had an altogether different set of standards on his mind. Noting that the medical profession had all but eliminated "the quack in that field," he went on to assert that "university education in business will be incomplete in a vital respect if our studies of the field of business do not recognize the obligations of these schools to aid in raising the standards of business conduct." And for the Boston University business school dean Everett Lord, the responsibility that businessmen bore for causing the Great Depression simply underscored that business had yet to become a profession proper. "If we accept the standards generally recognized," Lord told the AACSB, "that a profession is a vocation for which technical preparation is necessary and in which the motive of action is service rather than profit, we may realize that our schools have done . . . very little toward the latter."[17] In 1931, fifty years after the Wharton School opened, over 15 percent of the U.S. workforce languished without jobs, roughly 8 million people, and many had been laid off by exactly the kind of large-scale industrial enterprises business school grads were, allegedly, being trained to lead. But in 1931, business schools seemed further away than ever from producing professional men of business, the ones who put social purpose above private profit and behaved ethically and responsibly. Certainly, the business quacks had not been eliminated.

If business schools played little part in shaping the New Deal, they certainly understood that they would have to react to it. More specifically, leaders at business schools realized that the New Deal was redefining the relationship between government and the private sector and that any business education would have to include some acknowledgment of this changed circumstance. That was the message Leverett Lyon delivered when he opened a session titled "The New Deal in Relation to the Problem of Business Education at the College Level" at the AACSB convention in 1934. Lyon, who as we have already seen had established himself as a leading expert on business education, now worked at the Brookings Institution and had a front-row seat as the New Deal unfolded in Washington. "Perhaps most significant for the collegiate school of business," he told the AACSB, "is the set of intellectual notions which are prominent in the New Deal. They are important both because they are different from those to which economists have become accustomed and because they are obtaining a popular currency and probably a popular acceptance that surpasses anything we have seen for many decades." Lyon's remarks implicitly suggested that the New Deal's "intellectual notions," while they had come from elsewhere, had arrived on campus, and if collegiate business schools failed to reckon with them, they did so at their peril.[18]

The following year, Wharton's Dean Willits echoed the sense of inevitability and the need for business schools to adapt. "Whatever one's attitude towards the 'New Deal,'" Willits told an audience in 1935, "no one would gainsay the fact that as we move further and further from the pioneer society and more and more into an integrated, interdependent society, our political system and our economic system will mesh more and more. The role of the state will expand and will touch business at a greater number of points." Willits then issued a gentle warning. "The point of all this emphasis upon the expanding role of government is that the increased role of government in economic and social affairs is as likely to be as harmful as it is helpful . . . if the instruments of public administration are not fundamentally improved."[19]

Two years later, Willits put his money where his mouth was. Or rather, he put Samuel Fels's money there. Fels, president of the Fels-Naphtha soap giant in Philadelphia, donated money to Penn to create a school of public administration housed within the Wharton School. Willits may have cast a worried eye toward Washington in his 1935 talk, but Fels wanted his money to be put to more local use. Fels believed that the people who set about reforming local government "are either amateurs who give but a portion of their time or politicians to whom such affairs are viewed chiefly from a political angle." More specifically, Fels hoped his new school would train managers who would bring professionalism to the ranks of state government in Pennsylvania. Corruption in Harrisburg existed on an epic scale (it still does), and a document from the time on "Institute of Local and State Government" concluded, "There is little evidence that the new political forces in power in Pennsylvania will be any more inclined to stop using appointments as political rewards and to develop a real Civil Service than have the political machines which preceded them."[20] In Philadelphia, at least, the Great Depression prompted people to think about using business schools to train people for jobs outside the private sector. Farther north in Cambridge, Harvard's dean, Wallace Donham, miffed probably that so many of FDR's advisors had come from Columbia University and not from Harvard and certainly not from his B-school, announced the creation of a new course "designed to train students for 'brain truster' careers."[21]

As dean of perhaps the most prestigious business school of the era, Donham spoke with a particular authority. While he was no apologist for the behavior of many businessmen in the face of the economic crisis, he was also not an enthusiastic supporter of the New Deal.[22] Less than two years after the New Deal began, Donham began to issue cautions. He favored work programs over "charity to the unemployed," but by fall 1934 he had become more concerned with deficit spending. "The Government's ability to continue work relief," he said, "depends on the attitude it takes toward managers of business. Unless business starts up, Government credit must crack under the cost which is twice the cost of subsistence relief."[23]

Two years later he took to the pages of the *Saturday Evening Post*. By 1936, the *Post* had emerged as one of the New Deal's chief antagonists, especially through the regular columns of Garet Garrett. So there was a certain oppositional significance when Donham's piece "The Class of 1936 Seeks a Job" appeared there. And just in case readers missed the magazine's editorial point of view, the first few columns of Donham's essay ran above an angry (and alas, unfunny) anti–New Deal cartoon on the page.[24]

It is a lengthy piece written in an almost avuncular tone and designed to be reassuring to the *Post*'s middle-class, middle-brow readership. Donham announced that he was "more optimistic than for some years" about the job prospects of college graduates. But he quickly qualified what he meant with a bit of finger wagging. College men of "ability, energy and good personality" would find jobs; "men who lack these qualities" would probably not. With that distinction made, Donham went on with a series of buck-up-America! bromides and chirpy paeans to traditional American virtues: Don't be persuaded by the "malcontents with the present order of things who would have us believe that opportunities for youth are at an end." No,

Donham insisted, "there is and will be opportunity for youth," because "America is a great heritage" and not "an arena of class and race strife." He acknowledged the need for a few good, well-trained men to enter the public sector: "We must have men of ability and training in Government service, for wisdom and balance are essential to popular government," though he did predict that "it will be a sad day for America if the present wave of popular criticism and bureaucratic regulation stops able youth from seeking outlet for imaginative leadership in industry and business." And so the essay went. It measures as nicely as anything how far the business school enterprise had traveled from the days when Simon Patten and Scott Nearing taught at Wharton.

Yet underneath the platitudes Donham's essay seems a bit confused. At one point he cheers that "an index of the greatness of our heritage [is] that the principal executives of our industries, large and small, are mostly common folk who secured their training by hard work and their education by the personal sacrifice of their parents; who hold their positions by sheer force of ability, energy, dependability and integrity," even while referring repeatedly to the value of college training that in the 1930s was certainly not common among the "common folk." And it wasn't clear whether his view of the employment situation reached much beyond the Charles River and his Harvard B-school campus. He boasted, "Through the six and one-half years of this depression a large percentage of our own graduates have found openings." Which I'm sure came as a relief to readers in Toledo, where unemployment had reached a mind-boggling 80 percent in 1933. Finally, however, Donham concluded the entire essay by saying, "Jobs for college men in 1936 will go to men who seek apprenticeship," hardly a stirring, or even particularly insightful, way to end.[25] In fairness, Donham was writing for a mass-circulation magazine and addressing a general readership, not writing for an academic journal or speaking to a professional organization. Still, Donham's essay despite its length offers remarkably little of any substance. At the moment of the greatest crisis U.S. business had ever faced, the senior voice of business education in the United States had very little to say.

The Great Depression provided an opportunity, or so some people hoped, for business schools to make good on their original promise, to hit the reset button and get back to the purpose of instilling values in future professionals. They had failed to turn business into a higher calling with a social purpose, and if the Great Depression demonstrated nothing else, it measured just how far American business was from a real profession. Horace Stern spoke to students at the Wharton School in 1934 and urged them to recognize this. "The Wharton School was never intended to be, and it never has been, a mere vocational trade-school, the exclusive, or even the dominant object of which was to equip young men to make a better living for themselves in a materialistic or worldly sense." One wonders how many of them were nonplussed by his exhortation. He went on, "On the contrary the founder stressed that the purpose was primarily to benefit the community and the nation as a whole by qualifying students to solve the economic and social problems incident to civilization and by teaching them to create wealth by service rather than by filching it from their fellows through guile or ruthlessness. . . . To be a Wharton School man, therefore, is to be a person selected and specially trained for communal service and leadership." As he surveyed the economic wreckage, Stern saw that "all the old confidence, the arrogance, the smugness, are gone, and that in their place stands a chastened world, a world of humility, a world vacillating and hesitant, a world not only ignorant but *conscious* of its ignorance as never before in the history of mankind. . . . We know our business men are not certain, our college professors are not certain, and our politicians and statesmen are far from certain."[26]

But Stern did not precisely know of what he spoke. He had graduated from Penn in 1899, not from Wharton but from the college. From there, on to Penn law and a distinguished career as a jurist, eventually rising to become chief justice of the Pennsylvania Supreme Court. He was not ever a businessman.

In truth, and despite the optimism that Stern and others retained toward a business school education, it is probably fair to say that for the most part inside collegiate business schools, business went on remarkably unchanged. As far as I can determine, the Great Depression caused no fundamental rethinking of the business curriculum, much less of the way business itself operated. "Commerce courses . . . were kept up to date with all the rapid changes of the New Deal" at Ohio State, but no one suggested that the courses were doing anything more than keeping up.[27] While economists struggled over big economic ideas and how to turn them into national policy, business school faculty went about their work as if unfazed. The *Journal of Marketing*, an academic publication, collected examples of marketing studies from universities around the country in its January 1938 issue. The first report in its "Progress in Marketing Research" came from the University of Arizona and announced that "Professor Edwin G. Wood's study of 'Salad Eating Habits of the People of Tucson, with Special Reference to Avocados,' mentioned in the July issue of the JOURNAL, is now available in summarized form."[28]

Circling the B-school Wagons

In 1938 the Alfred P. Sloan Foundation made a grant to the business school at the University of Denver. The Sloan Foundation had been established just four years earlier and certainly as a reaction to the New Deal. The University of Denver used the grant to create a Department of Government Management within the school of business. The goal, according to Sloan, was to create literacy about the finances of local government that would enable people to better understand how their taxes were spent. "The new department at the University of Denver," Sloan announced when the grant was made, "is an effort to aid the average citizen to understand the close interrelationship between the activities of his local government and his own well-being." When the first classes of students graduated from the new program in 1940 and 1941, *Business Week* called them "efficiency experts" for local government, trained to sniff out where the tax money had gone.[29]

Alfred P. Sloan himself, of course, had not gone to business school. He trained as an engineer at MIT and then moved into and up the executive ranks in the automobile industry. He became president of General Motors in 1923 and then chairman of its board in 1937. Under his leadership GM became the largest automaker in the world and one of the largest corporations altogether. He demonstrated his debt of gratitude to MIT with gifts not to the engineering programs but to the business school; MIT, in return, named the school after Sloan in 1964.

Among the industrial titans of his generation, Sloan was perhaps more low key and less flamboyant than many. He hated labor unions as much as his fellow carmaker Henry Ford, but preferred to attack them through subterfuge rather than with violent confrontations. And in his understated way, Sloan was part of a circle of right-wing, free-market evangelists who coalesced in the 1930s. Sloan created his foundation in large part to spread the gospel

of the unregulated free market against what he saw as the government in-
trusion of the New Deal. Run by Alfred's brother Harold, the foundation's
purpose was to promote "wider knowledge of basic economic truths"[30]

Most infamously, Sloan sat at GM's helm when the auto giant did business with Hitler's Germany under GM's Opel division. Hitler himself ad-
mired the deeply anti-Semitic Ford and kept a portrait of him on his desk.
But General Motors provided key technologies to the Nazi war machine
without which Hitler would have not invaded Poland, according to Albert
Speer. Senior GM executive James Mooney received the Grand Cross of the
German Eagle for "distinguished service to the Reich" in 1938. The following year Sloan defended GM's operations in Nazi Germany to concerned
shareholders, insisting that German internal politics should "not be considered the business of the management of General Motors" and that the German market was "highly profitable."[31] The moral bankruptcy of such "basic
economic truths" staggers the imagination.

Back at home, Sloan helped fund the American Liberty League, a coali-
tion of leading business figures and politicians joined in their opposition to
the New Deal. The Liberty League had at least some interactions with business schools and with individual faculty. Neil Carothers, for example, delivered a radio talk for the league in November 1935 titled "Inflation Is Bad
for Business" in which he predicted ruinous inflation because of New Deal
spending. When he delivered the talk Carothers was serving as director of
Lehigh University's business school and the Liberty League republished the
address as a pamphlet and then distributed it nationwide. (For the record,
inflation never became a problem during the 1930s, though many did begin
to worry about the economic consequences of deflation.) The Sloan Foundation insisted that once its grants were made the foundation would not med-
dle with the project or program, and I have no reason to doubt the sincerity
of that. At the same time, Alfred Sloan's personal politics shaped the very
nature of the foundation's mission, and the grant to the University of
Denver was among the first it awarded. Sloan was hardly a disinterested
philanthropist.[32]

Which is worth keeping in mind when thinking about the program at
the University of Denver. While the department that Sloan's money helped
create focused on local government administration and finance, that money
also enabled Denver's school of commerce to hold several conferences just before the war that had a more national profile. The first "Citizen's Confer-

ence on Government Management" was held in Estes Park, Colorado, in June 1939. The event brought together businessmen and government officials for wide-ranging discussions of government management, efficiency, and financing. The *New York Times* reported, "Some 250 bankers, lawyers, accountants, merchants, industrialists, editors and railroad and public utility executives are taking a week from their desks to discuss government spending with men responsible for it."[33]

The tone of the event serves as a reminder that once upon a time and not that long ago Americans could debate political and policy disagreements in serious and respectful ways. But I think it is also fair to say that the underlying assumptions of the conference, as evidenced in the five-day program, reflected Sloan's hostility to the New Deal and the threat he perceived it to be to his vision of free enterprise in the United States. That tone was set when the University of Denver's chancellor, David Shaw Duncan, opened the proceedings by reminding those gathered that Thomas Jefferson "held that the national government should look primarily after foreign affairs; the states should look after domestic relations. . . . To see how far we have gone, one has only to think of what functions have been and are being exercised by the national government in our day."[34] Five days later, the last word at the event was given to the general counsel of the National Association of Manufacturers, James Emery, who underscored the anti–New Deal agenda of the conference with a bit less circumlocution.

As Emery saw it, three things threatened the very foundation of American society: government spending (too much of it); taxation (too much of that too); and the National Labor Relations Act, because "it has developed discord, friction and class feeling." He laid out the stakes in stark terms. Some Americans, he announced, "continue to demand and support private enterprise and free economy," while others believe "we must now accept a politically planned economy of master federal authority and subordinated individualism." And then, in a ham-handed evocation of Abraham Lincoln, he exhorted, "We cannot be a mongrel society—half collective and half individualistic." Emery concluded by circling back to the Founders again. Speaking for those millions of Americans whose lives had been disrupted or ruined by the Great Depression, he assured the conference, "Many Americans are dubious today, not because of the anxiety of an anxious people to find social security, but because they fear that in reaching for it they may disregard and abandon teachings of 150 years of political security and economic progress enduring through panics, depressions, and war, and surviving through all the preserved freedom and accomplishment of individual enterprise."[35] If nothing else, you have to admire Emery's chutzpah.

Students of U.S. conservatism will recognize much here that is familiar: states' rights as a refuge from the overreach of the federal government; the anger at taxes; the hostility toward organized labor; reimagining the Founding Fathers as laissez-faire, small-government capitalists; and even the Turnerian myth of "the earthy intelligence of the frontier," as University of Denver's Dean Kaplan put it when welcoming delegates to Estes Park. That all this should have been on display at a conference sponsored by a business school, however, reminds us of the prepositional problem we touched on in chapter 2. Early in the twentieth century, business schools wrestled with whether their teaching and research should be *about* American business or *for* American business. After the First World War they chose the latter. Faced with the collapse of business in the 1930s, therefore, business schools had little to offer by way of critique or alternative. All they had was more of the same.

Inner City Economic Blues

George Shultz founded the Careers for Negroes in Management at the University of Chicago's Business School in part because of what he saw happening on the South Side of Chicago in the early 1960s. Sterling Schoen saw it too, remembering that "while I was at the University of Chicago on a postdoctoral fellowship in 1962–63, I witnessed the burning of Chicago. And, at that time, Saul Alinsky was sounding the call for a more widespread and active civil rights agenda."[36] Schoen, as we saw in chapter 4, took his experiences to St. Louis and began the Consortium for Graduate Study in Business for Minorities; the Careers program began in 1964.

And in 1964 riots broke out in North Philadelphia and in Harlem. The Long Hot Summers had begun.

It is no accident that many of the nation's most prestigious universities sit in the middle of its major urban centers. Industrialists made their money in those cities. That money, in turn, transformed U.S. higher education in the latter part of the nineteenth century, whether at new institutions like Hopkins, Berkeley, or Chicago or at older ones—Harvard, Yale, Columbia—that emerged as the modern, dynamic, research-driven places we know today. By the 1950s, however, those universities, and others besides, looked out more and more nervously at the cities that surrounded them, increasingly impoverished and in many cases increasingly black. By the 1960s those urban areas seemed ready to explode, and as the decade wore on many of them did. Several city-based universities seriously contemplated leaving their urban neighborhoods altogether and moving to the suburbs like everyone else.

In retrospect, it is easier to see that what happened across much of the urban United States in those decades after the Second World War amounted to a perfect storm. The tsunami of deindustrialization crashed on the shores of this country's ongoing racial tragedy. Some observers in the 1960s did see all the forces at work; many, including well-meaning ones, did not. The results, in any event, were easier to tally than to predict: vanishing jobs and abandoned neighborhoods and all the crime, hopelessness, and despair that followed.

The urban crisis of the 1950s and 1960s would seem a problem tailor-made to be addressed by business schools. Or at least by business schools as they liked to describe themselves. They allegedly produced leaders who could navigate the tricky and complicated world of business, uniquely trained to respond to the difficult challenges brought by rapidly changing economic forces, and even if they had been unprepared to assume that leadership role in the 1930s, surely they would be ready now. On top of that, in Philadelphia, in Chicago, in New York, and elsewhere the collapse of urban economies unfolded in real time just down the street from some of the most well-regarded business schools.

1969 was a rough year on many campuses around the country, but particularly those located in big cities. During the summer, Wharton's Dean Willis Winn sent a tired-sounding memo to his faculty. "The start of another regular academic year is only 8 weeks away, little enough time at best to plan for campus contingencies. With a view toward identifying potential crisis situations and at least exploring some possible options for dealing with such matters, I have listed the following 'Pressure Points' for discussion." [37] Those "pressure points" included demands for more black student enrollment, controversies surrounding ROTC (Reserve Officers' Training Corps), and objections to chemical warfare research.

Beyond the demonstrators he could hear and see out his office window, Winn had also read a manifesto issued by some faculty and staff at Penn earlier that year: "A New Mission for the University of Pennsylvania: Its

Response to the Crisis in the Relationship between Urban Universities and Their Communities." He might well have felt besieged on all sides.

The big issues that drove the tumult of the late 1960s often found local expression on college campuses. Students and faculty began to question the university's role in the military-industrial complex, for example, and Dean Winn found himself at the center of that controversy. In December 1968, Winn corresponded at length with H. D. Doan, president of Dow Chemical, producer of napalm. Dow's presence to recruit Wharton students (and other Penn students) had generated protests, and Winn wondered what might be done about that. In the end, Doan insisted to Winn, almost channeling Alfred Sloan's defense of GM's involvement with Hitler, "We must, I believe, stay with our fundamental decisions on napalm. We must, I believe, defend our right and responsibility to recruit [at Penn and elsewhere] as long as this is the common practice." But he also promised, "We can do both of these in ways that cause a minimum of disturbance and we will try to do so."[38] In 1968 *someone* needed to stand up in defense of napalm, and Doan bravely took on the task.

Activists also directed their anger at university-sponsored urban-renewal projects. Using federal money, and judicial power, many educational and medical institutions gobbled up surrounding real estate for their own expansion, often displacing poorer, blacker residents as a consequence. The frictions those projects caused, both off campus and on, forced universities, however haltingly, to reexamine their relationship with the neighborhoods of which they were a part. "Our conclusion," the authors of "A New Mission for the University of Pennsylvania" wrote, "is that the University of Pennsylvania must put behind it its custom of reacting defensively to the community's demands upon its capabilities as these demands arise; instead, it must gear itself psychologically, intellectually and organizationally to a new definition of its role, in which it anticipates and accommodates these demands as aggressively as it confronts the frontiers of scholarship and science."[39]

Wharton had already taken what it saw as steps in this direction the previous fall. Even before the term began Winn circulated an intramural memo asking for some feedback. "Your reaction to an idea," he wrote, "as to how Wharton (and ultimately the University as a whole) might contribute significantly to the alleviation of the Urban-Race-Poverty problem would be very much appreciated."[40] That idea was called the Community-Wharton Education Program (CWEP).

In broad strokes, the CWEP brought Wharton faculty together with residents of surrounding neighborhoods to teach courses in business and management. Faculty member Julius Aronofsky reported back to Winn after the initial meeting in September, "Much of the excitement over the program stemmed from the idea that it would be managerially oriented rather than training for specific technical jobs." Vocational training was often the thrust of many local and federally sponsored job training programs, but with the CWEP, "the idea of management training was emphasized because relatively few of the Black Community are in supervisory or managerial positions."[41] That observation, as we've seen already, was unarguably true in the late 1960s.

What happened at Penn in response to the urban crisis happened almost in parallel on the other side of the country at Berkeley. Berkeley was an epicenter of student unrest without question, but the campus also sits three or four miles straight up Telegraph Avenue from downtown Oakland. That city struggled with its own version of the economic crisis hitting other industrial centers, even if its troubles were not quite on the scale of Detroit or Chicago.

By 1968, Berkeley had a "decidedly negative reputation among many elements of the Bay Area minority community," which reputation, in turn, "frequently engendered suspicion and hostility regarding the intentions of the University." The geography of the East Bay didn't help relations any either. The trip on Telegraph Avenue from Oakland to Berkeley is all uphill, and among Oakland residents the university stood as the "White Citadel on the Hill," as Berkeley's Edwin Epstein put it. In response, as one of the first initiatives of his tenure as the new Berkeley president, Charles Hitch created the Urban Crisis Program in 1968 and housed it in the president's office. He also recalled Berkeley's DC lobbyist, Mark Ferber, from Washington and put him in charge of the program.[42]

The characterizations about Berkeley's relationship with its surrounding neighborhoods might have described virtually any of those between urban universities and their host cities at that moment: Yale and New Haven; Columbia and Harlem; Chicago and the South Side. And historically, if we are frank, on their best days town-gown relationships in places like those might be described as indifferent coexistence. Things were often much worse. As early as 1824, hundreds of New Haven residents laid siege to Yale College for two days after someone at Yale dug up a recently buried body for use at the medical school. What had changed in town-gown dynamics by the 1960s was a shared sense of urgency. Urban universities had to acknowledge that their fate and future was bound up with the fate and future of the cities in which they resided; cities, in turn, looked to universities for help of any kind but especially with their increasing economic desperation and social unrest.

After conducting a campus-wide survey to discover what initiatives already existed, Berkeley's Urban Crisis Program began to offer money for new ones. The grant program funded a wide array of projects from units around campus to engage with groups all over the Bay Area. The School of Business Administration received such a grant, for just over $27,000, effective January 1, 1969. The school, in turn, created its own Office of Urban Programs (OUP) as the locus for its community engagement activities.

In announcing all this to "interested members of the Bay Area and University Communities," OUP's director Edwin Epstein explained that "ghetto" residents wanted three things with which the business school might be able to help: the creation of minority-owned businesses, jobs for neighborhood residents, and the retention of money "within the community rather than having it go for the benefit of others." In other words, the business school wanted to use its expertise to promote economic development in struggling urban neighborhoods because "economic development is viewed . . . as a prime ingredient of overall social betterment." Epstein did not use the phrase "black capitalism" but that was, in effect, what he was describing.

These were not entirely uncharted waters for the business school, but Epstein did acknowledge that "to date, the efforts of the Schools of Business Administration in the Ghetto have been sporadic and *ad hoc*." More damning of the business school in an age when "action-oriented" students demanded "relevance" from their education, Epstein wrote that "the educational program of the Schools . . . has not emphasized to any great extent actual student involvement with current social problems."[43] Epstein then outlined a remarkably broad set of goals and objectives and a project to be pursued by the OUP, all intended "to combine the trinity of functions espoused by this University: public service, teaching and research." And while the OUP "cannot hope to undertake at one time all of the possible programs which could contribute" to the economic development of surrounding urban areas, Epstein thought that four ought to be implemented promptly: a technical assistance project, run by students, to help "aspirant minority businessmen"; a business skills clinic; development of a "technical assistance pool" of businessmen and faculty "who are willing to provide technical assistance to present and aspirant minority-owned businesses"; and a liaison service to serve as an "honest broker" between "minority community organizations and business-men and the Bay Area business community."[44] Epstein's sketch of what his office might do is even more ambitious given that the university grant lasted only eight months, and he had been hired for a two-year term as director.

In the event, OUP's university grant was extended for an additional academic year, but the president's money was not going to last forever. In April 1970 the office drafted a more formal proposal for its "technical assistance, research and education" program. Less ambitious perhaps, certainly less breathless than Epstein's memo from the year before, the proposal focused on three programs. The student-run technical assistance office was already up and running and with good results. In addition, the proposal called for creating a "program in management development," involving a set of courses offered over a two- to three-week session. The program mashed together the idea of university extension courses and the management courses offered to business executives. Finally, the proposal pitched expanding the research dimension of OUP's work to foster investigations by faculty and graduate students.[45]

Back in Philadelphia, the CWEP resembled the program started by George Shultz at Chicago and the consortium founded at Washington University. Wharton's effort, however, did not recruit students nationally. Rather, it targeted high school graduates from nearby neighborhoods to enroll in evening classes. If they did well, they were promised admission to Wharton proper and full scholarships. After organizational meetings in fall 1968, the program launched early in 1969. "Ghetto Youths Begin Classes," a newspaper headline announced on January 27.[46]

A week later, 250 people gathered under the auspices of the Wharton MBA Association to discuss "Wharton and the Community." The "lively" discussion served as a public unveiling of the CWEP. A Wharton professor, Russell Ackoff, one of the school's leading intellectual lights and a driving force behind the CWEP, told the crowd that a "lack of managerial skills" in poor neighborhoods stifles any economic development. CWEP, he explained, was an attempt to address that problem. Some in the auditorium pushed back. They reminded panelists that because there were so few black students or faculty at Wharton, and because of tensions between town and gown more broadly, the CWEP would be greeted with suspicion by many in the university's surrounding neighborhoods. To which the Wharton professor George Taylor replied, "If I were you students, I would stop dreaming of utopias and pick out an area within my own competence and try to push the ball forward a little bit, maybe."[47] Good advice to be sure, though probably not what students wanted to hear.

Though the program had been initiated by Wharton faculty, those faculty engaged both community leaders and business figures from the outset to help plan it. How invested the larger university was in CWEP is more ambiguous. By fall term 1973, 132 students were enrolled in twelve courses, all taught by Wharton faculty on a volunteer basis. But the financial aid promises the program had originally made proved more problematic. One of those involved with the program complained about Penn's indifference in a memo: "In the continuing absence of a University posture and mission respecting community service programs, it seems we must continue to handle this problem *ad hoc*."[48]

That complaint proved prescient in a way. By 1975 many programs at Penn found themselves struggling under a belt-tightening regime necessitated by the wider economic malaise of the 1970s, none more so than those that tried to address town-gown relations. "During the past academic year," Penn's student newspaper reported in April, "the University's austerity policy has taken its toll on relationships with the community, creating frequent tensions and disappointments for both administrators and community leaders." Forrest Adams told the paper that the university's administration "considers working with the community a luxury, and in this economic crisis we can't afford it."[49] Adams knew of what he spoke. He served as director of the university's Office of External Affairs, and in the spring of 1975 his office was closed.

There was some discussion of merging the program with the larger program of evening classes to cut costs. CWEP director Carolynne Martin, herself a CWEP graduate, thought this was a bad idea and reminded the higher-ups, "There is a definite dichotomy between the traditional adult student who enters Wharton Evening and the adult student who enters CWEP." CWEP survived this particular storm. Between 1974 and 1977 the program graduated sixty-eight students, and in 1979 Wharton Dean Donald Carroll issued his annual call for volunteer teachers, touting to his faculty that CWEP "has been one of the most successful community-related programs with which the University in general, and Wharton in particular, has been associated."[50]

Effie Brown grew up in a black neighborhood in West Philadelphia and as a kid sold homemade snow cones on the corner in her neighborhood in the summers. She was a strong student—"I had an A average in high school," she reported—but college was out of reach financially. She did what so many women, black and white, did in that era and became a secretary. She hated it; it bored her and she dreamed of a job where she could think. In the early 1970s she enrolled in the CWEP and did so well that she was offered a free ride to complete an MBA at Wharton. She turned that offer down, however, and went into business for herself instead. Ten years later she owned and ran a travel agency catering specifically to women and to black clients. "It has been a beautiful experience," she said of starting her own business, made even more beautiful by success.[51] Brown was certainly not alone in the success she achieved after participating in the CWEP. Several hundred students took the courses and then went on to careers in business, often opening their own businesses, often staying in Philadelphia. Those successes were real. For people like Brown they were life changing.

And yet when measured against the scale of the urban economic crisis of the 1960s and 1970s in Philadelphia—to say nothing of the rest of urban America—the CWEP seems inadequately small. Wharton, after all, stood among the top business schools in the nation—the world—with a network of alumni that included some of the most powerful and influential men in the private sector. But its response to the urban crisis in the form of the CWEP was entirely local and might be categorized as good works rather than a more systematic attack on a complex problem. The CWEP, for all its virtues, remained on the margins of Wharton's activities. So too did the urban crisis. The same might be said of Berkeley's program on the other coast.

Wharton professor George Taylor was certainly right that teaching management was an area within the competence of Wharton faculty and that doing so to constituencies that otherwise would not have access to Wharton expertise was a small step in the right direction. Dean Winn might have inadvertently revealed part of the conceptual problem in his memo when he talked about the "Urban-Race-Poverty problem," an unholy trinity that may have made it harder to disentangle what was happening in U.S. cities in ways that could have led to more comprehensive solutions. Tellingly, Winn didn't call the tectonic shifts taking place in the urban economy a "business problem." The urban crisis might have caused people at Wharton to reexamine the school's racial inclusion or the nature of the school's relationship with its host community, but it does not seem to have forced any fundamental questioning about the nature of the American private sector and the role it should play in the nation's hurting urban centers.

Manning the Barricades to Defend Free Enterprise

On May 5, 1970, students in business school at Berkeley voted 126 to 46 to boycott classes "until such time as the government of the United States does cease and desist the crime of intervention in the internal affairs of Southeast Asia"[52] The date here is full of significance: the vote and declaration came the day after the murder of four students at Kent State University by Ohio National Guard troops.

And on the same day, 3000-plus miles to the east, faculty and students at Harvard's business school met to draft an open letter to Congress and to Richard Nixon. They issued their letter on May 8, and in it they announced that the

> faculty and officers of the Graduate School of Business Administration, acting as individuals, declare our support for the following resolution adopted by a substantial majority of over 1,300 members of the Harvard Business School community in a public meeting on May 5, 1970: We condemn the administration of President Nixon for its view of mankind and the American community which:
>
> 1. Perceives the anxiety and turmoil in our midst as the work of 'bums' or 'effete snobs';
> 2. Fails to acknowledge that legitimate doubt exists about the ability of black Americans and other oppressed groups to obtain justice;
> 3. Is unwilling to move for a transformation of American society in accordance with the goals of maximum fulfillment for each human being and harmony between mankind and nature.
>
> In particular and most urgently we call for an end to the escalation of war in Southeast Asia and for the withdrawal of American forces from that region. In the United States we demand an end to the use of blind force as a means to resolve legitimate disagreement.[53]

The Vietnam War did find its way to the business school corner of campus, as these two episodes of collective outrage and despair indicate. But by and large, when we think of the campus convulsions of the late 1960s and early 1970s, Berkeley business school dean Earl Cheit was probably right when he recollected, "The general unrest affected the business school, but not necessarily as much as other parts of the campus. Business students were probably as idealistic as any other students, but they were more focused on their education than some of the leaders of student movements from other departments." Students at the University of Chicago also staged a general strike after the Kent State shootings—except those at Chicago's business school. Feeling pressure from other students and after the university's administration had suspended classes, they decided to join the strike. Profiles in courage they were not.[54]

In fact, Berkeley's Dean Cheit may have exaggerated the "idealistic" part in describing his students. A 1970 survey of Berkeley's MBA graduates found that "more men indicate a high priority on 'knowledge' and 'personal satisfaction' as their goals, and few regard 'socio-political' as an important goal, but 'income,' 'personal influence,' and 'future prestige' all ranked high."[55] Campuses might have been swarming with long-haired peace activists in the 1960s, but it is probably safe to say that not many of them were enrolled in business schools.

Even as the Vietnam War wound down and the U.S. war effort slouched to its inglorious end, the American economy entered another period of protracted dysfunction. The recession of the 1970s officially began in 1973 and ended in 1975 and was the consequence of several factors, including the Nixon Shock of 1971, in which he essentially dissolved the Bretton Woods system of international financial exchange; the Organization of Petroleum Exporting Countries oil embargo of 1973, which sent U.S. energy prices through the roof; and the inflationary spending on the war itself.

The Nixon recession also added a new word to our economic vocabulary: stagflation. As defined by one wag, stagflation described an economic condition in which everything that should go up goes down and everything that should go down goes up. Mostly what that meant was that the unemployment rate *and* inflation rose dramatically and simultaneously, something the standard economic models failed to predict and struggled to explain. Unemployment peaked in 1975 at 9 percent, the highest rate Americans had experienced since the Great Depression, and while the economy started to grow in 1976, inflation remained stubborn. The great postwar economic boom was over.

The Age of Stagflation was a different kind of economic crisis than the Great Depression had been, but some of the reactions to it by business seem remarkably the same. Some conservative business leaders and their political handmaidens worried not so much about runaway prices or the rising number of Americans without jobs but instead about the reputation of business itself. On college campuses, the war had caused at least some number of students and faculty to question the ethics and morality of the military-industrial complex. The economic crunch of the 1970s broadened that dissatisfaction and mistrust. A Harris poll conducted in 1976 found that the number of Americans who had "a great deal of confidence" in the leaders of major corporations stood at an underwhelming 16 percent. Just ten years earlier, in 1966, that figure had been 55 percent.

For U.S. business, then, the twin crises of Vietnam and stagflation did not represent ethical failures or corporate dysfunction but rather a problem of marketing. How to restore the faith of the American people in their corporate leaders? And more to the point, how to make sure that those 84 percent of Americans who did not express "a great deal of confidence" in corporate America did not demand any significant political action as a result of their dissatisfaction?

The National Association of Manufacturers (NAM) had been involved in a variety of educational—or proselytizing if you prefer—ventures since at least the 1950s. Across that decade, NAM sponsored a speakers service to provide lectures on college campuses. The speakers came from a roster of businessmen assembled by NAM and as one advertising flyer described the program: "The speakers listed in this brochure are volunteers in a most important task. They hope that through their efforts and your cooperation, students will gain increased knowledge and understanding of business practices." NAM's Walter Cooper described the lecture series in a memo as having three primary goals: (1) to have businessmen "become interested in education and educational institutions"; (2) "to add reality to course content by discussing actual business practice and problems with students"; and (3) "to present the viewpoints of businessmen and industrialists on a number of business, economic and social problems." And as he put it later in that memo, "The College Speaking Program will serve two primary groups—teachers colleges and schools of business administration." NAM worked with campus chapters of Delta Sigma Pi to coordinate and facilitate the speakers program.[56]

NAM also busied itself putting together extensive prep materials for high school and intercollegiate debate teams on topics, including "Resolved: That the Requirement of Membership in a Labor Organization as a Condition of Employment Should Be Illegal" and "The Argument against Federal Aid to Education." Beginning in 1949, NAM also sponsored an Annual Congress of American Industry to which it invited forty-nine college students (one per state plus Washington, D.C.) to a series of panel discussions with business leaders and business school professors. NAM also recognized the importance of business schools to promote its brand of free-market corporate capitalism. In 1964 it established the NAM Council of Business School Deans, whose purpose "is to provide an avenue of direct, two-way communication and information between industry and those most closely related to the production of future business executive personnel."[57]

With the civil rights movement in full swing and with baby boomers arriving on college campuses in their multitudes, people inside NAM sounded panicky in the early 1960s. Austin Murphy, the director of NAM's Education Division, sounded an alarm in a memo outlining some "educational objectives" for the organization. First, Murphy proposed, "we must educate our own members to the need for developing an effective opposition to the prevailing theory of the omnipotent state and to the most effective means of mounting and sustaining such an offensive." Second, "we must reach the colleges and universities where ideas germinate and develop a positive program to obtain better than a hearing for ideas of individualism and the free enterprise economy." And Murphy continued in a way that sounds positively Leninist in its strategy: "We must reach college and university students; college and university faculty; college and university administrators; college and university trustees. . . . Our governing aim should be to direct the resources of industry (whether in the form of gifts to college development programs; establishment of teaching 'chairs'; gifts and grants for scholarships and fellowships; gifts to foundations; grants and direct payments for research; purchases of advertising in college and university publications) toward our friends and away from our enemies in the ideological struggle between government enterprise and individual enterprise."[58]

The tone of Manichaean hysteria here is startling, though not really surprising. After all, Robert Welch, the conspiracy-crazed founder of the John

Birch Society, had once been on NAM's board of directors. Murphy's memo does, however, reveal just how early NAM had identified college campuses as front-line battlegrounds in its war against the creeping theories of the "omnipotent state," how NAM saw ways to manipulate colleges to promote its particular agenda, and how it saw business students as foot soldiers to enlist "in the ideological struggle between government enterprise and individual enterprise."[59] Murphy, in fact, had been the dean of the business school at Seton Hall University.

By the late 1960s, however, NAM recognized that changes were blowing in the wind, and they tacked accordingly. No more dark and dire warnings about impending socialism, at least not on campuses. Instead, NAM worried that young people were simply walking away from the business life and that business needed an image makeover. In 1966, NAM's Women's Department sent out program kits to its member clubs titled "Thunder on Campus." Designed as a response to campus unrest and to the lack of interest in business, these canned programs addressed "what is behind the protests, their cause, who is doing the protesting, and how industry is meeting the challenge of today's students." More conciliatory in tone than the previous "educational objectives," each of the programs was supposed to conclude with a talk titled "Industry Meets the Challenge of Today's Students." The takeaway? "This then is the picture of industry today. Students have a social concern, a search for a meaningful task, and need to be and find themselves. Industry is answering the challenge."[60] NAM had decided that the kids were all right after all. Provided they chose a career in business.

In 1969 Lee Hamilton, the NAM vice president for education and a former University of Miami business school professor, summed up NAM's worries in a speech he gave at Youngstown State University. "Opinion research polls over the past several years," he informed the students, "seem to suggest that there is an amazing lack of interest in business careers on the part of college students. The Lou Harris Poll, among other things, showed that 50% of college seniors believe business careers are financially rewarding, but only 20% consider such careers challenging. Only 11% feel a business career is creative. Only 7% consider a business career to be intellectually stimulating. Only 1% feel a business career offers the chance to help others. . . . As one pundit recently stated: 'Unfortunately, college students don't dislike American business; they just ignore it.'"[61]

This was the private sector's public relations problem on campuses in a nutshell. As campuses heated up across the 1960s, growing numbers of students rebelled against the white-collar, gray flannel world of their fathers and imagined lives for themselves doing something more compelling than moving up the corporate ladder. Hamilton, however, wanted to tell them that careers in business would allow them to do good by doing well. "I am saying that there is no real conflict," he went on that evening, "between making a profit and meeting legitimate social needs. . . . We may, in fact, see the formation of profit-seeking companies whose purpose will be to become deliberate instruments of social change."

That was Hamilton's concession to the civil rights revolution, the antiwar movement, and everything else that convulsed campuses in 1969. The corporate world was changing—or it might. But he was quick to defend the private sector's track record from the slings and arrows it was enduring. "Contrary to the views of sidewalk social critics, men engaged in business careers have served mankind quite well—and they will continue to serve society. In fact, there is considerable evidence that suggests to me that businessmen in the course of seeking a profit have served society's needs far better than those who deliberately set about to do good deeds."[62] Not everyone, I suspect, would have agreed.

The U.S. Chamber of Commerce, another enormous and influential business lobby group, also worried about those poll numbers suggesting that the nation's youth were turning their backs on business. Starting in 1962 it began to sponsor College-Business Symposiums through its local chapters. A 1970 organizational pamphlet explained the purpose of these get-togethers. "Symposiums go a long way toward closing the communications gap between the business world and the academic community," the chamber believed, "and they often provide surprises for the participants." The chamber wanted to bring the two worlds together: "Face-to-face confrontations between student leaders from college and university campuses and successful businessmen do much to improve mutual respect. Attendance at a Symposium may be an eye-opener for students who have accepted the cliché-ridden, stereotype of the American business executive—a Babbitt from the pages of Sinclair Lewis, motivated solely by profits, lacking ethical knowledge, or moral commitment."[63]

The chamber was also prepared to concede misunderstandings in both directions. "Too many collegians hold a distorted view of businessmen and their pursuits," the chamber opined. "And businessmen's enthusiastic responses to Symposiums often stem from discoveries that not all collegians are 'mop-topped beats' whose passport to the world is a beard, electric guitar, and collection of folk songs."[64] Never mind that by 1970 the world of folk-song-singing Beats had long passed—one wonders as well how many college students were reading Sinclair Lewis in 1970—the conciliatory, almost avuncular tone of this brochure underscores that the chamber, like other business groups in the 1960s and 1970s, believed that the only reason college students were walking away from U.S. business was a failure of presentation and communication. As James Kilpatrick fumed in an essay responding to yet another survey indicating that Americans had a jaundiced view of business, "American businessmen, who pride themselves on being able to sell anything, have not sold business."[65] No one seems to have entertained the idea that students understood exactly what was being sold and they just did not want to buy or that the student critique of U.S. business practice might have merit.

Harvard certainly failed to make that acknowledgment in its own attempt to address student attitudes about business. In 1967, it ran a summer program for fifty "top undergraduates" from twenty-five colleges and universities, mostly on the East Coast, to intern in large corporations. The ten-week summer began with a two-week crash course in business education at the B-school followed by eight weeks working in a placement. "We wanted to start a dialogue with them [students]," B-school professor Charles Orth explained, "to find if exposure to business by experience would change their opinions about business." Harvard's Dean George BakXer also described the project as something of an experiment: "We hear a great deal about the fact that students don't want a business career," he told the press at the beginning of the summer. "Well, we don't know exactly what the score is, and we're . . . hoping to find out."[66]

The results of the experiment were underwhelming. Some of the participants discovered what so many others have: summer internships often deliver far less than promised. One student complained that he was asked to write a report for his employer about recruitment but that no one ever read it. Kenneth Steinglass, who was placed in the marketing department of a large company, summed up his summer as "passing out spoons and sticking pins in maps." But more to the point, the experience of working for companies like Proctor & Gamble and John Hancock Insurance did not really dispel the perceptions the students already had about business, and in some cases it reinforced them. Several of the students reported that they found an atmosphere of stultifying conformity at their placements. It wasn't just that they all had to wear the same uniform—several were called out for wearing sport-coats to work and appearing in shirts other than white—"there seemed to be a conformity of ideas," according to Boston University student Thomas Mesenbourg, who spent his summer at Bankers Trust. He went on, "There were no intellectual conversations, no discussions of the war in Vietnam. It was all business, and it got boring after a while." Boring on a good day, according to another student. "If I were to generalize from my experience," he reported, "I would say that I am astounded at the tremendous range of mediocrity." If the students had been led to believe that life in the corporate world ran on high-stakes, high-speed decisions, they were disappointed here too. As one student put it, "The only real split-second decision-making we saw was in deciding to pass the buck."[67] Harvard initiated the program believing that unfamiliarity with U.S. business had bred the contempt in which some students held it. Familiarity, it turned out, did not do much to change that.

Recognizing that young people had soured on the corporate world, NAM set up a new task force in the early 1970s to foster better "student and industry relations." A 1972 pamphlet outlined a Student-Industry Plan for Action describing "how NAM members can improve student industry relations by establishing contact with business student members of the Delta Sigma Pi business fraternity at 151 universities in forty states."[68] This effort was of piece with others. As the 1960s stumbled into the 1970s, beleaguered businessmen galvanized themselves to build a movement to reassert a conservative political agenda.

Movement was exactly what the National Leadership Methods organization had in mind when it began sponsoring the Students in Free Enterprise competitions in the 1970s. The competitions started in Texas, where National Leadership Methods was based but then spread around the country. The group described its goals as twofold: "To encourage and help young people anticipating business careers to commit themselves to a movement of their own creation to: 1) speak up for our American free enterprise system which, even with its imperfections, has brought us to the highest standard of living human history has ever known, and 2) help preserve for themselves the opportunity to bring to the system new life and new leadership for its continued improvement and progress." No one at National Leadership Methods apparently saw the irony that they were using handsome corporate sponsorship to have U.S. business students create a movement of their own.

In 1976, National Leadership Methods approached the business school at Ohio State University, asking the dean there to promote the competition to be held in Cleveland (and funded locally by Standard Oil of Ohio). Writing to the OSU dean, Edward Bowman, Robert T. "Sonny" Davis boasted, "By the end of this coming school year we anticipate that 150 colleges of business throughout the United States will be participating in this program." But then he cut to the chase, explaining that "approximately half of them [are] including the program under a seminar for up to three hours college credit. We would strongly suggest that the program be worked into such existing seminars since it lends itself well to this type of course." Unlike the civil rights movement or the movement against the Vietnam War, the movement to promote free-market capitalism that the National Leadership Methods hoped to generate could be counted toward graduation.

To its credit, OSU was not prepared to give away its academic integrity quite so easily. Associate Dean Robert Georges responded to Davis by saying, "We agree thoroughly with the proposition that one of the best long-term solutions to the problems of free enterprise and the growth firm is through collegiate programs which can provide a substantial foundation for public understanding of the economic system and how to help it perform more effectively." But he went to add that "our objective is to assure free enterprise responsiveness to growing public concerns for economic and related social issues associated with society's aspirations for the future. . . . If as a function of our regular programs you feel we can also compete in your program, we would be happy to discuss it with you."[69] Georges's letter reveals that at least some business schools felt caught betwixt and between in the 1970s. On the one hand, they remained committed, as they had been since the 1920s, to corporate capitalism the way it was presently organized and remained unwilling or unable to offer any alternative ideas or even serious critiques of it. On the other, they recognized that those commitments might put them at odds with "public concerns for economic and related social issues associated with society's aspirations for the future."

Some business schools did try to adjust to the temper of the times by making some space for those public concerns. Students at Stanford's business school created the Committee for Corporate Responsibility in 1970 both to push for and to assist with developing more socially conscious initiatives in the private sector. They started by sending out a questionnaire to four hundred corporations to survey what companies were already doing to address environmental, racial, and other issues. They heard back from only eighty, and only sixty of those responses were deemed "substantive." Still, the Stanford students found a number of companies eager to do something but at a loss to know just what or how.[70] Vanderbilt University had a chance to build these concerns into the very architecture of its business school. Vandy's B-school opened in 1969. Part of the impetus behind it was to "stem the drain of young managerial talent from the South." But under its founding dean, the mathematician and physicist Igor Ansoff, the school hoped to distinguish itself from other schools because "its special niche" would be "the management of change." Ansoff made it clear as the school swung open its doors that he wanted to attract "the campus activist as well as the organization man."[71]

Other schools responded to student interest in "occupations that are more socially oriented" and to students who wanted to "express this societal interest in education, government, welfare and health" by adding courses focused on nonprofits to their curricular portfolios. Wharton, for example, began offering an MBA specifically in health care administration in the early 1970s. Samuel Sapienza explained to *MBA* magazine, "In the past, schools of management devoted little attention to the not-for-profit area. A few graduates, it was known, would enter this field. Even though they had no training in [the] specific area they would face, it was assumed they carried with them the general tools, the techniques of application, and the theory of management to sustain a career and make a contribution. . . . We must educate people to meet the challenges of the public sector."[72]

Wharton and others might have begun programs in nonprofit management as a response to more "socially oriented" students, but William Pounds, the dean of the Sloan School at MIT, put the matter quite the other way around. "The primary function [of business schools]," even in the new environment, "is still to assist in the intellectual and emotional development of people to run large institutions." What had changed, Pounds said, was that business schools "have begun to acknowledge that hospitals, schools and governments have the same problem as industry."[73] The question left unasked, as business schools tried to respond to a new generation of students, was whether by embracing the nonprofit sector B-schools would become more socially engaged or whether nonprofits would come to resemble corporations more and more.

Bad for the Economy, Good for Business (Schools)

The editors of *Nation's Business* probably did not see the subtle irony when they juxtaposed two articles in their May 1974 issue.

The first was written by none other than Barry Goldwater. In it he warned readers with his characteristic hyperventilation that "the threat of crippling anti-business legislation is now greater than at any previous time in my experience." American business, Goldwater thundered, "faces the fight of its life." Goldwater did acknowledge that this "drive against business is fueled by public anger," especially against the oil industry, though he failed to acknowledge that public sentiment might have a role in shaping legislation in a democratic society. But then in a sleight of logic also too often characteristic of Goldwater's style, he blamed the legislative threat on a "leftist-liberal cabal."[74]

The very next article, however, was considerably more upbeat. Even in the midst of the economic downturn that was fueling all that pernicious public anger, "demand for this spring's class [of MBAs] is up about 10 per cent on average." What's more, the average starting salaries for those newly stamped MBAs was up 5 percent. William Baughn, the dean at the University of Colorado business school, agreed that "pessimism in some quarters about the economy just isn't affecting the demand for M.B.A.'s." John Hennessey, the dean of the Tuck School of Business at Dartmouth, could barely contain his glee: "It's heartening to find that companies aren't going to stop recruiting M.B.A. talent. We don't see cyclical peaks and troughs for M.B.A.'s—just a growing demand." Despite the existential threat businesses allegedly faced from regulators and politicians, and never mind that the economy itself was in the midst of a protracted and painful recession, life at business schools was good in the 1970s.[75]

Even as he was launching the attitude adjustment internships in 1967, Harvard's Dean Baker thought reports of student antipathy toward business were highly exaggerated. After all, applications to the B-school had doubled in just the previous five years regardless of civil rights unrest or Vietnam protests. The admissions director Anthony Athos wondered what all the fuss was about and why the nation's titans of industry were behaving like Chicken

Little: "I have some trouble understanding why presidents of corporations are responding to things in the press." Perhaps, suggested *Business Week*, the problem was fragile egos and nothing more. "Businessmen, like everyone else," the magazine commented, "want to be liked, and the leaders of today's college generation don't seem particularly fond of the business world."[76]

College students might have expressed a certain disdain for the corporate world, but in the era of stagflation they were voting with their feet, and not just at Harvard. By the early 1970s, Wharton found itself bursting at the seams with students. In his annual report to his faculty for academic year 1974–75, Wharton Dean Donald Carroll reminded people that enrollments in the undergraduate program had grown 20 percent in just two years "as I assume you are painfully aware." Students not already in Wharton were also applying to transfer from other corners of the university in large numbers—a "45–50% increase over last year." This created what Dean Carroll called "a very strange situation." As the economic downturn of the stagflation years took its toll on the rest of the university, Wharton was thriving. Carroll wrote to the faculty, "We find ourselves prosperous, and increasingly prosperous, amid university stringency. In a sense, this puts us on a collision course with our colleagues elsewhere in the University." But as Carroll was quick to add, "On the other hand, I prefer it be this way than sharing the stringency."[77]

The news was similarly rosy on the other coast. Enrollments at Berkeley's business school also began to rise. In 1970 Berkeley's Dean Holton told the school's alumni magazine, "Fall enrollment in courses offered by the Schools of Business Administration were surprisingly large. . . . More majors from other departments are choosing electives in Business Administration." Two years later, the acting dean Berkeley, Dow Votaw, told the same publication that the numbers kept going up and that "there is other substantial evidence to support the conclusion that this trend is not the result of a temporary fluke but of a major change in student goals and interests." By 1973's spring semester, 726 students were enrolled, Associate Dean Epstein reported, the highest figure since 1957 and an increase of nearly 150 over 1971. In fact, when the University of Denver's Peter Firmin did a national survey in 1974 he found that "the national trend has reflected sharply *increased* enrollments in business programs throughout the nation." This was true on his campus as well. By 1977 business surpassed education as the single largest category of undergraduate major. One out of every six bachelor's degrees now went to a business major.[78]

The economic crisis of the early 1970s made enrolling in business schools more attractive not less, and at least at Wharton it solved the Botany Bay problem that had plagued business schools from the very beginning. Carroll reported that as applications continued to climb, Wharton could be more and more selective in its admissions. "Quality is up," he told the faculty and later repeated that "the quality of the applicants continues to be excellent." Quality went up too at the University of Denver, or at least the admission rates started to drop. The business school accepted over three-quarters of its applicants in 1973 but only two-thirds by 1977.[79] Starting in the 1970s, business students were no longer the least accomplished, least talented ones on campus. Business schools could thank stagflation for that.

In the end, the much-discussed disenchantment that the sixties generation felt toward business was either highly exaggerated or it evaporated pretty quickly. In 1975 the Institute of Life Insurance piloted a program to put insurance executives on college campuses to live, teach, and go to classes. When one such executive, stationed at Bryn Mawr College, was asked whether he found the students to be "anti-business," he replied, "I don't really get that impression."[80] Whatever the level of their skepticism with the establishment or whatever their level of anger at The Man, college students in the late 1960s and early 1970s did not express it by walking away from business schools. In 1970, Roy Raymond, a student at Stanford's business school who sported long hair and a drooping mustache and who prowled the campus in sandals, explained his brand-new Jaguar XK-E. "I find no conflict," he told a reporter fifteen years before Don Henley and the Eagles would sing about seeing a Dead-head sticker on a Cadillac, "between the idea that I will make a lot of money and still be socially relevant."[81] Somewhere, the NAM's Lee Hamilton was smiling.

Going Global

Shortly after the Second World War ended and just as the Cold War had settled as a frost over much of the globe, the U.S. government created the U.S. Technical Assistance and Productivity (USTAP) program. The purpose of USTAP was to bring young management trainees from Western Europe, expose them to American business practices, and enroll them at the finest American business schools, including NYU, Columbia, Stanford, and Wharton. Started in 1949, USTAP by 1954 was bringing as many as seventy-five Europeans to this country each month.[82]

USTAP can surely be seen as part of a panoply of programs developed after the war to use soft power in the Cold War struggle, the Marshall Plan for Western Europe foremost among them. But the timing here is unintentionally ironic. USTAP offered Europeans a U.S. business education precisely at the moment when Americans were beginning to acknowledge just how dreadful that education was.

USTAP started before the Ford and Carnegie reports came out. The British *Report on Higher Education* appeared after those two. Issued in 1963, it was the first study of its kind—a comprehensive survey of British higher education and recommendations about where it ought to go. The committee heard from British business leaders who fretted that British business could not compete in the postwar economy unless it began more formal programs in management training. They suggested establishing several comparable to "the great business schools of the United States." The committee took notice and recommended in its report the creation of "at least two major graduate schools of business, together with an expansion of business studies in other universities and scientific and technological institutes."[83]

Either Lord Robbins, the chair of the committee, was unaware of the Ford and Carnegie studies, unlikely as that seems, or he and his committee did not much care about them. U.S. business schools were becoming an international model, never mind the decidedly mediocre report card they had just received. USTAP had brought Europeans to the United States in the 1950s to introduce them to business schools; by the 1960s Europeans decided to develop their own management schools; and in the 1960s and 1970s, America business schools themselves started to look abroad. The traffic in business education was now transatlantic.

In 1966, *Business Week* called the move of U.S. business education to Europe an "invasion," perhaps an ill-advised term given what other invasions the United States was engaged in at that moment. Nor did *Business Week*'s reporter seem to realize the accidental reference he made to Taylorism when he wrote, "American scientific management is providing European business with the essential framework, the common language, and the harmony that is still the distant goal of the Brussels Eurocrats." Invasions and time-motion studies notwithstanding, "Management schools are being created as fast as funds and faculty can be found," and *Business Week* reported that some of those schools were recruiting faculty from the United States. And why not? "Teaching the American way of doing things in Europe has become a major attraction for American professors of business administration. Many of them spend a large part of their time traveling as guest lecturers."[84] The following year, the same magazine announced that "the U.S. business school at long last is going global."[85] The AACSB caught up with this invasion when it amended its accreditation standards to mandate that "students be exposed to the international dimensions of business" in 1974.[86] As early as the 1967–68 school year, business students at the University of Denver were being introduced to international business, and within a decade the school was offering a degree in "international management." An internal study at Wharton in 1973 identified "international management" as one of two key areas the school needed to develop, and thus on July 1, 1974, the Wharton School's International Office opened "to act as a focus for the international activities of the School."[87]

Business schools and their faculty had been involved in overseas projects since the end of the Second World War or, more to the point, once the Cold War started. As the Michigan State University business school dean Donald Taylor sketched it, "Throughout the nineteen fifties and early nineteen sixties many Schools of Business Administration were involved in international projects, ranging from institution building endeavors to strictly research efforts or faculty and student exchange programs." He noted, "These efforts were generally jointly funded, with the U.S. effort wholly or in part funded by the U.S. government or U.S. foundations." Wharton, for example, had engaged in a business education project in Karachi, Pakistan, in the 1950s that was funded by the International Cooperation Administration, another U.S. government program.[88]

But, Taylor continued, that government and foundation support faded by the mid-1960s and as a consequence so did the international activities of American business schools. "The gradual withdrawal of U.S. government and foundation support," he wrote, "particularly in the area of business, resulted in a reduction of School of Business activities abroad beginning in the late nineteen sixties." Thus, the invasion that *Business Week* reported in 1966 was more a resumption than a new assault but one without as much government sponsorship. "In the early nineteen seventies the U.S. multinational corporation, long a participant in the U.S. international relations, stepped to the forefront as a major arm of American involvement in foreign cultures." They did so, in Taylor's estimation, not simply to plant the corporate flag overseas but because "the increased concern for social responsibility on the part of business at home also affected the outlook of corporate managements as they moved overseas."[89] Some multinational corporations saw themselves as having multinational social responsibilities.

Taylor wrote his report in 1976, as that concern for social responsibility was already waning, and he wrote, therefore, with a different concern. Given that profit-making corporations, rather than government or philanthropic foundations, might set the agenda and not simply pay the bills, Taylor thought that AACSB needed to establish some sort of code of conduct for business schools to follow when they worked internationally. He wasn't alone. Almost ten years earlier, the Columbia business school dean Courtney Brown had warned a conference on international business education that "the multinational corporation, which is not always compatible with national interests, is going to emerge as a powerful force."[90]

In the end, however, American business schools and the business school model have expanded internationally at an astonishing rate. One study found over 1600 business schools operating in over a hundred countries around the world by 1999, and they had achieved a kind of hegemony. That study concluded that "the MBA and B-Schools have achieved rule-like status in global society as the primary program and institution of educating and producing professional managers needed to lead increasingly universalistic and standardized forms of business around the world." The authors continued, "Despite criticisms and controversies, the MBA and B-Schools have diffused to a majority of countries worldwide, and it is extremely challenging to find a society that is immune to this trend."[91] It isn't clear whether Taylor ever got the code of conduct he advocated for, but in 1997 AACSB accredited its first business school outside North America. The organization felt compelled to change its name to the American Association of Collegiate Schools of Business *International*.

U.S. business schools had little to say about the economic crisis of the 1970s, just as they had had little to offer during the Great Depression, just as they had little to offer to their own urban neighborhoods as many of those neighborhoods imploded. Even while the steel industry collapsed in Pittsburgh and automakers in Detroit found themselves looking at ruin, U.S. business education became a major export product. Across the twentieth century, business schools failed to anticipate crises, and they had little by way of solutions to them. But they did demonstrate an ability to turn these crises to their own advantage.

Chapter 6

SAME AS IT EVER WAS

How Business Schools Helped Create the New Gilded Age

Practices and processes inside the B-school buildings have changed over the course of more than one hundred years without question, but the continuities are just as striking. Most of the refrains we have heard in the previous chapters continue to be sung: Do business schools produce graduates fitted for jobs in business? Is that the job of business schools in the first place? What, exactly, is the value and purpose of a business degree?

One thing has changed, at least from my review of the evidence: Business schools themselves have stopped trying to answer, or even ask, some of these basic, foundational questions. As recently as the 1970s, according to one observer, "no one—neither the students, nor the schools, nor the public—had yet decided just what the purpose of business school was."[1] A remarkable comment, given how long and how hard business schools had been at it. When Lyman Porter and Lawrence McKibben undertook a study of business schools in 1988, the first comprehensive such study since the bombshells of 1959, they came to that conclusion. "We observed that there is a high level of satisfaction *within* schools about the quality of the job they are doing in educating students for productive careers in the business world," but they added, "We came away from our university interviews concerned that there may be too much overall *complacency and self-satisfaction. . . . The consequence of this self-satisfaction is that currently within universities and their business/management schools there is little perceived need for major changes in the way in which collegiate management education is carried out.*"[2]

Complacency and self-satisfaction. Yet amid their disappointment and disapproval, Porter and McKibben seemed to have missed an important point. After all, business school classrooms continue to burst at the seams, the donor money rains down more and more torrentially, their graduates land lucrative jobs, and faculty salaries grow apace. Why on earth would business schools shake that complacency and undergo "major changes" if everything seems to be going so well?

So in this final chapter I want to see how business schools figured out what their purpose was, to bring some of the stories we have been charting forward to the present or near present, to look at what has changed and how, and to look at what has not.

The Stars Align, Finally

From the outset, as we have seen already, business school leaders insisted that a collegiate business degree trained businessmen (yes, almost entirely men— we've discussed that already too) who put social responsibility before mere moneymaking, the public good before private gain. That theme emerged in earnest before the First World War, and it was echoed loudly during the Great Depression. Social responsibility, the lesson went, and ethical behavior are what distinguish business school graduates from ordinary profit seekers: a sermon that may well still be preached today. Whether or not those educational instructions yielded measurable results as students moved into the business world is difficult to say, though the repeated exhortations over the decades that business schools needed to drum this recitation more loudly suggest that they weren't particularly effective. Either way, we can date, at least symbolically, the moment when the very idea of corporate social responsibility began to wither: September 13, 1970.

On that Sunday Milton Friedman published his essay "The Social Responsibility of Business Is to Increase Its Profits." Any corporate executive who talked about the "social conscience" of business, Friedman charged, or about its social responsibility—and we've seen that such talk was thick in the air in 1970—was really advocating "pure and unadulterated socialism." People may, or may not, feel some sense of social obligation, Friedman averred, but not organizations. (Friedman had to fudge the most peculiar fact of U.S. business life: that corporations are legally considered people.) Corporate executives were employees of the shareholders, who owned the corporation. Any time they did something to promote some social cause or other, they were "spending someone else's money for a general social interest." In doing so, Friedman's logic continued, the executive became "in effect a public employee, a civil servant, even though he remains in name an employee of a private enterprise." Thus, and the title of his essay summarized it with admirable efficiency, Friedman concluded that corporations had only one responsibility: make as much money as possible for shareholders.

Friedman was already a towering figure at the University of Chicago when he wrote that essay, and his neo-laissez-faire economic ideas had been circulating for some time. What made Friedman different from most other Chicago School economists and their devotees was the relish he took in acting as a public provocateur. He was good at it too. His face wound up on the cover of *Time* magazine in 1969, and in 2006 that same magazine described him as the most influential economist of the second half of the twentieth century. "The Social Responsibility of Business Is to Increase Its Profits" appeared in the *New York Times Magazine*, not in an academic journal.[3]

Friedman did not use the phrase "shareholder value" in "The Social Responsibility of Business Is to Increase Its Profits"—the phrase itself does not seem to have come into wide circulation until the turn of the millennium—but that was essentially what he was describing. And corporate America took heed.

Change didn't happen overnight. As late as 1990 the Business Roundtable, a conservative business lobby group made up of corporate CEOs, still insisted that "corporations are chartered to serve both their shareholders and society as a whole." The Roundtable specified why "society as a whole" mattered: "The central corporate governance point to be made about a corporation's stakeholders beyond the shareholder is that they are vital to the long-term successful economic performance of the corporation. . . . The thrust of history and law strongly supports the broader view of the directors' responsibility to carefully weigh the interests of all stakeholders as part of their responsibility to the corporation or to the long-term interests of its share-holders."[4] Shareholders and stakeholders could coexist in a model like this.

Seven years later, however, that "broader view" had been chucked. In 1997, the Business Roundtable issued another statement: "In the Business Round-table's view, the paramount duty of management and of boards of directors is to the corporation's stockholders; the interests of other stakeholders are relevant as a derivative of the duty to the stockholders." And in a line that could almost have been lifted straight from Milton Friedman's 1970 essay, "the notion that the board must somehow balance the interests of other stake-holders fundamentally misconstrues the role of directors."[5]

Much went out with the bathwater in 1997. Like "long-term interests," replaced now by an obsessive focus on quarterly earnings reports. Like work-ers and the communities in which they live—all now just stakeholders no longer of concern to any corporation. And notice the almost breathtaking arrogance of rejecting public obligations, given how much corporations de-pend on—demand—public supports of one sort and another, from the pub-licly granted charters that create them to that legal status of personhood, to the legal swaddling of bankruptcy laws and bailouts that insulate them when they fail. Think of it as cradle-to-grave security. Of course, U.S. businesses had a similar "we take, you give" attitude toward the public during the first laissez-faire Gilded Age too.

Just as astonishing was the rationale used by the Business Roundtable to get to its conclusion about the primacy of shareholder value. "The weakness of the stakeholder model is the absence of an overall objective function which implicitly or explicitly specifies the trade-offs from expenditures on various items, including the firm's stakeholders." That meant, in turn, that "there is no way to measure and evaluate the performance of managers." Worse still, and once again channeling Milton Friedman, "managers are then left free to exercise their own preferences and prejudices in the allocations of the firm's resources with no logical way to hold them accountable." Thus, for want of a metric, did any sense of corporate social responsibility die.

In walking away from corporate social responsibility, the Business Round-table wasn't so much staking out a well-reasoned principle as throwing up its hands. The issues the Roundtable raised as it dismissed stakeholders are challenging to be sure. In its statement the Roundtable announced that stake-holder interests no longer mattered "because [they] would leave the board with no criterion for resolving conflicts between interests of stockholders and of other stakeholders or among different groups of stakeholders," but that does not mean that such criteria cannot ever be found. After all, stakeholders mattered to corporations during the postwar boom years, and U.S. corporations somehow managed to be profitable. The statement really admits that the issues are complicated, too hard, apparently, for the Roundtable's CEOs who just couldn't be bothered to sort them out.[6]

In other words, making a fetish of shareholder value, turning it into the only objective for those who run corporations, is intellectually (and morally) lazy. But it is also brilliant in its simplicity. It reduces all the variables that might be involved in running a large, complex organization to a single one. And as any high school kid taking algebra will tell you, solving a problem with one variable is a whole lot easier than solving a problem that involves many. It reduces a potentially bewildering array of choices a corporate executive might make down to only those that increase shareholder value, and damn the consequences. I won't insist that the cult of shareholder value that has come to dominate corporate America is the most pernicious development of the last generation, but only in such a world is the measure of a successful airline journey that you arrive with all your teeth intact.[7]

For our story, however, the triumph of the shareholder-value view of the world represents, finally, a perfect synergy between economists, the corporate world, and business schools. It has served as the Big Idea that connects these three constituencies more tightly than ever and gives the business school curriculum a coherence it had not had before.

The task of translating Milton Friedman's moral exhortations into business-school speak was taken up by Michael Jensen, a product of Friedman's own University of Chicago. After taking a job at the business school at the University of Rochester, Jensen wrote a paper titled "Theory of the Firm: Managerial Behavior, Agency Costs and Ownership Structure," which took Friedman's call for corporate amorality and drew a road map for businesses to achieve it. As one commentator described it, the paper "laid the groundwork for the most radical change in the hierarchy of power in corporate America since the robber barons had given way to professional managers."[8]

Give Jensen his due. While many of the era's leading free marketeers had their economic thinking shaped by the third-rate novels of Ayn Rand, Jensen's literary taste ran to something more highbrow.[9] He liked to tell the story of George Bernard Shaw propositioning a woman to sleep with him for a million dollars. She said yes, and then Shaw immediately changed the terms of the deal to ten dollars. Insulted, the woman refused, asking Shaw what kind of woman he thought she was. To which he replied, "We've already established that. Now we're just haggling about the price."[10] Jensen used that ditty to conclude that, in the end, we're all just prostitutes, haggling over prices. This "insight," if that's quite what it is, became hugely influential, and it made Jensen a star. Suitably starstruck, Harvard's business school hired him, on terms unusual even by B-school standards, and Jensen decamped from Rochester. From Harvard Jensen's ideas spread throughout the B-school world like kudzu vine, and from there to boardrooms and executive suites everywhere.

The dogma of shareholder value served a purpose on campus much in the way it functioned in the corporate world. It made things easy. It swept away ambiguities and nuance and ethics and substituted a mantra in their place, one that could be chanted in any or all business school classes. Here, finally, was the glue that held the curriculum together, the center around which it would revolve, and understanding how to achieve it became the most important task for students to master. It took an idea originally generated by economists, created an applied version of it to teach to business students, and validated the way many corporations were already behaving. A Grand Unified Theory of business school education, and with it business schools became a crucial part of the "neoliberal thought collective."[11]

Students certainly got the message. In the early years of the twenty-first century the Aspen Institute conducted a series of surveys with MBA students at fifteen different business schools. In response to the question "What do you believe are the primary responsibilities of a company?" more than 70 percent of the respondents in 2002 ticked "maximize value for shareholders." By contrast, 25 percent of them answered "create value for the local community in which it operates." And lest there be any question about what happened to corporate social responsibility in the Age of Shareholder Value, 75 percent of those students responded that companies benefit from fulfilling their social responsibilities primarily because it creates a better corporate image. That figure rose to over 80 percent in the 2007 survey.[12] Professors of marketing have done their job well.

Looking out at the MBA landscape at the turn of millennium, Harold Leavitt, who taught at Stanford's business school, saw mercenaries rather than prostitutes. He thought that "the new professional MBA-type manager began to look more and more like the professional mercenary soldier—ready and willing to fight any war and to do so coolly and systematically, but without ever asking the tough path-finding questions: Is this war worth fighting? Is it the right war? Is the cause just? Do I believe in it?" Prostitutes, mercenaries, take your pick. Either way, the business school graduate of the early twenty-first century looked nothing at all like the well-rounded, civic-minded professional that business schools had promised to create in the early twentieth century and that they promised over and over again to create across the twentieth century.[13]

The Irrelevance of Ethics

Business students did not have answers to Leavitt's questions, because those questions had rarely been put to them and certainly not in deep and challenging ways. They are the sorts of questions that get asked in discussions of ethics and values, and as we have seen, ethics in business schools has been a topic always on the verge but never quite arriving. In virtually every decade of the twentieth century commentators, educators, and even businessmen have called for teaching ethics in business schools. That those calls continued across the century only underscores that business schools have been unable or uninterested in answering them. So, speaking to Wharton graduates in 1934, Horace Stern reminded them that if businessmen really wanted to be considered professionals like doctors and lawyers were "there is an inescapable corollary which must be accepted by the business man, and that is that the high standards and the codes of ethics which have always lent distinction to the professional world must now be adopted in the business world as well."[14] But that admonition went largely unheeded. By 1976, forty years or so after Stern spoke, ethics in the Wharton curriculum consisted of a single elective course. It had certainly not been woven into the fabric of a Wharton education. Ethics in business schools has always been put on the agenda for the *next* meeting.

Which may help explain the grant application the American Philosophical Association made to the National Endowment for the Humanities in 1977. The APA was housed at that moment at the University of Delaware, just down I-95 from Philadelphia, and APA leadership had some correspondence with Wharton. The APA recognized two things in 1977. First, the reputation of U.S. business practice, as we discussed in chapter 5, was at a historic low among the American public. Second, business schools had very little by way of ethics on offer in their course catalogs. The APA proposed to solve those problems.

Because Americans no longer trusted big business, the APA explained to the NEH, "business schools are being forced to introduce courses in business ethics even though business schools are not really prepared to offer them." The problem, according to the philosophers, was that "although both representatives of business schools and business leaders recognize the need for courses in ethics, they admit they need assistance in preparing them." That's where the APA could step in. At a moment when academic jobs in the humanities were drying up, the APA thought it had hit on a win-win idea. Business schools would finally get genuine curriculum in ethics, and philosophy students with doctorates would get jobs.

However brilliant this idea, the NEH, alas, was not impressed. In a letter to the APA's Norman Bowie, Stephen Miller, an NEH program officer, agreed with the basic premise of the proposal but wasn't entirely convinced that APA's project would do the job. "If I may raise some larger questions," Miller wrote, "though it is true that everyone is concerned about the conduct of businessmen, it is not clear from your proposal just how businessmen could be helped by a course in 'business ethics' rather than, simply, 'ethics.'" Asking just what the distinction was between business ethics and plain old ethics seems a fair question, but Miller wasn't finished. He concluded a bit more sharply, "Let me say finally, that there is some concern among reviewers and members of the Council that the humanities *not* be understood as somehow providing a quick 'values fix' for society." [15]

The NEH reviewers had a point. U.S. businesses faced growing public hostility, and they wanted business schools to fix their problem. Business schools, in turn, ran to philosophers to come up with a crash course in ethics. There is something vaguely insulting about that. Still, the APA had identified a genuine problem and designed a proposal that, while it would probably not have solved it conclusively, was surely a good step in the right direction. After all, call it "business ethics" or just "ethics," business schools didn't teach it and didn't know how to, and businesses themselves seemed sorely in need of sorting that out.

In the event, NEH did not fund this project, and ethics remained on the periphery of business school curricula. Surveys done in 1982 and again in 1985 revealed a tepid enthusiasm for ethics courses at business schools. Indeed, that

1985 tally counted less than 50 percent of schools polled offering such a course.[16] By then, of course, the public perception of business had changed in Ronald Reagan's America. Suspicion was out; greed was good.

In 1986, even before the hangover of the Reagan party had set in, the University of Denver's business school started to respond to the wretched excess of the decade. There people began to discuss overhauling the MBA curriculum to put a central stress on ethics, social responsibility, and community welfare. Two years later, cable TV magnate and Denver alum Bill Daniels put $10 million behind the effort. By 1991, after several of the Wall Street swashbucklers of the 1980s had lost everything or were facing indictments or both, after the deregulated savings and loan industry collapsed and required a public bailout, and as the post-Reagan recession had settled in, ethics came back to business school campuses. Another survey of B-schools discovered that over 90 percent of those schools offered business ethics. The survey authors wrote, "New accounts of check-kiting schemes, defense contract fraud, cover ups of health risks, unfair takeover tactics, insider trading and product adulteration appear as weekly items in the news. Consequently, business ethics has now become a prime academic growth area, spawning new textbooks, research, and scholarly articles."[17] No coincidence that the journal *Business Ethics Quarterly* published its debut issue in 1991.

That sounded like good news. The bad news about teaching ethics, however, was that the American Association of Collegiate Schools of Business members surveyed reported that they still—after all these years!—did not know "how to do it, and where to put it" in the curriculum. The solution in the early 1990s was the same as it had always been—a one-off, often-elective course in ethics. Fewer than 10 percent of the schools thought integrating ethics more broadly into the curriculum was a good idea; a majority, however, thought "a joint effort with their philosophy department" might be. The APA may just have been onto something in 1977 after all.[18]

More troubling, though, the authors found that a renewed focus on ethics "is not accompanied by evidence of effectiveness." They continued, somewhat bloodlessly, that in their "search of the literature on ethics instruction, no studies were found that reported significant relationships between ethics teaching and the incorporation of ethical considerations into decision making."[19] Apparently, one course in business ethics didn't really make much difference in how businessmen behaved. That may be connected to the ethics taught to these students by their faculty. One scholar observed that any discussion of business ethics "is remarkably devoid . . . of specific real-world policies or practices on the part of businesses, or the outcomes these have generated in the aggregate." [20] A business ethics with all the ramifications, implications, and consequences stripped out. Maybe the NEH program officers evaluating the APA grant application had been right after all.

Wash, rinse, repeat. After the foam had evaporated on the frothy 1990s, after the dot-com bubble burst, after Enron collapsed, after Tyco and Parmalat and all the rest, business schools once again asked whether they were doing enough to instill ethics into their charges and how they might better do so. Yet another survey, this one in 2007, found yet another increase in ethics courses taught at B-schools. This time around at least one commentator wondered whether the solution to the problem of the lack of ethics in business "might be more complex" than offering elective courses in the subject. [21] And note the date on the survey: the information was collected shortly before the housing market collapsed, taking so much else down with it.

But if Michel Anteby's observations are correct, B-school students learn their ethics primarily through a process of routines and expectations, not through any formal instruction. Anteby was a new professor at Harvard's business school when he decided to do an "ethnography" of, yes, the Harvard Business School (this presumably cut down on his research commuting time). Finding daily life at the business school "as exotic as [Bronislaw] Malinoski's experiences in the Trobriand Islands"—a comparison some Trobrianders surely found insulting—Anteby viewed the business school as a remote tribe, passing on its culture in inexplicit, often unspoken ways to its newest members. Anteby titled the book that resulted from this fieldwork in his own office *Manufacturing Morals*. But he sidestepped the biggest question his own work raises: What is good and what is bad, and how is that distinction drawn by the natives on the Charles River? "The term *moral*," Anteby writes, "is here defined as what a given community deems appropriate." So it isn't morals (or ethics) that are manufactured at Harvard but norms, and there is precious little evidence that those norms ever get questioned. Au contraire, the initiates who succeed best are the ones who internalize the norms fastest and most fully. [22]

In fact, it isn't at all clear that business schools are successful even at getting their students to behave ethically while still *in* school, much less once they leave it. A study published in 2006 found that 56 percent of MBA students cheated in their classes. (Another survey comparing the ethics of MBA students and inmates at a minimum security prison found that the latter held higher standards.)[23] While the report appeared in an academic journal, it created a great deal of buzz in the public and much hand-wringing among B-school leaders. Did MBA programs attract amoral people or perhaps students who had cheated their way to the top as undergraduates? Since many MBAs had already spent a few years working in the private sector, had they brought the get-ahead-at-all-costs attitudes of the private sector with them, or did business schools themselves do something to students to make them dishonest?[24] Was amorality one of those unspoken norms passed on from B-school generation to B-school generation? Whatever the answer, students at the Fox School of Business at Temple University can be forgiven if they tossed the memo from Dean Moshe Porat about ethical behavior. In the summer of 2018, news broke that the Fox School had consistently and pervasively falsified the data it submitted to *US News and World Report* for its annual carnival of rankings. Porat ceased to be dean once the scale of the fraud became known but, as of this writing, remained a tenured member of the faculty.[25]

Things don't appear to get much better once business school grads, MBAs in hand, leave campus: 40 percent of the CEOs cited in the 1999 *Fortune* article "Why CEOs Fail" had "MBA" on their resumes. And that raises the question business schools have avoided perhaps more than any other: Just how accountable should they be for the performance of their graduates?

On one hand, none of the robber barons whose money helped reshape U.S. higher education in the late nineteenth century went to business school. They didn't need shareholder value theory to brutalize their workers, to despoil the environment, or to crash the economy repeatedly. Rapacious greed does not require a business school degree.

On the other, the number of business school heroes who have wound up jailed or fined or who should have faced some combination of both for their misbehavior is truly stunning. Harvard's high-flying Jeffrey Skilling, who helped wreck Enron, went to jail. So did Rajat Gupta. That conviction must have hit close to home at Harvard, since Gupta went on from the business school there to lead McKinsey before landing in a federal prison. Not to be outdone, the Wharton School can go toe-to-toe with Harvard for members in the B-school Hall of Shame. In 2011 Raj Rajaratnam, Wharton '83, went to jail in the biggest insider trading conspiracy since the 1980s. One of the

iconic figures of that earlier era, of course, was Michael Milken, also a holder
of a Wharton MBA. He went to prison too. Ivan "greed is good" Boesky,
another icon of the go-go 1980s, never went to business school. But he did
teach at one—Columbia's—before heading off to do time. At Ohio State
University, the hotel and conference center attached to the business school is
named after Roger Blackwell, an internationally renowned professor of marketing who pledged $7 million to the project when it was being built in
2001. Late in 2005 he stood before a federal judge to receive a six-year sen-
tence for insider trading.

And on and on and on it goes. Lindsey Naegle, a hard-charging Wharton grad, had her dinner date interrupted by a call from her lawyer inform-
ing her that she too was under indictment. Naegle is a character on *The Simp-
sons* (the date was with Ned Flanders). That such a scene could be played for
laughs only underscores how common such scenes have become. *US News
and World Report* has not, to my knowledge, published a list of business
schools ranked by the number of graduates who break the law (or more to
the point, get caught breaking the law), though I suspect that list would look
eerily like its ranking of "best" business schools.

The point of rehearsing all this malfeasance is simple: business schools
have, from the very beginning, aspired to turn business into a profession and
to make professionals out of businessmen. Yet no other profession produces
felons in quite such abundance. Look at it this way: if senior doctors at the
Harvard and Penn medical centers, also among the finest in the world, went
to jail in the same numbers for killing patients or falsifying research, there
would be investigations and hearings, and those places would probably be
shut down.

Any sense of accountability for what business schools create, however, is
so rare it can't be turned into a tradable commodity even by Wall Street financial alchemists. Not inside business schools where critical analysis and self-
reflection have never been in much demand, nor from the universities
themselves, who one would think might grow tired of all the black eyes they
get as a result of their business schools. Quite the contrary, a certain brazen
shamelessness prevails. I asked someone at Ohio State whether it wasn't em-
barrassing to have a hotel named after a convicted felon and was told that
the university feels it has "developed a good brand" and thus the Blackwell
name stays. Having been released from prison, Roger Blackwell picked up
his teaching and hit the lecture circuit as if nothing had happened.

That combination of arrogance and obtuseness was never better on display than in a speech delivered by the Harvard business school dean Jay Light in October 2008 as part of the B-school's hundredth-birthday celebrations. With the flaming wreckage of the Great Recession still falling from the sky, Light enumerated all the things "we failed to understand," including "how much [the financial system] had changed in the past 15 years or so." That seems particularly daft given how much Harvard faculty and graduates had contributed to those changes. Light went on to say, "We will leave the talk of fixing the blame to others. That is not very interesting." Not to Light, perhaps, given where the fingers might wind up pointing, but most of the rest of us did want to know who was responsible, and we still do. Then Light issued his battle cry: "We must be involved . . . in fixing the problem."[26] In 2008, Light's "I'm from the business school and I'm here to help" offer rang a bit like that arsonist who sets fire to your house and then offers to bring you a bucket of water.

There is plenty of blame to go around for the Great Recession and its aftermath to be sure. But business schools deserve a great deal of it. Vast enterprises dedicated to studying American business and training the people who run it, the business schools failed to see what was coming and failed to see the severity of it. Today, they have had little to offer to address the two pressing issues of the age: climate change and economic inequality.[27] No, instead what is "trending" at business schools as I write this in 2018 is "business analytics." At least according to Joyce Russell, the dean of the business school at Villanova University, who explained in an interview, "Our undergrads all take analytics. That's really hot."[28] She was not referring to rising global temperatures.

By extension, business schools bear some measure of responsibility, therefore, for the toxic politics—called by many "populist"—that swept across the United States and Great Britain (and other places besides) in the wake of the economic meltdown. It seems incontrovertible now that the long, lingering anger caused by the Great Recession helped fuel Brexit and the rise of *Trumpismo*.[29] That anger stemmed not only from the damage itself—the lost jobs, homes, retirement savings, and the rest—but from the fact that no one was held accountable for the recklessness, the fecklessness, and the greed. I am not suggesting at all that business school deans or their faculty should have gone to jail for business malpractice, though some people surely should have. However, the blasé attitude toward it all expressed by Harvard's Jay

Light bespeaks an utter cluelessness inside business schools about the social, political, and economic consequences of what gets taught inside their gilded halls and a head-in-the-sand refusal to take any responsibility for it.

None of this inspires much confidence, needless to say, in the ethical center of B-schools, but it does demonstrate that, as they chant the mantra offered to them by Milton Friedman, business students have found that maximizing shareholder value begins at home.

A Meeting of Business Minds

The causal connections are not straightforward, nor are they simple. But the questions can be framed this way: Are business schools responsible for the tectonic shift as the U.S. economy morphed from the industrial capitalism of the mid-twentieth century to the finance capitalism that took over beginning in the 1980s? Or were they just beneficiaries of a shift that would have happened anyway?[30]

Whatever the answer, happy beneficiaries they certainly were. The rise of finance capitalism has created a bonanza of jobs under the heading of consulting, and in, well, finance. Many of those jobs went to business school graduates. The numbers tell their own story. McKinsey, the trend-setting consulting giant, decided that it would hire not just MBAs but Harvard MBAs starting in the 1950s. By 1967 one-third of McKinsey consultants were Harvard products. It was surely just coincidental that Marvin Bower, the long-time managing director of McKinsey, was himself a Harvard B-school grad. The cozy relationship exists to this day. In 2010 roughly five hundred Harvard business school alums were working for McKinsey, making the firm far and away the single largest consumer of the Harvard business school product.[31]

Jobs in consulting and finance are the back-end analogues to shareholder value curriculum. They provide an almost logical outlet for an education focused on that single goal. As we have already seen, businessmen complained repeatedly across the twentieth century that business school graduates did not know anything genuinely useful. Consulting makes a virtue of that vice. Rather than learn about businesses specifically—about producing steel or selling sneakers or marketing organic produce—MBA students cum future consultants learn about Business generically. In this sense, consulting rhymes perfectly with an education based on case studies. It is predicated on drawing a certain set of lessons from some specific situation and applying them to any, and it surely isn't coincidental that Harvard, where the case-study curriculum was born, should produce so many consultants.

For consultants, therefore, the dogma of shareholder value means that when they walk into a specific suite of offices it does not really matter much what kind of business gets done in them. Matthew Stewart, who worked for a New York consulting firm at the turn of the twenty-first century, saw the absurdity—and the arrogance—of people like himself hired by some business to tell it what to do, and paid handsomely at that. With his $75,000 per year starting salary, and billing clients to the tune of half a million a year, Stewart could never shake the feeling that he was "a snake oil salesman without snake oil," nor did he ever lose "the sensation that [he] was just making it up as [he] went along."[32] But then Stewart was not the holder of an MBA, from Harvard or anywhere else. He got into the consulting business as an unemployed—unemployable by his description—PhD in German literature. He had not drunk the B-school Kool-Aid.

The task for any upper-level manager or consultant is always the same: figure out how to maximize shareholder value. The way to do that, often enough, was to focus on a corporation's "core competency"—what it did best and where it had a competitive advantage. That phrase first appeared in a 1990 article written by the University of Michigan Business School professor C. K. Prahalad and Gary Hamels, who got his doctorate there. And having figured out its core competency, a corporation should outsource everything else. The idea swept through management courses around the country and became central to what future managers and management consultants learned in B-schools. Along with shareholder value it constitutes a major ingredient in the Kool-Aid.

If the question now is always the same, then so too are the answers: mergers, acquisitions, asset stripping, layoffs, plant closures and consolidations, and all the rest. All good for short-term shareholder value, but to gauge the larger effects of such myopic decision making consider the story of two janitors. In the 1980s, Gail Evans went to work for Kodak in Rochester, New York, cleaning Building 326. She was a Kodak employee, which meant that in addition to benefits and vacation time, she took advantage of Kodak's program to help her further her education. She took some computer classes, and when she completed her degree in 1987 she was promoted into a professional-track job in information technology at Kodak. She's been in senior executive positions ever since.

Marta Ramos cleans up after Apple employees in Cupertino, California. She is not an Apple employee because Apple contracts out all those services to other businesses. Ms. Ramos receives no Apple bonuses or vacation time or any help with education. She'll never move up the Apple ladder because she doesn't work for Apple in the first place, and given what she makes it's hard to imagine that she'll move up any ladder no matter how hard she works. Cleaning is not, after all, a competency at Apple's core, and the company surely pays less for that work than if it hired its own janitors. That makes shareholders happy no doubt, and as I write this Apple has just become the first company whose stock valuation reached $1 *trillion*. But the tens of thousands of workers like Marta Ramos have had their futures sacrificed on the altar of shareholder value.[33]

The Triumph of Finance Capitalism (Education)

The intertwining of business schools and the Wall Street world of finance also has its roots in the postwar period. In 1954, for example, the investment firm Kidder Peabody presented the Wharton School with $10,000 as seed money to endow a professorship in investment banking. A prospectus was then sent out to a variety of financial firms asking them to contribute. "From the October, 1929, crash until the recent post-war years," the brochure read, "'Wall Street,' and all that it connotes in the popular mind in terms of investment and finance was a favorite whipping boy. Today, with few exceptions, the climate has changed to one of confidence and good will ... [but] the 'Wall Street' myth has not been completely discredited and eliminated. ... The number of college graduates seeking careers in investment banking and related activities is not keeping pace with the need for trained manpower in these important aspects of our economic life."[34] It is hard to fathom that at one time Wharton graduates did not flock to Wall Street. But by the end of the twentieth century they, along with the graduates of other high-end business schools, surely did. By the first years of the twenty-first century two-thirds of Harvard MBAs, give or take, took jobs in finance or consulting.

The Italian city of Genoa lays claim to being the home of the world's first bank, founded in 1407, and for several centuries they operated roughly the same way. They collected money in the form of deposits and distributed it in the form of loans. They took a percentage of those transactions as their profit. Banks made it possible for people to buy houses and for businesses to start or expand. No one would deny the necessity of banks in this or any other economy, and they still justify their role in society on these terms.

But the old, distributive model of banking, the one that had prevailed since the fifteenth century, went into rapid eclipse in the last quarter of the twentieth century. Now banks, the big ones especially, have reinvented themselves as trading machines. They make trades on virtually anything and everything and at increasing speed and at staggering volume. These trades make money by moving money, not by financing other things. By the early twenty-first century, these financial trades made banks more and more money. In 2010, for example, Morgan Stanley generated more than a third of its revenue by executing those kinds of trades, while only 15 percent of it came from more traditional banking functions. Goldman Sachs made only 13 percent of its revenue in conventional financing and a whopping 63 percent in the trading world.[35] These tremendous profits have pressured banks to invent even more financial products to sell in order to satisfy their shareholders' demands. A few of these have proved useful for the rest of society; many of these financial instruments have been dubbed "exotic"—one of my favorite euphemisms since it makes these baroque, opaque, and often-destructive financial confections sound like fun vacation destinations. Yet even here, business school graduates have not been the innovators, though that is no black mark against them to be sure. As has been well reported, the transformations in the world of finance—the high-speed trading, algorithmically based decision making, even engineering of the asset values that create more and more financial products—have been generated by the quants, not the MBAs or the finance majors.[36] Those latter simply hired physicists, mathematicians, and computer scientists to work on Wall Street and gave them their marching orders, which, in turn, helped take the global economy off the cliff. Black marks after all.

Like the world of consulting, the new finance capitalism fit hand in glove with the business school emphasis on the techniques of maximizing shareholder value. Profit has always been at the center of capitalism, and finance was the means to that end. Invest in a new widget company; the company sells lots of widgets; enjoy the fruits of that investment. Now moving money around has become the end unto itself, not the means with which to invest in something else. Students of finance need only learn how to go through these algorithmic motions. They no longer need to think about the connection between money and everything else or about the consequences of all these financial shenanigans. And as with consulting, there may well be no there there in the upper altitudes of finance capital. No question it has produced profits in astounding volume, but all this financial wheeling and dealing, as much as 30 percent of the U.S. economy, has nothing to do with building, buying, or selling anything tangible. Nor is there any evidence that this kind of financial activity indirectly increases the overall size of the U.S. economic pie.

Oh, the irony! By the turn of the twenty-first century, business school education had aligned itself with the demands of business more than at any time since Wharton began offering classes in 1881. But it did so by divorcing itself from the rest of American society. Here it achieved a union with economics departments. If people have complained that all those abstract equations in economics books had little to do with how people actually lived, then the world of finance has become similarly unhinged from anything real. There is much to suggest that finance capitalism, as practiced on Wall Street by those trained at business schools, constitutes, in the memorable phrase of Adair Turner, chair of Britain's Financial Services Authority, "socially useless activity."[37]

In fact, that characterization might be entirely too generous. Evidence piles up that the operations of finance capitalism—especially the vulture capitalists of private equity firms, venture operations, hedge funds, and the rest—have been deeply destructive not only to the U.S. economy but to American society as a whole. You can hear the anguish in Allan Ardis's voice. Ardis once ran a company that provided services to KB Toys. KB had been founded in 1922 in Pittsfield, Massachusetts, and was a profitable operation. This venerable company once had over 1100 stores nationwide and roughly 8000 employees. Once it was "discovered" by Bain Capital, Bain bought up a controlling interest in the company, immediately saddled it with huge debt, using it to buy back stock. By 2009, unable to keep up with the debt, this beloved toy company was shut down. KB had weathered the Great Depression and the Second World War and the economic malaise of the 1970s, but it could not survive the predations of vulture capitalists of the sort being minted in MBA programs. The thousands who once worked for KB were not the only ones who lost out, of course. "My service business depended on KB as its main customer," Ardis wrote in 2016, adding, "It is gone now, too, along with 70 workers." If Bain rings a bell, it may be because that's where 2012 Republican presidential nominee Mitt Romney once worked. For gutting KB Romney made $86 million. As Ardis put it, "KB Toys, and my business, were just more lambs ready for slaughter in Romney's view."[38] Is it even worth noting that Romney too is the holder of an MBA from Harvard?

Lancaster, Ohio, is a town roughly the size of Pittsfield. In 1947 *Forbes* magazine devoted its thirtieth-anniversary issue to Lancaster because, in its editorial view, Lancaster was the all-American city. Much of the reason for that was the symbiotic and mutually beneficial relationship the city had with its largest employer, Anchor Hocking Glass. Lancaster and Anchor had invested in each other over the decades and each enriched the other. As kids, Anchor executives had often gone to high school with guys who wound up working the furnaces and molding machines. As adults, they drank together in the same bars after work.

That lasted until the 1980s, when the vultures started to circle overhead. Beginning with Carl Icahn, the original corporate raider, and then proceeding through a dizzying number of corporate owners and executive teams, mergers and failed mergers, acquisitions and failed attempts at buyouts, layoffs, and worker concessions, Anchor wound up a shell of its former self. And to be clear, Anchor's products remained competitive in the market. You may have one or two in your kitchen even today. Anchor didn't suffer because of trade deals or cheap Mexican labor or cheaper Chinese imports. Anchor was ruined by a deliberate and repeated strategy of loading it with debt in order to extract profits for investors. From the vantage point of a finance class, Anchor is a real success story.

The results in Lancaster, as the journalist Brian Alexander has achingly chronicled, have been predictably devastating. It isn't simply the economic loss, grim as that has been. That loss, in turn, has torn the social fabric that once knitted Lancaster together. Seventy years after *Forbes* featured Lancaster, that all-American city now sits squarely in the middle of what people call the Heroin Heartland.[39]

The lesson of Pittsfield and Lancaster and who knows how many other places is that the decline of well-paying manufacturing jobs, and the destruction of communities that follows, may have as much to do with maximizing shareholder value as with any of the usual suspects blamed for the crisis: China, the North American Free Trade Agreement, technology, the inevitable and inexorable workings of "the market." In that sense, we can lay the fault for the crisis at the feet of business schools that not only teach the executives-to-be the rationales and techniques to take the money and run but give the whole enterprise a shiny academic imprimatur. After all, it's what they teach at Wharton and Harvard, isn't it?

Business Schools R Us

I gave a draft of this book to a friend to read, and he asked, "If they're such terrible failures, then why do they keep flourishing?" Why indeed? It's a good question, and so let me offer some thoughts by way of an answer. A few easy answers offer themselves immediately.

One constant in the history of higher education since the Civil War has been that universities expand. They have enrolled more students, built more buildings, offered more degrees, and opened more units from one decade to the next. Business schools are simply a part of this bigger story about higher education in the United States: as its turf expands, its brief enlarges and its vision grows ever more expansive. When Joseph Pulitzer offered substantial money to Harvard and Columbia to start schools of journalism in the 1890s, both universities scoffed at that idea. Now the Columbia School of Journalism stands as one of the ornaments of Columbia's campus. There is almost no endeavor now that hasn't been turned into a university degree. So while business schools don't provide professional training in the way that law schools and medical schools do, the notion of what constitutes a profession has become so elastic that business schools have, in essence, moved in that direction simply by standing still.

Likewise, the fact that business schools have thrived even while they have failed is a testament at one level to the power of institutional inertia. Once a new department or school or program is launched on campus it can be devilishly hard to close it or even change it significantly. Deck chairs can sometimes be rearranged, after committees have deliberated and reports have been issued, but the boat continues to head largely in the same direction. That's true everywhere on campus.

Business schools are perhaps more impervious to change than the other professional schools with which they want to be compared because they don't have to respond to the external pressures put on other professional schools by more robust professional organizations. If the American Bar Association calls for changes to the way future lawyers are taught, law schools take notice. There is no analogy for business schools, as I have discussed already. So if there is no external pressure to change, and if universities themselves don't provide much pressure for business schools to reform, why on earth would they?

Plenty of people explain the continued success of business schools, fittingly and self-servingly enough, by attributing it to market forces. Business schools sell what students want to buy, and they do so more effectively than, say, the classics department. This is unarguably true. If students didn't flock to business schools—for both undergraduate and graduate degrees—they would not loom as large as they do on campus. And I acknowledge that some of this increased enrollment has come from women who, while not represented in business schools in anything like their proportion on the rest of campus, started arriving in business schools in larger numbers in the 1970s.

There is a first-order problem with this explanation, despite how often it gets invoked: there is no such thing as a "free" market except in the parlor-room games of some economists and faculty at business schools. All markets are structured, one way or another, to favor certain outcomes over others. The academic "market" on campus is shaped, among other ways, by graduation requirements, and over the last few decades those requirements have been recalibrated to favor the practical arts over the liberal ones. In the struggle that has always existed between the practical and the ornamental, university administrators have chosen sides and students have responded accordingly.[40]

More than that, however, the success of business schools, at least as I see it, is driven by variations of greed and anxiety—two sides of the same coin really—and in this women are no different from men. As we have seen, despite whatever beating the reputation of U.S. business took during the stagflation years of the 1970s, students responded to that economic malaise by heading off to the B-school; the safest port, as they saw it, in the economic storm and the fastest route to the largest salary. In fact, enrollments did decline a bit in the late 1990s when the Clinton economy revved hottest and students felt more secure about their employment future. But economic insecurity has predominated in the twenty-first century. The students starting their college careers as I write this were born as the dot-com bubble burst and had their formative years during the Great Recession. Plenty of evidence—from delayed marriage rates to an aversion to buying houses—suggests just how damaging those experiences have been to the psyches of many young people. And to their parents'. I've lost count of how many students I've talked with who admitted that they were majoring in business because their parents told them to, not because they have any real interest in doing so.

Yet even while business schools have become more popular with students, and even while admissions standards have risen as a consequence—a trend that we saw began in the 1970s—the education students receive there does not seem to have improved much at all. In their blockbuster 2011 study of what college students learn, the sociologists Richard Arum and Josipa Roksa found that business students routinely did less work, were held to less rigorous academic standards, and simply learned less than students in the arts and sciences. For example, "students concentrating in business coursework reported lower levels of reading requirements and higher frequency of having experienced neither the reading nor the writing requirement."[41] Joseph Alutto must have thought the students at Ohio State's business school were working too hard, so as dean (1991–2007) he reduced the writing requirement and eliminated the foreign language requirement altogether. This while at the same time slapping the word "global" on everything the business school did. It is a feat of successful marketing, to be sure, that business students have been persuaded to pay in order to get *less* education than their peers on the other side of campus. The irony is delicious because it seems lost on business school students, their parents, and at least some of their faculty.

In a sense, the economic anxiety that makes business schools so seductive for students is a reflection of the larger drift of American society since the 1970s. As I've described in this chapter the greed-is-good, maximize-shareholder-value ethos that triumphed in the 1980s created a perfect synergy with what business schools taught. That hasn't changed. (I've been assured by several business school faculty that shareholder value is being supplemented now with stakeholder value, but I'm not sure the substitution of two consonants will really accomplish very much.) Students in business schools see the world off campus mirrored inside their classrooms. As Joel Podolny put it, "The way business schools today compete leads students to ask, 'What can I do to make the most money?' and the manner in which faculty members teach allows students to regard the moral consequences of their actions as mere afterthoughts."[42] Podolny ought to know. He served as the dean of Yale's business school from 2005 to 2008.

And that leads us, finally, to another problem of prepositions.

A century ago Thorstein Veblen wrote about universities run *by* business-men, and he did not have charitable things to say. More recently, a small bookshelf has been filled with titles decrying the "crisis" of the contemporary university.[43] More than a few read almost like end-of-days jeremiads: "the last professors" announces the title of one; "the end of the American university" reads the subtitle of another. Each of these books offers its own diagnosis of what ails higher education—from the growing phenomenon of contingent labor to the incoherence of the curriculum—and I don't want to conflate them all unfairly. Still, most share in common the complaint that American universities have uncritically imbibed "corporate values," that they now run themselves *as* a business. Or at least as business schools think they ought to be run.

I'm largely persuaded by much of what these authors write because I have seen it all myself. Even so, jeremiads are stories of decline, and declension stories posit some sort of prelapsarian golden age. I don't think the history of U.S. higher education supports the weight of that nostalgia. 1970 was the last year more students graduated with arts and sciences degrees than with occupational ones, and by the turn of the twenty-first century the fields of the traditional arts and sciences saw declines even while enrollments grew by 50 percent.[44] Besides, if there were such a moment, Veblen reminds us that businessmen were in charge even then. The modern university was founded on a set of contradictions, competing claims, and compromised positions. That much hasn't changed.

Two things have changed over the last few decades, however, at least in my reckoning. The first involves the erosion of the democratic impulse of American higher education. The promise of higher education, whether or not it has ever been fully kept, has been to marry education useful for making a living to education necessary to train citizens and to make that education broadly accessible. Now that promise appears on the verge of being broken altogether on campuses where occupational degrees—and business schools are at the vanguard of the triumph—have conquered the arts and sciences. As a consequence, the liberal arts may only be preserved and fostered at small colleges and a handful of elite universities, while various kinds of job training will predominate everywhere else.[45] The democratic dream of making college education in philosophy and history and literature available to everyone will have died, and business schools will be a major accomplice in the killing.

The second change is the growing influence of business-school think on the way universities do their own business. Not surprisingly, the anschluss of business school ideas into the offices of central administration gathered steam in the 1990s at the same moment that they aligned themselves so neatly with the developments of finance capitalism. I'll touch on three areas where universities have come to resemble, if not so much business, then business school curriculum.

First, finance. Finance, crudely put, is the alchemy of turning every conceivable thing in the galaxy into an asset, fixing a value to that asset, and then making a profit from the purchase or sale of it. For universities since the 1990s that wizardry has been translated into three letters: RCM. Those letters stand for "responsibility center management," often translated by the more jaded among us as every-tub-on-its-own-bottom budgeting. It can be said to have made its national debut with the publication of Edward Whalen's book *Responsibility Center Budgeting: An Approach to Decentralized Management for Institutions of Higher Education* in 1991.

Whalen was an economist at Indiana University, and his book was a report of a kind on Indiana's experience in decentralizing its budget and making individual units at the university responsible for generating their own revenues. Whalen wrote about the shortcomings of the experiment along with its successes, but university administrators elsewhere apparently didn't read those first bits. RCM quickly became the budget model for universities across the country.

How, you might ask, is an academic department supposed to generate revenue?[46] The RCM regime turns students into assets, and departments earn money by enrolling students in their classes. Which is why the most jaded among us also refer to RCM as warm-butts-in-seats budgeting. The equation is brutally simple: more students equals more money for departments; fewer butts-in-seats equals less money. Less money, of course, ultimately means fewer faculty, fewer resources for research, and a host of other consequences.

Putting aside the ethics of treating students as monetizable assets, there are two obvious problems with RCM. First, since the total number of students on any campus is finite, RCM puts every department in a competition with every other department to attract them. One student in your class means one student *not* in my class. So much for the *uni*versity, in this tweed-jacketed Hobbesian world where the budgetary stakes are high. Second, because RCM creates a system of departmental winners and losers, enrollments become the metric by which the university decides what its academic and intellectual priorities are. Taken to its extreme—and RCM is moving in this direction in a number of places—whole bodies of knowledge could cease to exist on a campus if students don't show up for the classes. Like philosophy. Or Russian literature. In effect, RCM allows the shape of the very education on offer in the first place to be determined by the choices made by students not yet old enough to drink legally. Whatever you think the purpose of higher education ought to be, that is hardly the way to achieve it.

Second, management. Management's contribution to maximizing shareholder value has been to preach the gospel of core competency. Do what you do best, outsource everything else to someone else. Costs are cut, efficiencies are achieved, profits are increased. Universities, no less than the private sector, have enthusiastically practiced what their management faculty have been preaching.

Universities require all sorts of employees to do things other than teaching and research—groundskeepers, building maintenance crews, housekeepers, for example. There is a financial logic to outsourcing these functions as a way of reducing a university's expenses. But, as with so much else about the shareholder value economy, those savings allow the university to ignore the costs—"negative externalities" in the lingo—created elsewhere.

Consider another janitor: Larry. Larry the Janitor. I never learned his last name, but he cleaned the building that houses the history department at Ohio State University when I worked there. Larry was a nice guy with a lot of miles on him, a toothless Appalachian refugee who, like so many others, had left West Virginia or Kentucky to find a job in Columbus, Ohio. Larry found himself working for a janitorial contractor the university had hired as it phased out employing its own cleaning staff. I call him toothless not to be snide but because his teeth were, in fact, in terrible, painful condition. But Larry's employer didn't provide any dental insurance. We in the building—faculty and staff—took up a collection to help pay for a dental procedure. The fact that my building was equidistant from OSU's dental school, where Larry couldn't afford his treatment, and the business school, where students were learning the techniques to create more and more workers like Larry, was bitter beyond irony.

That isn't even the worst of it. Honest people can disagree, I suppose, over whether Apple owes Marta Ramos anything more than what she gets as a subcontracted worker cleaning up after Apple employees. But Ohio State University was founded, as were all the great public universities, precisely to provide the Larrys of the nation a chance at higher education. A generation ago, his work would have been done by someone employed by OSU, with access not only to health benefits but to discounts on university classes and a chance to earn a college degree. As an outsourced employee, he'll never get any of that.

Third, marketing. If finance people look at the world and see nothing but assets, marketers see nothing but brands. So when universities hire marketing and public relations consultants, as they have started doing regularly, they hear the same mantra over and over: Maximize the brand!

The message is the same whether at Oregon State or Oklahoma State or Ohio State and thus so are the campaigns launched after the consultants have cashed their checks. Homogenize all the "messaging," proliferate the "branded merchandise" (deploy university lawyers to police that branding vigorously, lest some company begin to sell its own OSU sweatshirts in Corvallis, Stillwater, or Columbus), and come up with a catchy ad slogan around which to organize it all: things like "Out There" (Oregon State) and "America's Brightest Orange" (Oklahoma State) and "Do Something Big" (Ohio State). For marketers, students aren't assets, they're customers, and in the imperatives of marketing they must be advertised at and sold to at every opportunity. (In this model, staff and faculty pretty quickly become customer-service associates.)

If it all starts to seem numbingly the same—the bumper-sticker slogans and branded beer mugs—that's because it is. Marketing is about surfaces and facades, about appearances and illusions. There isn't anything substantive in any of this because there isn't supposed to be. "Out There" might well be used as a slogan for a company selling adventure vacations, and if the folks in Stillwater tire of "America's Brightest Orange," the marketing consultants can sell it to a citrus conglomerate. Marketers want you to buy, not to think. Universities, of course, are places of thinking, but the administrators who hire the marketing consults don't seem to have thought to ask the question Why? Why should we turn our institution into a product and package it like fast food or pickup trucks? What is to be gained from an ad campaign other than telling the trustees, some number of them holders of business school degrees, that you have an ad campaign?

We might look at other areas where the syllabi of the business school have come to shape the way universities are run. Like leadership programs routinely run on campuses that borrow their agendas from leadership courses, despite the fact that there is no good evidence that leadership can be taught. Like the cult of administration that permeates campuses, as presidents are seen now as CEOs and compensated accordingly. Like the very language routinely spouted by those same administrators that comes directly from the world of business—words like "excellence," "eminence," "productivity," and the rest that are simultaneously stripped of their meaning and Orwellian in their insidiousness.[47]

In the end, business schools have succeeded because they have brilliantly straddled the contradictions inherent in U.S. higher education since the end of the Civil War despite their manifest failure to achieve any of the goals their promotors set for them. They fit nicely on the landscape of campus because they mirrored the rest of the university in many ways. And they continue to thrive because the rest of campus now more closely mirrors them. That feat has surely been among their greatest successes.

Donald Trump went to Wharton.

Depending on your point of view you are either nodding your head in affirmation or crying out, "Cheap shot!" So let me hasten to say that it is entirely unfair to blame Wharton for Trump's pathological narcissism, his gargantuan vulgarity, or maybe even his repeated failures as a businessman, though that one is a bit more head-scratching. After all, Newt Gingrich received a doctorate in history and Joseph Goebbels one in literature, and no one would blame those two disciplines for the kind of figures they went on to become.

And yet Trump exemplifies exactly the kind of man for whom the collegiate business school was created in the late nineteenth century. Deeply and transparently insecure, Trump has reminded his supporters over and over that he went to Wharton and that means he's really, bigly smart. Trump sees his Wharton degree as giving him social status and intellectual credibility. That Wharton degree is a credential rather than an accomplishment, and he believes that it signals that he knows what he's talking about, even when it is risibly obvious that he doesn't. At the turn of the twentieth century, one function of the new business schools was to give the sons of the new industrial titans a respectable patina, to launder their wealth by scrubbing it with a college degree. And so it is for Trump, inheritor of a business his father built.

What Trump may or may not have learned at Wharton is entirely beside the point. And not just Trump and not just at Wharton. Jack Welch, who had his own, let's say checkered, career as a corporate CEO, told students at MIT's Sloan School that they should spend their time networking. "Everything else you need to know you can learn on the job," he advised, because the academic part of the MBA was "a waste of time." Sloan's dean stood there looking stunned.[48] Business schools have attempted to teach knowledge both useful and ornamental, to conjure Benjamin Franklin again. The record would suggest that they have failed in both directions.

So the story ends largely where it began. Business schools continue to struggle with their basic purpose on almost exactly the same terms as they did a century ago. They still don't know which preposition they ought to be using: do they educate *about* American business? Or *for* American business? Are they a truly academic enterprise or merely a training ground for U.S. corporations? Thus, one senior business school professor could write in 2009 that the two foundation reports issued in 1959 ruined business schools by making them too academic. That prompted the MBA holder and former Bowdoin College president William Enteman to reply that business schools were not nearly academic enough and that, as servants of the shareholder-value ethos, business schools "become mere training programs in the latest tactics." Ten years later, Martin Parker, surveying this existential confusion, acknowledged that both sides had a point but that ironically they reinforced rather than contradicted each other. Yes, the business school has come to resemble the rest of the university by demanding research and publication from its faculty, but "because it borrows the gown and mortarboard of the university, and cloaks its knowledge in the apparatus of science . . . it is relatively easy to imagine that the knowledge the business school sells and the way it sells it [is] somehow less vulgar and stupid than it really is." All the window dressing of academia without any of its substance. Parker concluded, "Having taught in business schools for 20 years, I have come to believe that the best solution to [the] problems is to shut down business schools altogether."[49]

And just as the foundational dilemma of business schools remains unresolved, so too some of their sharpest critics, like Parker, are insiders, as was the case a hundred years ago. Business schools have always been filled with individual faculty who do smart and important research, and they graduate thousands of students who go on to have productive careers. But when one of their own can describe the business school as "a cancerous machine spewing out sick and irrelevant detritus," it is probably fair to say that, as institutions, business schools have become indifferent to criticism and immune from serious reform.[50] Plus ça change and Leviathan rolls on.

Business schools have failed to live up even to their own promises, to say nothing of the expectations the rest of us ought to have of them. And for nearly a century and a half they've made a tremendous success of that failure.

Acknowledgments

We authors save writing the acknowledgments for last because, while much can be fun and exciting about writing a book, by the time we get to the end it has become exhausting. Looking back with gratitude on all those people who helped is just the thing to rejuvenate a writer. I'll start with all those who made my research possible: Mark Lloyd and Tim Horning at the University of Pennsylvania archives; Jennifer Comins at Columbia University; Halle Mares at Ohio State University; Jacqueline Johnson at the university archives at Miami University; Kathi Neal at the University of California, Berkeley, university archives; Kate Crowe at the university archives at the University of Denver; and Lisa McCown at Washington and Lee University who helped long-distance as did Hanna McCleod at the American Association of Collegiate Schools of Business. This book also relies on archival research done at several foundations, but I was able to do that research only because the staff at each were so generous with their assistance. Thanks, then, to Renee Pappous at the Rockefeller Archive Center, Susanne Pichler at the Mellon Foundation Archives, and Nate Williams at the Alfred P. Sloan

Foundation. A special thanks to the Hagley Museum and Library, and to Lucas Clausson there, for providing me with a research grant to work with their extraordinary collections in a setting equally as wonderful.

One definition of a true friend is someone you impose on who doesn't think it's an imposition in the first place. I have imposed on many doing this book, but I need to thank Bill Childs, Susan Schulten, and David Steiger-wald in particular. I owe Jonathan Zimmerman twice over. Not only did he encourage me to do this book but he read an early draft of it, made it better, and then introduced me to Michael McGandy at Cornell University Press. A thank you to Michael for getting this book finally between covers. Thanks as well to Don Fehr, who helped me think through the book more closely. The production of this book began as soon as I arrived in the history department at Miami University, and I want to thank everyone there for the warm, generous welcome they have given me. I am also grateful to the College of Arts and Sciences for a semester of research leave. Zach Logsdon helped speed this along by providing research assistance that was as thorough as it was timely.

My parents, Terry and Peter Conn, cheered this book on with all the enthusiasm with which they have always supported me. And as I grow older the achievements of their lives strike me as more and more remarkable. My son, Zachary, read this book while he was still in high school, and his stamp of approval meant more to me than he knows. My daughter, Olivia, went off to college while I wrote this and her experiences have helped me think more about what higher education means these days. In the time it has taken me to finish this book my wife, Angela Brintlinger, has done a great deal more. She remains my best interlocutor, my best reader, and my best friend.

NOTES

Introduction

1. Bledstein, *Culture of Professionalism*, 6. In his book Burton Bledstein notes how different this made U.S. colleges and college graduates. "A man with a Cambridge or an Oxford education," he wrote, "seriously considered the harmful effect that entering the common world of business might have upon his status" (6).

2. These figures come from two graphs in Cheit, *Useful Arts and the Liberal Tradition*, 92–93; and from Brossard and Dewhurst, *University Education for Business*, 256.

3. "Ewald T. Grether, Dean of the UC Berkeley Schools of Business Administration 1943–1961," oral history, 1993, vol. 1, Regional Oral History Office, University Archives, Bancroft Library, University of California, Berkeley, 448.

4. Veblen, *Higher Learning in America*, 206.

5. Fitzpatrick, "University's Service to Business," 189.

6. For a good overview of this, see Zimmerman, "Uncle Sam at the Blackboard," 47–48.

7. Charles Franklin Thwing, once the president of Western Reserve University in Cleveland, looked back on one hundred years of German-American educational interchange in 1928. Thwing, *The American and the German University*.

8. Fiske, "University Reform," 292.

9. Laurence Veysey's *Emergence of the American University* remains an indispensable guide to the evolution of U.S. higher education. In it, he notes that Hopkins's first president, Daniel Coit Gilman, was never quite as keen or consistent about the notion of "pure" research as he and others at Hopkins often maintained. Julie Reuben has examined how the growth of the research university created a sharp division between a nineteenth-century conception of truth, rooted in religious values and traditions and scientific fact taken to be value-free. Reuben, *Making of the Modern University*. For a comprehensive history of higher education, see Dorn, *For the Common Good*.

10. Hofstadter and Hardy, *Development and Scope of Higher Education*, 90.

11. Thwing, *The American and the German University*, 174.

12. The off-the-cuff remark came in a speech on January 30, 2014, in Wisconsin, and he graciously apologized for it shortly thereafter.

13. See Brint, "Rise of the 'Practical Arts,'" 231–59.

14. Hofstadter and Hardy, *Development and Scope of Higher Education*, 92.

15. James, "Origin and Progress of Business Education," 52; Prickett, *Collegiate Schools of Business*, 15 (emphasis in source).

16. Fussell, *Class*, 43.

17. Porter and McKibben, *Management Education and Development*, 302.

18. David Labaree calls collegiate schools of education the Rodney Dangerfields of higher education in *The Problem with Ed Schools*. Thanks to Jon Zimmerman for pointing this out to me.

19. McCraw and Cruikshank, *Intellectual Venture Capitalist*, 27.

20. Veblen, *Higher Learning in America*.

21. See Hall, "Noah Porter Writ Large?," 217.

22. Veblen, *Higher Learning in America*, 68.

23. Parker, "Why We Should Bulldoze the Business School."

24. Far and away the best book on the history of business schools that I have come across is Rakesh Khurana, *From Higher Aims to Hired Hands: The Social Transformation of American Business Schools and the Unfulfilled Promise of Management as a Profession*. As the subtitle of the book suggests, Khurana tells a rise and fall story of the attempt to turn management into a profession. I rely on it a great deal, especially in chapter 1. Carter Daniel's *MBA: The First Century* is useful but not as deeply analytic as one might have wanted. For its centennial celebration, the Wharton School commissioned Steven Sass to write a history. However, *The Pragmatic Imagination: A History of the Wharton School* turned out to be a serious piece of historical work rather than a celebratory piece of self-promotion. So too did Michael Sedlak and Harold Williamson's *The Evolution of Management Education: A History of the Northwestern University J. L. Kellogg Graduate School of Management, 1908–1983*, which examines the tension between the demands of businesses and the desires of academics to shape the education on offer there. The McCraw and Cruikshank book, *Intellectual Venture Capitalist*, is certainly an example of puffery—it is even printed on thick, glossy paper. Two other books worth noting are Gabriel Abend, *The Moral Background: An Inquiry into the History of Business Ethics*, a smart sociological study of philosophy and history; and Mie Augier and James March, *The Roots, Rituals, and Rhetorics of Change: North American Business Schools after*

the Second World War. This last focuses on what the authors see as the "golden age" of business schools between 1945 and the 1970s. There is another genre of business school history that we might call the exposé. Duff McDonald's *The Golden Passport: Harvard Business School, the Limits of Capitalism, and the Moral Failure of the MBA Elite* is one of those. Philip Delves Broughton's *Ahead of the Curve: Two Years at Harvard Business School* is too, but it could also be called a kiss-and-tell since Broughton received a Harvard MBA before writing his very funny book. A trenchant critique of business schools comes from the business school professor Martin Parker, *Shut Down the Business School.* While the book is not strictly speaking a history, it covers much historical ground in making the case to rebuild business education entirely.

25. This is certainly the conclusion Michael Sedlak and Harold Williamson come to in their study of Northwestern University's business school. The academics there "argued that the primary purpose of institutions of higher business education was to develop 'executives' and that exposure to theoretical and analytical disciplines provided the most valuable training" for that goal. Employers and students, on the other hand, wanted "technical skill development . . . in specialized business functions in order to familiarize students with business methods." Sedlak and Williamson, *Evolution of Management Education*, 161.

26. In fairness, engineering programs are still overwhelmingly male.

27. "A Program for the Wharton School," MS, 1957, Wharton School Dean's Records, UPB 5.4, box 59, folder 18, University Archives, University of Pennsylvania.

28. Porter and McKibben, *Management Education and Development*, 314–15.

1. The World before (and Shortly after) Wharton

1. Sass, *Pragmatic Imagination*, 21–23.

2. Léautey, *Enseignement Commercial et les Ecoles du Commerce en France et dans le Monde Entier.* Léautey arranged his book by country. For the section on the United States, see 673–757. All quotes are my translation. Roger Geiger counted 263 by 1890 in "Era of Multipurpose Colleges," 130.

3. For a quick review of this early history, see Herrick, *Meaning and Practice of Commercial Education*, 178–79.

4. "Mercantile Education," 144–45.

5. "Commercial Colleges," 413.

6. Roger Geiger has called these "multipurpose colleges" the "missing link in the evolution of American higher education." Geiger, "Era of Multipurpose Colleges" and "Crisis of the Old Order."

7. There has been a little historical scholarship on these schools. See, for example, Olegario, *A Culture of Credit*, especially 106–7. She counts roughly twenty such schools in operation by 1850.

8. "International Business College Association," 654.

9. The story here is a bit murky, and I rely on the not fully sourced account from Herrick, *Meaning and Practice of Commercial Education*, 183–86.

10. "Biographical Album of Lancaster County Nebraska," NEGenWeb Project, Resource Center, On-Line Library, accessed October 2016, http://www.usgennet.org/usa/ne/topic/resources/OLLibrary/pbal/pages/balc0140.htm.

11. *Student's Guide to the Theoretical Department of the United States College of Business and Finance,* n.p.; *Student's Guide to the Theoretical Department Eastman National Business College,* 5 (emphasis in sources).

12. Charles, "Fair Cincinnati," 16.

13. Hodges, "Commercial Education," 464.

14. Quoted in Léautey, *Enseignement Commercial,* 712, 707.

15. Mussey, "Business as a Learned Profession," 4.

16. Garfield, "Elements of Success," 2–3 (emphasis in source). The publication date of 1881 suggests that this was published after Garfield's assassination as a memorial gesture.

17. *International Business College Association,* 8–9; Mussey, "Business as a Learned Profession," 3, 5.

18. See Burton, *City of Detroit,* 768–69.

19. James, "Commercial Education," 7. Craig Honick recounts reform efforts directed at proprietary colleges in "Chronic Scandal in the American Proprietary School Sector."

20. *What Business Education Means in Peirce School,* 5.

21. Ashley, "Universities and Commercial Education," 2; Haskins, "Business Education," 1688.

22. Glade, "Present State of Business Education," 652–53.

23. Smith, "Commercial Education," 53, 55.

24. "Mercantile Libraries," 437.

25. "Cultural Cornerstone."

26. For descriptions of this project, see "Useful Public Library," 504–5; and Dana, "Relations of the Library to the City," 314–17.

27. *What Business Education Means in Peirce School,* 9.

28. I have written extensively about the Philadelphia Commercial Museum, including chap. 4 in *Museums and American Intellectual Life;* "Epistemology for Empire," 533–63; and "Museums by Commerce." What follows draws from all that work.

29. Hoyle, "Philadelphia Commercial Museum," 107.

30. Plehn, "Address."

31. Wilson, *World's Trade,* 2.

32. "The Philadelphia Museums," Pepper Papers, 6:1094–98, Department of Special Collections, Van Pelt Library, University of Pennsylvania.

33. Cortelyou, "Some Agencies for the Extension of Our Domestic and Foreign Trade," 2.

34. Herrick, *Meaning and Practice of Commercial Education,* 287.

35. Wanamaker, "John Wanamaker Commercial Institute," 151–54.

36. Lyon, *Education for Business,* 361.

37. Wanamaker, "John Wanamaker Commercial Institute," 152.

38. Wanamaker, 151, 154.

39. Wanamaker, 151–52.

40. "Training Their Own Employees," 10.

41. Schwedtman, "Experiment in Practical Commercial Education," 330, 332.

42. Beatty, "Comparative Study of Corporation Schools," 25; *Papers, Reports, Bibliographies and Discussions.*

43. "Business Men in the Role of Pedagogs," 335; Patten, "University Training for Business Men," 219.

44. Lyon, *Education for Business*, 354, 359–60.

45. Harris, "You Can Grow Your Own Executives," 72–76.

46. Bennett, "Attitude of the National Association of Corporation Schools," 299.

47. Stewart, "National Association of Corporation Schools," 40.

48. "Business Men in the Role of Pedagogs," 335.

49. Beatty, "Comparative Study of Corporation Schools," 103.

50. *Commissioner of Labor.*

51. Beatty, "Comparative Study of Corporation Schools," 106.

52. Beatty, 108, 110.

53. "Business Men in the Role of Pedagogs," 35.

54. Wanamaker, "John Wanamaker Commercial Institute," 151.

55. James, "Relation of the College and University," 155; Herrick, *Meaning and Practice of Commercial Education*, 11; Anderson, "Educate Men Specially for Business," 556.

56. Marshall, "Relation of a School of Commerce," 84.

57. Glade, "Present State of Business Education," 656.

58. Sass, *Pragmatic Imagination*, 21.

59. Figures are from Geiger, "Crisis of the Old Order," 273.

60. Khurana, *From Higher Aims*, 49–50.

61. Haskins, "Business Education."

62. Norton, "Commercial Education," 423.

63. Stimson, "Need for Advanced Commercial Education," 244; Laughlin, "Higher Commercial Education," 679.

64. Wharton, "Business Men at School," 304.

65. Hodges, "Commercial Education," 465.

66. Haskins, "Business Education," 1705; Anderson, "Educate Men Specially for Business," 553.

67. Stone, "Dawn of a New Science," 449.

68. Stimson, "Need for Advanced Commercial Education," 241.

69. James, "Relation of the College and University," 151, 153–54.

70. Brett, "Need of Commercial Education," 730.

71. Glade, "Present State of Business Education," 654.

72. Waldo, "New Movement in Commercial Education," 798.

73. Stimson, "Need for Advanced Commercial Education," 240–41.

74. The figure of two hundred comes from Glade, "Present State of Business Education," 654.

75. Wheeler, "Public Concern in Improved Business Administration," 13–15; Herrick, *Meaning and Practice of Commercial Education*, 49–51.

76. Abend, *Moral Background*, esp. chap. 5 for the three case studies. "The data shows that higher-status periodical publications expressed moral expectations about the emerging business schools time and again" (Abend, 231).

77. Hotchkiss, *Higher Education and Business Standards*, 3–4, 12; Patten, "University Training for Business Men," 220; Anderson, "Educate Men Specially for Business," 555.

78. Jones, "College of Commerce," 181.

79. Schwedtman, "Experiment in Practical Commercial Education," 329–30.

80. Owens, "How to Get a Business Education," 214; Draper, "College Man in Business," 28; "Harvard Business School," 274.

81. Draper, "College Man in Business," 29.

82. Scott, "Training for Business at Wisconsin," 129.

83. The Yale and Amherst figures are cited in Herrick, *Meaning and Practice of Commercial Education*, 49; and in Draper, "College Man in Business," 28–29. Harvard's figure is from Khurana, *From Higher Aims*, 211.

84. Brandeis, *Business*, 1, 12.

85. Brandeis, 2, 4–5.

86. Those seventeen were Columbia, Cornell, Dartmouth, Harvard, New York University, Northwestern, Ohio State, Tulane, Berkeley, University of Chicago, University of Illinois, University of Nebraska, University of Pennsylvania (Wharton), University of Pittsburgh, University of Texas, University of Wisconsin, and Yale. That last one is curious, since Yale did not have a business school and wouldn't until the early 1970s. After attending this organizational meeting, Yale did not join the AACSB. I am taking most of my information about the history of AACSB from an in-house history printed for the organization's fiftieth anniversary: *American Association of Collegiate Schools of Business*.

87. Cited in Sharman and Shaw, "Education of Business and Professional Leaders," 383.

88. To pick one example more or less out of a hat: in late 2014 the board of United Technologies forced the retirement of CEO Louis Chenevert. "In 2014, UTC predicted annual sales approaching $100 billion by 2020; actual sales haven't come close. As the company's performance waned, the board of directors worried Chenevert might be too focused on the 110-foot yacht he was having built for himself in Taiwan. . . . UTC bid him farewell with an exit package valued at a little less than $200 million." Gruley and Clough, "Remember When Trump Said?" The mind boggles to think of what Chenevert might have earned had he performed successfully. Trump's claim, incidentally, was also not true.

89. The most energetic case made against the professions as antidemocratic is Burton Bledstein's *The Culture of Professionalism*, in which he argues that professions were driven almost entirely by middle-class status anxiety. See also Tim Harford, a columnist for the *Financial Times*, who argues much the same in *The Undercover Economist*. For a critique of Bledstein, see Tom Haskell's review "Power to the Experts," in the *New York Review of Books*, October 13, 1977.

90. See *American Association of Collegiate Schools of Business*, 187–95 (emphasis in source). In making this decision, they effectively dealt out what remained of business education at what Geiger called the "multi-purpose" institutions that developed in the last part of the nineteenth century.

91. Khurana, *From Higher Aims*, 292.

92. Vanderlip, *Business and Education*, 29–30.

93. "Private Business Schools," 200–201.

94. *American Association of Collegiate Schools of Business*, 8.

95. Anderson, "Educate Men Specially for Business," 556; Glade, "Present State of Business Education," 653.

96. Lyon, *Education for Business*, 280, 311–12.

97. Flexner, *Universities*, 162–64. Abraham Flexner dismissed undergraduate business education out of hand; he called Harvard's graduate—and thus professional—business program "pretentious and for that reason more dangerous" (163).

2. Teach the Children . . . What?

1. Brandeis, *Business*.

2. This is a good time to note that the most deeply conceived analysis of professionalism remains Andrew Abbott's *The System of Professions* and to acknowledge that I will not be engaging with the issues he raises here. Rather than focus on things like credentialing and associations or esoteric knowledge, Abbott instead sees professions operating in an ecology in which they establish jurisdiction, fight over turf, and struggle to maintain these in the workplace, the culture at large, and through establishing legal and administrative rules favorable to them. Tellingly, he mentions business education only once (206).

3. Bryce, "Commercial Education," 699; Wooster, "University Schools of Business," 48.

4. James, "Relation of the College and University," 152.

5. "Education of a Man of Business," 382–83.

6. "Circular of Information of the University of Denver and the Colorado Seminary," 1884–85, Special Collections, University of Denver, 22–27.

7. "Annual Announcement of the Wharton School of Finance and Economy," 1883, University Publications, Annual Announcements, UPL 10.3, University Archives and Records Center, University of Pennsylvania.

8. "Ewald T. Grether, Dean of the UC Berkeley Schools of Business Administration 1943–1961," oral history, 1993, vol. 1, Regional Oral History Office, University Archives, Bancroft Library, University of California, Berkeley, 471; Anderson, "Educate Men Specifically for Business," 554.

9. "Harvard Business School," 273–74; Hurley, *Awakening of Business*, 78–79; Chandler, *Visible Hand*, 467.

10. Brossard and Dewhurst, *University Education for Business*, 253.

11. Mears, "Teaching of Commerce and Economics," 648.

12. Christopher Loss discusses Scott in *Between Citizens and the State*, 31–33.

13. "Educational Activities of Chambers of Commerce," 1928, U.S. Chamber of Commerce Collection, box 79, 15, Hagley Museum and Library, Wilmington, DE.

14. Brossard and Dewhurst, *University Education for Business*, 50, 261.

15. Brossard and Dewhurst, 23, 115, 243.

16. Marshall, *Collegiate School of Business*, 27.

17. Scott, "Training for Business at Wisconsin," 128.

18. Brossard and Dewhurst, *University Education for Business*, 116–17; survey reported in "College Graduates as Business Sees Them," 35.

19. James, "Origin and Progress of Business Education in the United States," 55; Brossard and Dewhurst, *University Education for Business*, 221.

20. "Ewald T. Grether," Regional Oral History Office, 521. Dean Grether complained repeatedly in his oral history interview that Berkeley's College of Commerce stagnated between 1914 and his arrival as dean in 1941. He remembered that opening the bureau was his first move in reinvigorating the place.

21. Lough, "Reorganization of Instruction in Finance," 661.

22. Weaver, "Functions of a University Bureau," 49–50.

23. Fitzpatrick, "University's Service to Business," 188.

24. Secrist, "Round Table Conference," 229, 231.

25. Secrist, 229.

26. Weaver, "Functions of a University Bureau," 47–48.

27. Dickinson, "Bureaux for Economic and 'Business' Research," 402.

28. "Sees Bottom of Slump," *New York Times*, February 20, 1931.

29. See *Denver Clarion*, May 22, 1924; notes in Special Collections, University of Denver; Dickinson, "Bureaux for Economic and 'Business' Research," 408.

30. Dickinson, "Bureaux for Economic and 'Business' Research," 400; Ayres, "College of Money-Changing," 251.

31. See Dean's Reports, 1962–63, box 29, Special Collections, University of Denver.

32. Letter from James Yocum to Charles Truxal, May 18, 1964, UA.RG30.I.1.002, University Archives, Ohio State University.

33. "History of the College of Administrative Sciences," MS, University Archives, Ohio State University, UA.2017.0042.0008, 6.

34. Dickinson, "Bureaux for Economic and 'Business' Research," 400.

35. Calkins, *Business the Civilizer*, vi.

36. Stone, "Dawn of a New Science," 446.

37. Stone, 446–55.

38. Ayres, "College of Money-Changing," 250–52.

39. Secrist, "Round Table Conference," 225.

40. Lough, "Reorganization of Instruction in Finance," 656.

41. Lough, 654–55.

42. Donham, "Business Teaching by the Case System," 58. For a contemporary report on Harvard's decision to teach case studies, see Parsons, "Harvard Teaching Business," 166–73.

43. "Ewald T. Grether," Regional Oral History Office, 571–72.

44. Cherington, "Relations between Colleges and Business," 121.

45. Wooster, "University Schools of Business," 50; Young quoted in Calkins, *Business the Civilizer*, 288.

46. Jones, "Some Propositions concerning University Instruction," 195; Wolfe, "Undergraduate Economics Curriculum," 7–8 (emphasis in source).

47. Lough, "Reorganization of Instruction in Finance," 656; Calkins, *Business the Civilizer*, 279, 288.

48. Heilman, "Ethical Standards in Business," 19–23. Heilman was giving one of the William A. Vawter Foundation lectures at Northwestern.

49. Lockley, "Business Education and the Humanities," 418–19.

50. Kerr, "Schools of Business Administration," 73.

51. Kerr, 63.

52. "Ewald T. Grether," Regional Oral History Office, 304.

53. Pierson, *Education of American Businessmen*, 7–8, 42–43.

54. Kerr, "Schools of Business Administration," 63–65.

55. Letter from G. L. Bach to James Perkins, February 15, 1955, series 111.A, box 837, Carnegie Corporation records, Columbia University Archives.

56. Internal memo, May 17, 1956, Carnegie Corporation records, series 111.A, box 837, Columbia University Archives; resolution, Carnegie Corporation records, series 111.A, box 837, Columbia University Archives.

57. James Howell, "The Ford Foundation and the Revolution in Business Education: A Case Study in Philanthropy," MS, September 1966, FA739, box 284, Rockefeller Archive Center, Ford Foundation Records.

58. Internal memo from FJ, April 1957, Carnegie Corporation records, series 111.A, box 394, Columbia University Archives; Howell, "Ford Foundation and the Revolution," Ford Foundation Records; Robert Gordon, "Some Current Issues in Business Education," paper presented to AACSB, May 1958, FA739, box 50, Rockefeller Archive Center, Ford Foundation Records.

59. Norton-Taylor, "Business Schools," 138.

60. Letter from Frank Pierson to deans and department chairs, Carnegie Corporation records, series 111.A, box 837, Columbia University Archives.

61. Letter from James Perkins to Tom Carroll, May 22, 1958, Carnegie Corporation records, series 111.A, box 838, Columbia University Archives.

62. Gordon and Howell, *Higher Education for Business*, 6, 445; Pierson, *Education of American Businessmen*, x, 51–52.

63. Pierson, *Education of American Businessmen*, 51, 55; Gordon and Howell, *Higher Education for Business*, 125, 126; "Education for Business Administration," internal memo, November 28, 1956, Carnegie Corporation records, series 111.A, box 837, Columbia University Archives; internal memo from James Perkins, October 29, 1959, Carnegie Corporation records, series 111.A, box 838, Columbia University Archives.

64. Norton-Taylor, "Business School," 240.

65. Corrigan, "Whither Collegiate Business Education," 46, 47; "Popularity Swamps B Schools," 194; Lockley, "Business Education and the Humanities," 420; "A Program for the Wharton School," MS, 1957, Wharton School Dean's Records, UPB 5.4, box 59, folder 18, University Archives and Records Center, University of Pennsylvania, 6–8.

66. Pierson, *Education of American Businessmen*, 54.

67. Viegel, letter, 5.

68. "They Prescribe More Education Less Business," 84, 85.

69. Kirk, letter and response, 5.

70. "Foundation Director Raps Bizad Curriculum"; Lyle, "Wharton School to Revise Courses."

71. Letter from D. J. Hart, dean of University of Florida to Carnegie Corporation, May 13, 1960, Carnegie Corporation records, series 111.A, box 838, Columbia University Archives; letter from Richard Kozelka to John Gardner, May 9, 1960, Carnegie Corporation records, series 111.A, box 838, Columbia University Archives.

72. Internal memo, May 2, 1961, Carnegie Corporation records, series 111.A, box 838, Columbia University Archives.

73. Ford Foundation Records, FA732B, reel 2512, Rockefeller Archives Center.

74. Letter from Russell Wahlig to Theodore Holton, December 10, 1969, School of Business Administration Records, CU-29, carton 8, University Archives, Bancroft Library, University of California, Berkeley.

75. Howell, "Ford Foundation and the Revolution," Ford Foundation Records; letter from G. L. Bach to Thomas Carroll, September 20, 1960, FA 739, box 112, Rockefeller Archive Center, Ford Foundation Records.

76. Howell, "Ford Foundation and the Revolution," Ford Foundation Records.

77. Lee, "Diverse Views," 6, 7.

78. Foy, "Businessman Looks at Business Education," 18, 16.

79. Benton, "Failure of the Business Schools," 26, 74.

80. Benton, 26, 73, 74. McCaffrey quoted in Pamp, "Liberal Arts Training for Executives," 44–45.

81. Sheehan, "New Report Card on Business Schools," 149; Goldwin and Nelson, *Toward the Liberally Educated Executive*, viii.

82. Sheehan, "New Report Card on Business Schools," 148; Fisher, *History of AACSB International*, vol. 2, 30–31.

83. Hall, "Maligned Business School," 597–601.

84. Hall, 597–601.

85. "Wharton Copes with Its Identity Crisis," 49, 51.

86. "Worrisome Boom in Second-Rate B-schools," 82, 86.

87. "MBA Itch Is Mostly a Myth," 30.

88. "Worrisome Boom in Second-Rate B-schools," 86.

89. "The Future of Management Education and the Role of the American Assembly of Collegiate Schools of Business," December 5, 1975, Dean's Records, UPB 5.4, box 86, folder 11, University Archives and Records Center, University of Pennsylvania. I think this report was sent to all AACSB members.

90. Kerr, "Schools of Business Administration," 73.

91. "They Prescribe More Education," 86.

92. These figures come from a survey conducted by Thomas Wheelan and reported in "Top Managements' Perspective on Business Education," 289–91.

93. "Stumping the Deans," 106.

94. James Baugham papers, box 1, folder 23, Hagley Museum and Library, Wilmington, DE.

3. Dismal Science versus Applied Economics

1. Stone, "Dawn of a New Science," 449.

2. Hotchkiss, *Higher Education and Business Standards*, 44, 72, 99; Kennedy, "Wall Street and Academy Lane," 372. Willard Eugene Hotchkiss used the phrase "scientific method" twenty times in his book.

3. The summary of the Klein Committee of 1933 is recounted in Smith, *First Fifty Years of the College of Commerce and Administration*, 44–45.

4. See "Centennial History of the Department of Economics," University Archives, Ohio State University, 1. It isn't clear that this course was actually taught that year, but its inclusion in the roster, even if only as an aspiration, suggests the importance of political economy at that moment.

5. Ely, "American Economic Association," 70. In fact, political economy did not stand on its own at most places in the United States after the Civil War. According to A. W. Coats, as late as 1880 "there were only three men in the leading schools" whose primary responsibility was to teach political economy. Coats, "Educational Revolution and the Professionalization of American Economics," 345.

6. For the information about Harvard, see Mason, "Harvard Department of Economics," 384.

7. Ely, "American Economic Association," 67–71.

8. Hotchkiss, "Northwestern University School of Commerce," 199. Hotchkiss was the Johnny Appleseed of collegiate schools of business. After founding the school at the University of Minnesota, he moved to Evanston to start the school at Northwestern. His last stop was as the founding dean of Stanford's business school.

9. Mason, "Harvard Department of Economics," 407.

10. Pierce, *Negro Business and Business Education*, 253, 296.

11. Ely, "American Economic Association," 49.

12. For more on this connection, see Sass, "Uneasy Relationship," 225–40.

13. Sass, 236.

14. Sass, 232–36.

15. Sass, 237.

16. DuBois's study was published in the same year as John Dewey's *School and Society* and seems almost like a direct reply to it, though that certainly can't be the case. In his book, Dewey complained that U.S. education remained mired in a medieval scholasticism that valued intellectualism for its own sake and not for the work ideas could do in the world.

17. Patten, *Social Basis of Religion*.

18. Saltmarsh, *Scott Nearing*, 16–28. This remains the best of the Nearing studies.

19. Coats, "Educational Revolution and the Professionalization of American Economics," 358.

20. This figure and Nearing's quote are from Hughes, *Penn in Ink*, 101.

21. "Scott Nearing," 46.

22. Saltmarsh, *Scott Nearing*, 97.

23. Saltmarsh, 98.

24. Sass, *Pragmatic Imagination*, 126.

25. Mears, "Teaching of Commerce and Economics," 648–49.

26. Howard, "Economics and the Science of Business," 106.

27. Howard, 109.

28. Howard, 109–10.

29. McCrea, "Place of Economics in the Curriculum," 219–27.

30. Lough, "Reorganization of Instruction in Finance," 657, 661–62.

31. Woolley, "How Our Colleges Teach Business," 5–6.

32. McCrea, "Place of Economics in the Curriculum," 221.

33. McCrea, 220–21.

34. "Relationship between Departments of Economics," 73–84. This may not have been the first time the two groups got together to discuss the problem. See "Collegiate Schools of Business," 41.

35. Marshall, *Collegiate School of Business*, 16–17.

36. "Relationship between Departments of Economics," 75–76.

37. "Relationship between Departments of Economics," 74–75.

38. Towle, "Business Cycles and Business Men," 365–67.

39. Towle, 365–67.

40. Grether, "Development of the AACSB Core Curriculum," 147.

41. MacKenzie, "Development of AACSB Standards," 192 (emphasis mine).

42. Kerr, "Schools of Business Administration," 64.

43. Gordon and Howell, *Higher Education for Business*, 200.

44. Bernstein, *A Perilous Progress*, 101. As Julie Reuben notes, the commitment to value-free "science" was part and parcel of separating the secular university from religious pressures. Indeed, the Social Gospel movement and its impact on U.S. social science might well be the last example of a religious movement exerting a substantial influence on higher education. Reuben, *Making of the Modern University*, 132.

45. Bernstein, *Perilous Progress*, 106.

46. Department of Economics Self-Study, March 1, 1983, UA.2017.0042.0004, University Archives, Ohio State University.

47. Michael Bernstein writes, "Economists of the late nineteenth century would have looked with great satisfaction on the New Economists of the late twentieth." Bernstein, *Perilous Progress*, 126.

48. Coats, "Educational Revolution and the Professionalization of American Economics," 372.

49. The publication of Thomas Kuhn's *Structure of Scientific Revolutions* in 1962 marks a watershed in the way people understood the nature of scientific research. That it was published just as the neoclassicists were coming to dominate the economics profession is another irony of the discipline's history.

50. I have taken much of this discussion from Morgan and Rutherford, "American Economics," 1–26.

51. Two examples illustrate my point. Business schools are not mentioned at all as being significant for development or diffusion of economic ideas by Phyllis Deane in her study of the former or by David Colander and A. W. Coats in their study of the latter. Deane, *Evolution of Economic Ideas*; and Colander and Coats, *Spread of Economic Ideas*.

52. "Center Stage for Economic Education," 1962, National Association of Manufacturers Collection, series 1, box 58, Hagley Museum and Library, Wilmington, DE.

53. Goldberg, "Mathematics for Business Students," 67; Wheeler, "Development of AACSB Standards," 36.

54. "Economic Rebel," UA.RG30.I.1.002, University Archives, Ohio State University.

55. See James Howell, "The Ford Foundation and the Revolution in Business Education: A Case Study in Philanthropy," MS, September 1966, FA739, box 284, Rockefeller Archive Center, Ford Foundation Records.

56. Daniels College of Business Records, Dean's Report 1964–65, Special Collections, University of Denver.

57. "Ewald T. Grether, Dean of the UC Berkeley Schools of Business Administration 1943–1961," oral history, 1993, vol. 1, Regional Oral History Office, University Archives, Bancroft Library, University of California, Berkeley, 490–92, 539. The committee also recommended that the economics department no longer be involved in training students in the social work program.

58. Bell, *Reforming of General Education*, 204.

59. Siegfried and Bidani, "Differences between Economics Programs," 181.

60. "A Plan to Assure Academic Quality in Economics Programs at the University of Denver," June 1985, Department of Economics Records, box 2, Special Collections, University of Denver.

61. See memo from Irving Weiner, January 21, 1981; memo from William Burford to Roy Wood, February 22, 1988; memo from unidentified faculty member (emphasis in source), Department of Economics Records, box 2, Special Collections, University of Denver.

62. Memo from Caporaso to A. O. Pfnister, October 6, 1986, Department of Economics Records, box 2, Special Collections, University of Denver. Another memo, this one from William Zaranka, Arts and Sciences dean, to Roy Wood, Denver provost, January 27, 1988, lays out a chronology of this controversy.

63. "Report of the Ad-Hoc Review Committee," December 1988, School of Business Administration Records, CU-29, carton 6, University Archives, Bancroft Library, University of California, Berkeley.

64. Memo from Douglas Vickers to Dean Winn, December 4, 1969, Dean's Records, UPB 5.4, box 85, folder 43, University Archives and Records Center, University of Pennsylvania.

65. "Plan to Assure Academic Quality," Department of Economics Records (emphasis in source).

66. Clower, "State of Economics," 23. Clower's assessment was anticipated by several years by the comedic character Father Guido Sarducci. In Father Guido's "five-minute university" skit from the late 1970s, you learn in five minutes everything you will remember five years after you graduate from a four-year school. Economics is reduced to "supply and demand. That's it."

67. Colander, "Invisible Hand of Truth," 31.

68. Paul Krugman wrote a much-discussed column for the *New York Times*, "How Did Economists Get It So Wrong?," September 6, 2009.

4. It's a White Man's World

1. McGirt, "Why Race and Culture Matter in the C-Suite."

2. Léautey, *Enseignement Commercial et les Ecoles du Commerce en France et dans le Monde Entier*, 712.

3. "International Business College Association," 9.

4. Garfield, "Elements of Success," 7; Mussey, "Business as a Learned Profession," 6.

5. Nesbit, *History of Wisconsin*, 249–50.

6. Vecchio, *Merchants, Midwives, and Laboring Women*, 102.

7. *Haas School of Business*, 10.

8. Announcement 1918–1919, Special Collections, University of Denver.

9. *What Business Education Means in Peirce School*, 2.

10. See Wharton Annual Report 1954–55, 4; Wharton School Dean's Records UPB 5.4, box 81, folder 31, University Archives and Records Center, University of Pennsylvania; "Wharton School Course Will Open in September to Women Matriculates," *Daily Pennsylvanian*, February 22, 1954.

11. "Harvard and Radcliffe Launching Program in Business Administration for Women," 27.

12. Hughes, "A Woman's New York"; Norton-Taylor, "Business Schools," 238.

13. For a review, see Miller and Hamilton, *Independent Business School in American Education*, esp. 124–26.

14. Vinocour, "The Trend Is toward the Trained," 16–17.

15. "Circular of Information, 1887–8," Clark Atlanta University Archives.

16. Oak, "Business Education in Negro Colleges," 175.

17. *National Survey of the Higher Education of Negroes*, vol. 2, 12.

18. Pierce, *Negro Business and Business Education*, 240.

19. Pierce, 236, 254, 291, 316–17.

20. Pierce, 281, 283; Oak, "Our Aimless Business Education," 264–65.

21. This figure is cited in a memo from AACSB president V. K. Zimmerman to all AACSB-member deans, August 13, 1979, Wharton Dean's Records, UPB 5.4, box 36, folder 12, University Archives and Records Center, University of Pennsylvania.

22. Robert McKersie, *A Decisive Decade: An Insider's View of the Chicago Civil Rights Movement during the 1960s*, 74–75. McKersie, himself a Chicago Business School faculty member in the 1960s, wrote his memoir of his involvement in the civil rights movement there. Also see "Opportunities for Negroes in Management," *Chicago Tribune*, October 27, 1965.

23. For a good summary of Nixon's black capitalism agenda see Kotlowski, *Nixon's Civil Rights*, 125–56. For more on the intersection of business and black power, see Hill and Rabig, *Business of Black Power*.

24. Kinzer and Sagarin, *Negro in American Business*, i.

25. Sturdivant, "Limits of Black Capitalism," 123.

26. Fields, "Industry's Response to the Black MBA," 60, 66; Booms, "Black MBA," 47–53.

27. Harrison, "Role of the Negro Business School," 46.

28. Jones, *Leading the Challenge of Change*, 10–19.

29. Alfred P. Sloan Foundation Annual Report for 1969, Alfred P. Sloan Foundation, New York, 48. Nevins and Merryman, "Search for Black Management," 9.

30. The council is described in the Alfred P. Sloan Foundation's Annual Report for 1969, 47–49.

31. Nevins and Merryman, "Search for Black Management," 11; Panschar, "Businessmen, Educators, Move to Enlist Black Grads," 13; Booms, "Black MBA," 51.

32. Fields, "Industry's Response to the Black MBA," 66.

33. Nevins and Merryman, "Search for Black Management," 56; Fields, "Industry's Response to the Black MBA," 66.

34. Booms, "Black MBA," 52; Lee et al., "Relevance in Three Top Business Schools, Black vs. White," 44.

35. Alfred P. Sloan Foundation Annual Report, 1974, Alfred P. Sloan Foundation, New York, 16–17.

36. Panschar, "Businessmen, Educators," 16.

37. "Professor, Vice Chancellor, Dean, Vice President," oral history of Earl Cheit, 2002, University Archives, Bancroft Library, University of California, Berkeley, 283.

38. Moskowitz, "Best Business Schools for Blacks," 58.

39. "Survey Says Black Students Are Getting a Fair Shake," 24–25.

40. Moskowitz, "Best Business Schools for Blacks," 52.

41. Curtin and Gasman, "Historically Black College MBA Programs," 81.

42. Pierce, *Negro Business and Business Education*, 267.

43. "Changing the Face of American Business since 1966," The Consortium, accessed March 2017, http://cgsm.org/about-us/history/.

44. "Report of the Dean of the School of Business Administration," and Raymond Glos, "50 Years of Educational Excellent, 1987," MS, School of Business Historical Files, group 12BA, box 2, Special Collections, University Archives, Miami University.

45. *Haas School of Business*, 10; W. C. Pieper, "An Analysis of Applicants Admitted to the Master's Program of the Graduate School of Business Administration," Office of Institutional Research, 1969, MS, Bancroft Library, University of California, Berkeley, 42; "Ewald T. Grether, Dean of the UC Berkeley Schools of Business Administration 1943–1961," oral history, 1993, vol. 2, Regional Oral History Office, University Archives, Bancroft Library, University of California, Berkeley, 869.

46. Gordon and Howell, *Higher Education for Business*, 28.

47. Burns, "Women Find Difficulty in World of Banking."

48. "Why Women Need Their Own MBA," 102.

49. "Proposal," June 1973, Pace University Grant File 47300019, Andrew W. Mellon Foundation.

50. "Proposal," November 1973, Pace University Grant File 47300019, Andrew W. Mellon Foundation.

51. Internal memo from Claire List, January 23, 1975; report from Sandra Ekberg-Jordan, December 1975, Pace University Grant File 47300019, Andrew W. Mellon Foundation.

52. Hennig and Jardim Grant Application, FA732G, reel 2305, Rockefeller Archive Center, Ford Foundation Records; "Why Women Need Their Own MBA," 102; internal Ford memo, FA732G, reel 2305, Rockefeller Archive Center, Ford Foundation Records.

53. Internal Ford memo, FA732G, reel 2305, Rockefeller Archive Center, Ford Foundation Records.

54. Internal Ford memo from Alison Bernstein, April 14, 1987, FA732E, reel 4978, Ford Foundation Records.

55. Report from Sandra Ekberg-Jordan, December 1975, Pace University Grant File 47300019 (emphasis in source).

56. Letter from Nancy Levien Goodman, February 18, 1978, Pace University Grant File 47300019, Andrew W. Mellon Foundation (emphasis in source).

57. Letter from Carol Hasto, Pace University Grant File 47300019, Andrew W. Mellon Foundation (emphasis in source).

58. "Fast Facts about Delta Sigma Pi," Delta Sigma Pi, accessed March 14, 2017, https://www.deltasigmapi.org/about/fast-facts.

59. Grand Chapter Congress minutes, vol. 4, Delta Sigma Pi national headquarters, Oxford, Ohio.

60. This episode was recounted by his son: James Jacobs, "Nothing New about Deltasig Diversity," *Deltasig* 87 (Winter 1998): 2.

61. Morrissey, "Past Imperfect."

62. Congress minutes, 1949, Delta Sigma Pi; see also "The Royal Order of the Pink Poodles," *Deltasig* 94 (July 2007): 46–47.

63. Congress minutes, 1977, Delta Sigma Pi.

64. "Report of the Administrative Science Task Force on Affirmative Action," 1974; letter from Robert Georges to Joanne Murphy, April 4, 1977, UA1989.126.001, University Archives, Ohio State University.

65. Weiss, "Women Could Be Majority of Law Students in 2017"; Commission on Women in the Profession, "A Current Glance at Women in the Law."

66. See "The Times They Are A'Changing," *Decision* alumni magazine, Winter 1977.

67. Moran, "Women Now Make Up 40% of Students."

68. Taylor, "Diversity as a Law School Survival Strategy." Taylor, a law professor at St. Louis University, did this study in 2015 and made his research available online as a pdf.

69. For complete data on enrollments compiled by the Association of American Medical Colleges see "FACTS: Applicants, Matriculants, Enrollment, Graduates, MD-PhD, and Residency Applicants Data," accessed March 19, 2017, https://www.aamc.org/data/facts/.

70. Aranda, "In Most MBA Programs, the Diversity Trend Is Down."

5. Good in a Crisis?

1. Broughton, "Harvard's Masters of the Apocalypse."

2. Broughton, "Harvard's Masters of the Apocalypse."

3. Barnard, "In the Classroom and on the Campus."

4. Willey, *Depression, Recovery and Higher Education*, 472–73. This study, commissioned by the American Association of University Professors, is a remarkable source for studying how the Great Depression affected college campuses.

5. "College Varies Enrollment with Business"; for national figures, see Willey, *Depression, Recovery and Higher Education*, 250–51.

6. Blaug, "No History of Ideas," 161.

7. For events at Washington and Lee, see a series of articles in the student paper *Ringtum Phi*: April 14, 17, 21, and 24, 1931, and May 4 and 8, 1934, Washington and Lee

University's Special Collections, Lexington, Virginia. I am indebted to Lisa McCown for these.

8. MS, School of Business, Historical Files, group 12BA, box 1, Special Collections, University Archives, Miami University.

9. Adams, "A Test for American Business," 1.

10. Adams, 1. In fact, Adams may have exaggerated the problem. In his study of attitudes toward business between 1880 and 1940, Louis Galambos found that while the Depression could "have caused a decisive breakdown in the corporate culture," for the most part it didn't. There was a backlash against big business to be sure, but not as large as one would have expected and not as vibrant as in earlier decades. Galambos, *Public Image of Big Business*, chap. 8, 223. Galambos's findings have been challenged because of the way he chose to sample public opinion. I largely agree with those critiques.

11. Khurana, *From Higher Aims*, 181.

12. Grant Application, September 1932, Carnegie Corporation Grant Files, CCNY record series 111.A, box 14, Columbia University Archives.

13. Grant Application, September 1932, Carnegie Corporation Grant Files.

14. Grant Application, September 1932, Carnegie Corporation Grant Files.

15. MacKenzie, "Development of AACSB Standards," 90.

16. MacKenzie, 92.

17. Khurana, *From Higher Aims*, 181–82.

18. Leverett Lyon, School of Business, Historical Files, group 12BA, box 1, Special Collections, University Archives, Miami University.

19. Joseph Willits, "Business Schools and Training for Public Service," MS, Wharton School Dean's Records, UPB 5.4, box 61, folder 13, University Archives and Records Center, University of Pennsylvania.

20. "Institute of Local and State Government," Wharton School Dean's Records, UPB 5.4, box 54, folder 18, University Archives and Records Center, University of Pennsylvania. Eighty years later it is tough to argue that the situation in Pennsylvania is much better, though given the scale of the problem that can hardly be blamed on the Fels Institute.

21. "Collegiate World."

22. For an assessment of Donham during this period, see Khurana, *From Higher Aims*, 185–87.

23. Youngman, "Retrenchment in Relief Outlay Is Asked to Cut Deficit."

24. Donham, "Class of 1936 Seeks a Job," 27.

25. Donham, 27.

26. Horace Stern, "The Wharton School Man in the World of Today," Wharton School Dean's Records, UPB 5.4, box 61, folder 9, University Archives and Records Center, University of Pennsylvania.

27. "College Varies with Enrollment in Business."

28. "Progress in Marketing Research," 236.

29. "Grant for Teaching in Government Management at the University of Denver," 786–87; "Tax Bill Doctors," 30.

30. "Sloan Foundation," 23.

31. Dobbs, "Ford and GM Scrutinized for Alleged Nazi Collaboration." The fact that it took over half a century after the end of the Second World War for these U.S.

corporations to confront their involvement with Nazi Germany also speaks volumes about their sense of corporate ethics and responsibility. As with Swiss banks, their concern seems to have been to protect themselves from lawsuits seeking damages and reparations, not to acknowledge their complicity.

32. Sloan and his project at the University of Denver are surely a part of what Kim Fein-Phillips has called the "top-down revolution," a conservative backlash against the New Deal led by a loose collection of businessmen, politicians, and intellectuals. Fein-Phillips, *Invisible Hands* and "Top-Down Revolution.". See also Collins, *Business Response to Keynes*, though this book does not mention business schools.

33. "Denver University Aids Study of Taxes."

34. Duncan, "Chancellor's Greeting to the Delegates," 6.

35. Emery, "Freer Hand for Private Enterprise," 613–22.

36. Jones, *Leading the Challenge of Change*, 13.

37. Memo from Willis Winn to faculty, July 10, 1969, Wharton School Dean's Records, UPB 5.4, box 35, folder 37, University Archives and Records Center, University of Pennsylvania.

38. Letter from H. D. Doan to Willis Winn, December 18, 1968, Wharton School Dean's Records, UPB 5.4, box 84, folder 6, University Archives and Records Center, University of Pennsylvania.

39. "A New Mission for the University of Pennsylvania," 1969, Wharton School Dean's Records, UPB 5.4, box 35, folder 11, University Archives and Records Center, University of Pennsylvania.

40. Intra-Wharton memo, August 30, 1968, Wharton School Dean's Records, UPB 5.4, box 83, folder 34, University Archives and Records Center, University of Pennsylvania.

41. Memo from Julius Aronofsky to Willis Winn, November 18, 1968, Wharton School Dean's Records, UPB 5.4, box 22, folder 1, University Archives and Records Center, University of Pennsylvania.

42. Memo from Edwin Epstein to interested members of the Bay Area and university communities, March 11, 1969, bk 1, p. 4; unidentified announcement June 11, 1968, bk 1, p. 56, School of Business Administration Records, University Archives, Bancroft Library, University of California, Berkeley.

43. Memo from Epstein to communities.

44. Memo from Epstein to communities.

45. "A Proposal for Technical Assistance, Research and Education," April 23, 1970, bk 2, p. 104, School of Business Administration Records, University Archives, Bancroft Library, University of California, Berkeley.

46. "Ghetto Youths Begin Classes," unidentified newspaper clipping, Wharton School Dean's Records, UPB 5.4, box 22, folder 1, University Archives and Records Center, University of Pennsylvania.

47. Sholl, "MBA Association Debates Need for University Involvement."

48. Memo from John Hobstetter to Robert MacDonald and James Shada, August 23, 1973, Wharton School Dean's Records, UPB 5.4, box 88, folder 27 University Archives and Records Center, University of Pennsylvania.

49. Novack and DeAngelo, "Community Relations Reap Frustration, Hope."

50. Letter from Carolynne Martin to Donald Carroll, January 31, 1978, Wharton School Dean's Records, UPB 5.4, box 38, folder 32, University Archives and Records Center, University of Pennsylvania; letter from Donald Carroll to Calvin Bland, August 23, 1977, Wharton School Dean's Records, UPB 5.4, box 38, folder 34, University Archives and Records Center, University of Pennsylvania.

51. Severin, "Wharton Community Program Helps Disadvantaged Residents."

52. CU-29, carton 1, School of Business Administration Records, University Archives, Bancroft Library, University of California, Berkeley.

53. James Baugham papers, box 2, folder 21, Hagley Museum and Library, Wilmington, DE.

54. Cheit quoted in *Haas School of Business*, 20; The Chicago episode is related in "New Business Student," 76.

55. Cheit quoted in *Haas School of Business*, 20; Survey 1970, CU-29, carton 8, University Archives, School of Business Administration Records, Bancroft Library, University of California, Berkeley.

56. Memo from Walter Cooper to Ransom Rathbun (n.d.) NAM Collection, series 1, boxes 23 and 64, Hagley Museum and Library, Wilmington, DE.

57. NAM Collection, series 1, box 38, Hagley Museum and Library. NAM also had extensive programs targeting high school students and the public schools more broadly. That programming was geared toward "economic education" because NAM was deeply distressed that students were not getting such education in schools and thus they would enter the work force susceptible to pernicious influences. In the 1960s NAM tried to draft off the post-Sputnik urgency for science education. In a 1965 paper, "The Choice: Economic Ignorance or Understanding," NAM staff wrote, "The launching of Sputnik served to awaken much of the nation's school system to the necessity of upgrading scientific courses, but it may have obscured an equally important need for improving the social science offerings in the school system. Among the social sciences, economics has long been the forgotten or neglected step-child." By the end of May 1962, according to an internal NAM accounting, the organization had sent out over 1.3 million pieces of its educational material. NAM Collection, series 1, boxes 61 and 64, Hagley Museum and Library.

58. "Proposal Regarding Educational Objectives," April 1962, NAM Collection, series 1, box 61, Hagley Museum and Library.

59. Welch caused NAM some considerable embarrassment when he accused Dwight Eisenhower of being a communist. This forced NAM's board to adopt a resolution in September 1960 reaffirming its faith in the president. That is bizarre enough, but when United Press International reported some months later that NAM had, in effect, censured the John Birch Society, NAM's Kenneth Miller penned a somewhat tortured memo to department heads, regional managers, and committee executives declaring "the Board resolution . . . did not mention the John Birch Society and therefore was *not* 'in effect' a motion of censure." NAM Collection, series 1, box 99, Hagley Museum and Library.

60. NAM Collection, series 11, box 190, Hagley Museum and Library.

61. Lee Hamilton, "Why a Business Career?," March 6, 1969, NAM Collection, series 1, box 61, Hagley Museum and Library.

62. Hamilton, "Why a Business Career?"

63. "College-Business Symposiums," 1970, US Chamber of Commerce Collection, box 92, Hagley Museum and Library.

64. "College-Business Symposiums," US Chamber of Commerce Collection.

65. Kilpatrick, "Why Students Are Hostile to Free Enterprise," 12. In fact, James Kilpatrick's essay is a rant about the survey results. He made no attempt to explain "why."

66. Baker quoted in "Wooing the Disenchanted," 78; Orth quoted in "Top Students Sell Business Short," 134.

67. "Top Students Sell Business Short," 134.

68. NAM Collection, series 1, box 23, Hagley Museum and Library.

69. See letter exchange between Robert Georges and Robert T. Davis, September 11 and September 20, 1976, UA.1984.094.003, University Archives, Ohio State University.

70. "Lending a Hand with Social Ills," 106–7.

71. "B-school for Entrepreneurs of Change," 82.

72. Sapienza, "Wharton's Venture into Non-profit Management Course," 109.

73. "New Business Student," 76.

74. Goldwater, "Business Faces the Fight of Its Life," 32–33; "Upswing in the M.B.A. Market," 34–35.

75. "Upswing in the M.B.A. Market," 34–35.

76. "Top Students Sell Business Short," 136.

77. Wharton Annual Report 1974–75, University Archives and Records Center, University of Pennsylvania, 6.

78. See "Dean's Notes," *Decision*, Fall 1970 and Fall 1972 issues; memo from E. M. Epstein, Spring 1973 enrollments to faculty, 1973, CU-29, carton 8, University Archives, School of Business Administration Records, Bancroft Library, University of California, Berkeley. Peter Firmin position paper, February 1975, box 55, Daniels College of Business Records, Special Collections, University of Denver (emphasis in source). For 1977 figures see Geiger, "College Curriculum and the Marketplace," 6.

79. Annual Report, 1977–78, box 55, Daniels College of Business Records, Special Collections, University of Denver.

80. "Where Executives Are Building a Better Image for Business," 81.

81. "New Business Student," 76. Raymond went on to found Victoria's Secret, which I suppose is one sort of social relevance, but after he sold that to Les Wexner, he never found business success again. He killed himself by jumping off the Golden Gate Bridge in 1993.

82. McGlade, "Big Push," 50–65. Jacqueline McGlade reports that during the Korean War U.S. businesses began to have misgivings about USTAP because European firms often employed radical unions. Business schools, therefore, became even more central to the USTAP program. McGlade, "Big Push," 57. For another assessment of the globalization of business schools, see Moon and Wotipka, "Education, 1881–1999," 121–36.

83. *Educating Tomorrow's Managers*, 23.

84. "Invasion of the Business Schools," 120.

85. "How Business Schools Welcome the World," 118.

86. Fisher, *History of AACSB International*, 31.

87. Dean's Report, 1967–68, Special Collections, University of Denver; Wharton School Dean's Records, UPB 5.4, box 96, folder 44, and Wharton Annual Report, 1974–75, University Archives and Records Center, University of Pennsylvania, 13.

88. Donald Taylor, draft report on international education for AACSB, January 9, 1976, Wharton School Dean's Records, box 86, folder 11; for the Karachi Project, see Wharton School Dean's Records, box 57, folder 15, University Archives and Records Center, University of Pennsylvania.

89. Taylor, draft report, Wharton School Dean's Records.

90. "How Business Schools Welcome the World," 122.

91. Moon and Wotipka, "Education, 1881–1999," 135.

6. Same as It Ever Was

1. Daniel, *MBA*, 217.

2. Porter and McKibben, *Management Education and Development*, 298 (emphasis in source).

3. I am in no position to judge Friedman's economic ideas, but in much of his public writing he rehashed variations of the thesis first put forward to the American public by Friedrich von Hayek in *The Road to Serfdom*. In "The Social Responsibility of Business Is to Increase Its Profits," Friedman wrote that any attempt by corporations to exercise social responsibility would lead inevitably to the "iron fist of Government bureaucrats." That 2006 piece was an obituary written by Lawrence Summers, "Milton Friedman," 171.

4. Khurana, *From Higher Aims*, 320.

5. Khurana, 321.

6. This shift by the Business Roundtable is discussed in Khurana, 320–21.

7. I am referring to the April 2017 incident involving a passenger being dragged off an overbooked United Airlines flight and having his teeth smashed in the process.

8. McDonald, *Golden Passport*, 366. Duff McDonald's discussion of Michael Jensen is particularly good.

9. Alan Greenspan and former House Speaker Paul Ryan frequently fawned over Rand's books while they were in power.

10. I wonder if anyone had the heart to tell Jensen that the quote almost surely did not originate with Shaw, and Shaw may never, in fact, have told the story at all.

11. I've stolen this phrase from the title of Philip Mirowski and Dieter Plehwe's collection of essays *The Road from Mont Pelerin: The Making of the Neoliberal Thought Collective*.

12. I have taken these figures from "Where Will They Lead?" published by the Aspen Institute in 2008. The tone of the report is decidedly upbeat, suggesting that students in 2007 were a bit less crass than they had been in 2002; the report's authors also suggest that the increase of women in MBA programs was responsible for this small change in attitudes.

13. McDonald, *Golden Passport*, 382. This is a point that Khurana makes in *From Higher Aims*.

14. Horace Stern, "The Wharton School Man in the World of Today," Wharton School Dean's Records, UPB 5.4, box 61, folder 9, University Archives and Records Center, University of Pennsylvania.

15. Grant application; letter from Stephen Miller to Norman Bowie (emphasis in source), both in Wharton School Dean's Records, UPB 5.4, box 36, folder 36, University Archives and Records Center, University of Pennsylvania. The APA seems to have consulted with somebody at Wharton in preparing the grant proposal.

16. Hoffmann and Moore, "Results of a Business Ethics Curriculum Survey"; Hosmer, "Other 338."

17. Schoenfeld, McDonald, and Youngblood, "Teaching of Business Ethics," 237.

18. Schoenfeld, McDonald, and Youngblood, 240.

19. Schoenfeld, McDonald, and Youngblood, 238.

20. Marens, "Second Time as Farce," 457–58. The philosopher most cited by business ethicists in their published work is John Rawls, but Marens explains that they have more or less completely ignored the important points Rawls made.

21. Esther Roca argues in "Practical Wisdom in Business Schools" that business schools should drop the pretense that their curricula are morally neutral and suggests a way for the reintroduction of values in management education (607–20).

22. Anteby, *Manufacturing Morals*, 2.

23. Parker, "Why We Should Bulldoze."

24. The original study by Butterfield, McCabe, and Trevino, "Academic Dishonesty in Graduate Business Programs," was reported widely, including in Mangan, "Survey Finds Widespread Cheating," and McCabe, "MBAs Cheat. But Why?"

25. Moran and Snyder, "Temple Finds More Misreporting."

26. Broughton, "Harvard's Masters of the Apocalypse."

27. See, for example, Landrum, "US Business Schools Failing on Climate Change."

28. "Jane Von Bergen: Executive Q&A."

29. This is one of the points Adam Tooze makes in his book *Crashed: How a Decade of Financial Crises Changed the World*. White nationalist and Trump campaign manager Stephen Bannon has made this point in numerous interviews. Bannon holds an MBA from Harvard.

30. My colleague Youn Ki in her important dissertation blurs the distinction I've just made. She has traced how some of those older industrial firms were on the cutting edge of the finance revolution. Ki, "Large Corporations and the Rise of Finance in the United States."

31. For a really interesting history of consulting, see McKenna, *World's Newest Profession*, Harvard figure on 208. For an anatomy of the incestuous relationship between McKinsey and Harvard, see McDonald, *Golden Passport*, chap. 23.

32. Stewart, *Management Myth*, 5.

33. Irwin, "Great American Janitor Test."

34. "A Matter of Common Concern to the Investment Banking Industry," Wharton School Dean's Records UPB 5.4, box 57, folder 9, University Archives and Records Center, University of Pennsylvania. Wharton also hosted several conferences on investment banking during the 1950s.

35. Cassidy, "What Good Is Wall Street?"

36. See, for example, Zuckerman and Hope, "Quants Now Run Wall Street."

37. Zuckerman and Hope.

38. Allan Ardis, letter to the editor, *Tampa Bay Times*, June 10, 2016.

39. Brian Alexander's *Glass House: The 1% Economy and the Shattering of the All-American Town* is a gripping story of Lancaster, Ohio, whose fate has important implications for the rest of the nation.

40. This can take a variety of forms: reducing or eliminating entirely a foreign language requirement, reducing writing requirements, or making different requirements for students outside the arts and sciences that virtually exempt them from any exposure to a liberal arts education. In the last several years, admissions officers at Ohio State have been discriminating against applicants who indicate an interest in majoring in the humanities.

41. Arum and Roksa, *Academically Adrift*, 81. Social work and education students fare almost as poorly. Arum and Roksa also found that business students spent the fewest hours per week on coursework. Arum and Roksa's findings have certainly been challenged. See Lederman, "Less Academically Adrift."

42. See Podolny, "Buck Stops (and Starts) at Business School."

43. A short bibliography: Ellen Schrecker, *Lost Soul of Higher Education*, focuses her concern on what she sees as the erosion of academic freedom. *University, Inc.* is Jennifer Washburn's analysis of the way private sector money now drives university research and the hazards of privatizing that research. Bill Readings wrote that the university has become entirely unmoored from its traditional roots and now resembles nothing so much as a transnational corporation, leaving the university in ruins. Which is the title of his book. Frank Donoghue examines the issue of academic labor and predicts the demise of the traditional humanities in *Last Professors*. In it he "emphasize[s] the oppressive significance of the corporate vocabulary of efficiency, productivity, and usefulness" (xv), a statement with which none of these other authors would disagree. Nor do I.

44. Brint, "Rise of the 'Practical Arts,'" 232, 235.

45. This is Frank Donoghue's prediction in *Last Professors*.

46. Universities with large science, engineering, and, especially, medical and pharmacology programs aggressively promoted projects early in the twenty-first century that result in patents and products that can be sold. This has led to fights over who owns the intellectual property generated by university faculty in their research. Jacob Rooksby has explored this development in *Branding of the American Mind*.

47. For a wonderful essay detailing the deliberately obfuscating nature of the language used in the world of finance, see Lanchester, "Money Talks."

48. This story is told in Stewart, *Management Myth*, 7.

49. Daniel, "How Two National Reports"; Enteman's reply "Is Business Education Too Antitheoretical?"; Parker, "Why We Should Bulldoze." Parker elaborates on this and much more in his book *Shut Down the Business School*.

50. O'Doherty and Jones, *Manifestos for the Business School of Tomorrow*, 1.

BIBLIOGRAPHY

Archival Sources

Alfred P. Sloan Foundation, New York
Andrew W. Mellon Foundation, New York
Carnegie Corporation Records, Columbia University Archives
Clark Atlanta University Archives
Delta Sigma Pi national headquarters, Oxford, Ohio
Ford Foundation Records, Rockefeller Archive Center
Hagley Museum and Library, Wilmington, DE
Special Collections, University of Denver
University Archives, Bancroft Library, University of California, Berkeley
University Archives, Ohio State University
University Archives, Special Collections, Miami University
University Archives and Records Center, University of Pennsylvania

Published Sources

Abbott, Andrew. *The System of Professions: An Essay on the Division of Expert Labor.* Chicago: University of Chicago Press, 1988.

Abend, Gabriel. *The Moral Background: An Inquiry into the History of Business Ethics.* Princeton, NJ: Princeton University Press, 2014.

Adams, James Truslow. "A Test for American Business." *New York Times Magazine*, January 10, 1937, 1–2+.

Alexander, Brian. *Glass House: The 1% Economy and the Shattering of the All-American Town.* New York: Macmillan, 2017.

Allen, Thomas J. "The Proposed College of Commerce." *Education* 21 (March 1901): 442–43.

The American Association of Collegiate Schools of Business, 1916–1966. Homewood, IL: Richard D. Irwin, 1966.

American Management Association. *Education for Business: A Balanced Appraisal.* New York, 1963.

Anderson, Woodford. "Should Our Colleges and Universities Educate Men Specially for Business?" In *National Education Association of the United States—Addresses and Proceedings, 1900*, 549–55. Chicago: University of Chicago Press.

Anteby, Michel. *Manufacturing Morals: The Values of Silence in Business School Education.* Chicago: University of Chicago Press, 2013.

Aranda, Peter. "In Most MBA Programs, the Diversity Trend Is Down," September 8, 2015. http://cgsm.org/in-most-mba-programs-the-diversity-trend-is-down/.

Arum, Richard, and Josipa Roksa. *Academically Adrift: Limited Learning on College Campuses.* Chicago: University of Chicago Press, 2011.

Ashley, W. J. "The Universities and Commercial Education." *North American Review* 176 (1903): 31–38.

Aspen Institute. "Where Will They Lead?" 2008. https://www.aspeninstitute.org/publications/where-will-they-lead-2008-executive-summary-pdf/.

Augier, Mie, and James March. *The Roots, Rituals, and Rhetorics of Change: North American Business Schools after the Second World War.* Stanford, CA: Stanford University Press, 2011.

Ayres, C. E. "The College of Money-Changing." *New Republic*, January 28, 1925, 250–52.

Barber, William, J., ed. *Economists and Higher Learning in the Nineteenth Century.* New Brunswick, NJ: Transaction Publishers, 1993.

——. *From New Era to New Deal: Herbert Hoover, the Economists, and American Economic Policy.* Cambridge: Cambridge University Press, 1985.

Barnard, Eunice. "In the Classroom and on the Campus." *New York Times*, October 18, 1931.

Beatty, Albert James. "A Comparative Study of Corporation Schools as to Their Organization, Administration, and Methods of Instruction." PhD diss., University of Illinois, 1917.

Beck, Hubert Park. *Men Who Control Our Universities.* New York: King's Crown Press, 1947.

Bell, Daniel. *The Reforming of General Education.* New York: Columbia University Press, 1966.

Bennett, Charles. "The Attitude of the National Association of Corporation Schools." In *Manual Training and Vocational Education*, 299–302. Peoria, IL: Manual Arts Press, 1915.

Bennett, G. Vernon. *Vocational Education of Junior College Grade*. Baltimore: Warwick and York, 1928.

Bennis, Warren G., and James O'Toole. "How Business Schools Lost Their Way." *Harvard Business Review*, May 2005, 96–104.

Benton, William. "The Failure of the Business Schools." *Saturday Evening Post*, February 18, 1961, 26+.

Bernstein, Michael. *A Perilous Progress: Economists and Public Purpose in Twentieth-Century America*, Princeton, NJ: Princeton University Press, 2001.

Blaug, Mark. "No History of Ideas, Please, We're Economists." *Journal of Economic Perspectives* 15 (2001): 145–64.

Bledstein, Burton. *The Culture of Professionalism: The Middle Class and the Development of Higher Education in America*. New York: W. W. Norton, 1976.

Booms, Bernard. "The Black MBA: An Alternative to Black Capitalism?" *Business Horizons* 14 (1971): 47–53.

Bosari, Jessica. "Are Business Degrees Recession-Proof?" *Forbes*, September 14, 2012.

Bouman, Andy, and Ute S. Frey. *Haas School of Business: A Brief Centennial History, 1898–1998*. Berkeley: University of California Press, 1998.

Brams, Stanley H. "Manufacturer Sets Up Tech School to Beat Shortage." *Nation's Business*, July 1956, 14–15.

Brandeis, Louis. *Business: A Profession*. Boston: Small, Maynard, 1914.

Brett, George P. "The Need of Commercial Education." *Independent* 72 (1912): 728–30.

"Bringing Up the Boss." *Fortune*, December 1951, 118–19+.

Brint, Steven, ed. *The Future of the City of Intellect: The Changing American University*. Stanford, CA: Stanford University Press, 2002.

——. *In an Age of Experts: The Changing Role of Professionals in Politics and Public Life*. Princeton, NJ: Princeton University Press, 1994.

——. "The Rise of the 'Practical Arts.'" In *The Future of the City of Intellect: The Changing American University*, edited by Steven Brint, 231–59. Stanford, CA: Stanford University Press, 2002.

Brossard, James, and Frederic Dewhurst. *University Education for Business*. Philadelphia: University of Pennsylvania Press, 1931.

Broughton, Philip Delves. *Ahead of the Curve: Two Years at Harvard Business School*. New York: Penguin Press, 2008.

——. "Harvard's Masters of the Apocalypse." *Sunday Times* (London), March 1, 2009.

Brown, William. "The EEOC's Chairman Comments on the Persistence of Racism." *MBA*, January 1972, 10–11+.

Bryce, James. "Commercial Education." *North American Review* 168, no. 511 (1899): 694–707."A B-school for Entrepreneurs of Change." *Business Week*, April 25, 1970, 82+.

"Budget Cutters Worry B-schools." *Business Week*, December 26, 1970, 15.

Burnham, James. *The Managerial Revolution: What Is Happening in the World*. New York: John Day, 1941.

Burns, Kathleen. "Women Find Difficulty in World of Banking." *Chicago Tribune*, July 18, 1971.

Burton, Clarence M., ed. *The City of Detroit, 1701–1922*. Detroit: S. J. Clarke, 1922.

"Business Men in the Role of Pedagogs." *Survey* 32 (1914): 335.

Butler, Nicholas Murray, ed. *Education in the United States*. Albany, NY: J. B. Lyon, 1900.

Butterfield, Kenneth, Donald McCabe, and Linda Trevino. "Academic Dishonesty in Graduate Business Programs: Prevalence, Causes, and Proposed Action." *Academy of Management Learning and Education* 5, no. 3 (September 2006): 294–305.

Calkins, Earnest Elmo. *Business the Civilizer*. Boston: Atlantic Monthly Press / Little, Brown, 1928.

"Can You Teach Management?" *Business Week*, April 19, 1952, 126+.

Carothers, Neil. *Inflation Is Bad Business*. Washington, D.C.: American Liberty League, 1935.

Cassidy, John. "What Good Is Wall Street?" *New Yorker*, November 30, 2010.

Chandler, Alfred D., Jr. *The Visible Hand: The Managerial Revolution in American Business*. Cambridge, MA: Belknap Press of Harvard University Press, 1977.

Charles, Thomas Logan. "Fair Cincinnati." *Frank Leslie's Popular Monthly* 45 (1898): 16.

Cheit, Earl F., ed. *The Business Establishment*. New York: John Wiley, 1964.

———. *The Useful Arts and the Liberal Tradition*. New York: McGraw-Hill, 1975.

Cherington, Paul. "Relations between Colleges and Business." *Journal of Marketing* 5 (1940): 120–21.

Clark, Evans. "Business Men in Control of American Colleges." *New York Times*, June 10, 1917.

Clower, Robert. "The State of Economics: Hopeless but Not Serious?" In *The Spread of Economic Ideas*, edited by David Colander and A. W. Coats, 23–29. Cambridge: Cambridge University Press, 1989.

Coats, A. W. "The Educational Revolution and the Professionalization of American Economics." In *Economists and Higher Learning in the Nineteenth Century*, edited by William Barber, 340–75. New Brunswick, NJ: Transaction Publishers, 1993.

Colander, David, and A. W. Coats, eds. *The Spread of Economic Ideas*. Cambridge: Cambridge University Press, 1989.

Cole, Arthur. "Economic History in the United States: Formative Years of a Discipline." *Journal of Economic History* 28 (1968): 556–89.

"College Graduates as Business Sees Them." *Literary Digest*, June 16, 1934, 35.

"The College of Commerce at the University of Cincinnati." *School and Society* 3 (1916): 60.

"College Varies Enrollment with Business." *Lantern* (Ohio State University), October 6, 1933.

"Collegiate Schools of Business." *School and Society* 18 (July 14, 1923): 41.

"The Collegiate World." *Lantern* (Ohio State University), December 12, 1934.

Collins, Robert. *The Business Response to Keynes, 1929–1964*. New York: Columbia University Press, 1981.

"Commercial Colleges—Their Nature and Object." *Hunt's Merchant's Magazine* 39 (1858): 410–13.

Commission on Women in the Profession. "A Current Glance at Women in the Law." January 2017. http://www.americanbar.org/content /dam/aba/marketing/women/ current _glance_statistics_january2017.authcheckdam.pdf.

Conference on Commercial Education and Business Progress. Urbana-Champaign: University of Illinois, 1913.

Conn, Steven. "An Epistemology for Empire: The Philadelphia Commercial Museum, 1893–1926." *Diplomatic History* (Fall 1998): 533–63.

——. *Museums and American Intellectual Life, 1876–1926*. Chicago: University of Chicago Press, 1998.

——. "Museums by Commerce, Museums of Commerce, Museums for Commerce." In *Collector's Knowledge: What Is Kept, What Is Discarded*, edited by Anja-Silvia Goeing, Anthony Grafton, and Paul Michel, 345–58. Brill's Studies in Intellectual History, vol. 227. Leiden: Brill, 2013.

Corrigan, Francis. "Whither Collegiate Business Education." *School and Society* 83 (1956): 45–47.

Cortelyou, George Bruce. "Some Agencies for the Extension of Our Domestic and Foreign Trade." *Annals of the American Academy of Political and Social Science* 24, no. 1 (July 1904): 1–12.

Cowley, W. H. "The University and the Individual." *Journal of Higher Education* 2 (1931): 391–97.

Curtin, Meredith, and Marybeth Gasman. "Historically Black College MBA Programs: Prestige, Rankings, and the Meaning of Success." *Journal of Education for Business* 79 (November/December 2003): 79–84.

Dana, John Cotton. "Relations of the Library to the City." *American City* 7 (1912): 314–17.

Daniel, Carter. "How Two National Reports Ruined Business Schools." *Chronicle of Higher Education*, November 8, 2009.

——. *MBA: The First Century*. Lewisburg, PA: Bucknell University Press, 1998.

Davidson, H. Justin. "How Businessmen Can Help Schools of Business." *Nation's Business*, October 1975, 73–74.

Deane, Phyllis. *The Evolution of Economic Ideas*. Cambridge: Cambridge University Press, 1978.

"Denver University Aids Study of Taxes." *New York Times*, June 18, 1939.

Dickinson, Z. Clark. "Bureaux for Economic and 'Business' Research in American Universities." *Economic Journal* 35 (1925): 398–415.

Dobbs, Michael. "Ford and GM Scrutinized for Alleged Nazi Collaboration." *Washington Post*, November 30, 1998.

Donham, Wallace B. "Business Teaching by the Case System." *American Economic Review* 12 (1922): 53–65.

——. "The Class of 1936 Seeks a Job." *Saturday Evening Post*, May 23, 1936, 27+.

Donoghue, Frank. *The Last Professors: The Corporate University and the Fate of the Humanities*. New York: Fordham University Press, 2008.

Dorfman, Joseph. *The Economic Mind in American Civilization*. New York: Viking Press, 1959.

Dorn, Charles. *For the Common Good: A New History of Higher Education in America*. Ithaca, NY: Cornell University Press, 2017.

Draper, Ernest G. "The College Man in Business." *Outlook* 106 (January 3, 1914): 27–30.

Duncan, David Shaw. "Chancellor's Greeting to the Delegates." In *Government: The Citizen's Business*. Denver, CO: University of Denver Press, 1939.

Dunfee, Thomas, and Diana Robertson. "Integrating Ethics into the Business School Curriculum." *Journal of Business Ethics* 7 (1988): 847–59.

Economic and Business Research in American Colleges and Universities. New York: Business Research Council, 1932.

Educating Tomorrow's Managers. New York: Committee for Economic Development, 1964.

Education for Professional Responsibility. Pittsburgh: Carnegie Press, 1948.

"The Education of a Man of Business." *Hunt's Merchant's Magazine* 15 (1846): 381–84.

Ely, Richard. "The American Economic Association, 1885–1909." *American Economic Association Quarterly*, 3rd ser., 11, no. 1 (April 1910): 47–111.

Emery, James A. "A Freer Hand for Private Enterprise." In *Government: The Citizen's Business*, 613–22. Denver, CO: School of Commerce, Accounts, and Finance, University of Denver, 1939.

Engwell, Lars, and Vera Zamagni, eds. *Management Education in Historical Perspective.* Manchester, UK: Manchester University Press, 1998.

Enteman, William. "Is Business Education Too Antitheoretical?" *Chronicle of Higher Education*, December 14, 2009.

The Ethical Problems of Modern Finance. New York: Ronald Press, 1930.

Explorations in Citizenship. Denver, CO: School of Commerce, Accounts, and Finance, University of Denver, 1940.

Fein-Phillips, Kim. *Invisible Hands: The Making of the Conservative Movement from the New Deal to Reagan.* New York: W. W. Norton, 2009.

——. "Top-Down Revolution: Businessmen, Intellectuals, and Politicians against the New Deal, 1945–1964." *Enterprise and Society* 7 (December 2007): 686–94.

Ferguson, Harold. "Is the Business Education Department a Dumping Ground?" *Balance Sheet* 25 (January 1944): 200–202.

Fields, Charles. "Industry's Response to the Black MBA." *MBA*, April/May 1969, 60–66.

Fisher, Dale L. *The History of AACSB International.* Volume 2: *1966–2006.* Tampa, FL: AACSB, 2007.

Fiske, John. "University Reform." In The Miscellaneous Writings of John Fiske: With Many Portraits of Illustrious Philosophers, Scientists, and Other Men of Note, 271–312. Boston: Houghton Mifflin, 1902.

Fitzpatrick, Edward. "The University's Service to Business." *School and Society* 12 (September 11, 1920): 186–93.

Flexner, Abraham. *Universities: American, English, German.* New York: Oxford University Press, 1930.

Foy, Fred C. "A Businessman Looks at Business Education." In *Views on Business Education*, by American Association of Collegiate Schools of Business, 11–22. Chapel Hill: University of North Carolina at Chapel Hill School of Business Administration, 1960.

Friedman, Milton. "The Social Responsibility of Business Is to Increase Its Profits." *New York Times Magazine*, September 13, 1970.

Fussell, Paul. *Class: A Guide through the American Status System.* New York: Simon and Schuster, 1992.

Galambos, Louis. *The Public Image of Big Business in America, 1880–1940.* With Barbara Barrow Spence. Baltimore: Johns Hopkins University Press, 1975.

Garfield, James. "Elements of Success." Address at Spencer's Bryant & Stratton Business College, 1881. Washington, DC: Spencer's Bryant & Stratton Business College, 1881.

Geiger, Roger, ed. *The American College in the Nineteenth Century*. Nashville, TN: Vanderbilt University Press, 2000.

———. "The College Curriculum and the Marketplace: Academic Disciplines and the Trend toward Vocationalism in the 1970s." Yale Higher Education Research Group Working Paper, 1980.

———. "The Crisis of the Old Order." In *The American College in the Nineteenth Century*, ed. Roger Geiger, 264–76. Nashville, TN: Vanderbilt University Press, 2000.

———. "The Era of Multipurpose Colleges in American Higher Education." In *The American College in the Nineteenth Century*, ed. Roger Geiger, 127–62. Nashville, TN: Vanderbilt University Press, 2000.

"Girls' School for Boys?" *Literary Digest,* May 20, 1916, 1449.

Glade, Earl Jay. "Present State of Business Education in the United States and Some Recommendations." In *National Education Association of the United States—Addresses and Proceedings, 1914*, 652–56. Chicago: University of Chicago Press.

Goldberg, Samuel. "Mathematics for Business Students." In *Views on Business Education*, edited by Fred C. Foy et al. Chapel Hill, NC: AACSB, 1960.

Goldwater, Barry. "Business Faces the Fight of Its Life." *Nation's Business*, May 1974, 32–33.

Goldwin, Robert, and Charles Nelson, eds. *Toward the Liberally Educated Executive*. White Plains, NY: Fund for Adult Education, 1959.

Gordon, Robert Aaron, and James Edwin Howell. *Higher Education for Business*. New York: Columbia University Press, 1959.

Government: The Citizen's Business. Denver, CO: School of Commerce, Accounts, and Finance, University of Denver, 1939.

"Grant for Teaching in Government Management at the University of Denver." *School and Society* 47 (1938): 786–87.

Greenberg, D. S. "Consulting: U.S. Firms Thrive on Jobs for European Clients." *Science*, n.s., 162 (November 29, 1968): 986–87.

Grether, Ewald. "The Development of the AACSB Core Curriculum." In *The American Association of Collegiate Schools of Business, 1916–1966*, 146–57. Homewood, IL: Richard D. Irwin, 1966.

Gruley, Bryan, and Rick Clough, "Remember When Trump Said He Saved 1,100 Jobs at a Carrier Plant?" *Bloomberg Businessweek*, March 29, 2017, https://www.bloomberg.com/news/features/2017-03-29/remember-when-trump-said-he-saved-1-100-jobs-at-a-carrier-plant.

Haddon, T. W. "Higher Commercial Education." *School and College* 1 (1892): 169–71.

Hall, Charles P., Jr. "The Maligned Business School: What Is a Liberal Education?" *Journal of Risk and Insurance* 35 (1968): 597–601.

Hall, Peter Dobkin. "Noah Porter Writ Large?" In *The American College in the Nineteenth Century*, edited by Roger Geiger, 196–220. Nashville, TN: Vanderbilt University Press, 2000.

Hardy, Gordon, and Daniel Everett, eds., *Shaping the Future of Business Education*. London: Palgrave Macmillan, 2013.

Harford, Tim. *The Undercover Economist.* New York: Oxford University Press, 2006.

Harris, Herbert. "You Can Grow Your Own Executives." *Nation's Business.* April 1956, 72–76.

Harrison, Lincoln. "The Role of the Negro Business School in Promoting Black Capitalism." *Journal of Negro Education* 40 (1971): 45–47.

"The Harvard Business School." *Science*, n.s., 28 (August 28, 1908): 273–74.

"Harvard and Radcliffe Launching Program in Business Administration for Women." *National Business Woman* 35 (1956): 27.

Haskell, Tom. "Power to the Experts," *New York Review of Books*, October 13, 1977.

Haskins, C. W. "Business Education." *Harper's Weekly* 46 (November 15, 1902): 1688+.

Heilman, Ralph. "Ethical Standards in Business and in Business Education." In *The Ethical Problems of Modern Finance*, 3–27. New York: Ronald Press, 1930.

Herrick, Cheesman. *Meaning and Practice of Commercial Education.* New York: Macmillan, 1904.

Hill, Laura Warren, and Julia Rabig, eds. *The Business of Black Power.* Rochester, NY: University of Rochester Press, 2012.

Hills, Gerald. "Graduate Business Schools and Minority Integration: The Black MBA." *AACSB Bulletin*, April 1973, 28–43.

Hodges, James. "Commercial Education." *North American Review* 144 (1887): 462–70.

Hoffmann, M., and J. M. Moore. "Results of a Business Ethics Curriculum Survey." *Journal of Business Ethics* 7, no. 2 (1982): 81–83.

Hofstadter, Richard, and C. DeWitt Hardy, *The Development and Scope of Higher Education in the United States.* New York: Columbia University Press for the Commission on Financing Higher Education, 1952.

Honick, Craig. "Chronic Scandal in the American Proprietary School Sector: A Historical Perspective on Why Treatments Have Not Provided a Cure." Paper presented at the Annual Meeting of the American Educational Research Association, April 22, 1992.

Hosmer, L. T. "The Other 338: Why a Majority of Our Schools of Business Administration Do Not Offer a Course in Business Ethics." *Journal of Business Ethics* 4 (1985): 17–22.

Hotchkiss, Willard Eugene. *Higher Education and Business Standards.* Boston: Houghton Mifflin, 1918.

——. "The Northwestern University School of Commerce." *Journal of Political Economy* 21, no. 3 (February 1913): 196–208.

Howard, Earl Dean. "Economics and the Science of Business." *Journal of Political Economy* 25 (1917): 106–10.

"How Business Schools Welcome the World." *Business Week*, December 9, 1967, 118–19+.

Hoyle, W. E. "The Philadelphia Commercial Museum." *Museums Journal* 1 (1901–1902): 107.

Hughes, Alice. "A Woman's New York." *Washington Post*, May 31, 1937.

Hughes, Samuel. *Penn in Ink: Pathfinders, Swashbucklers, Scribblers & Sages. Portraits from the Pennsylvania Gazette.* Philadelphia: Xlibris, 2006.

Hurley, Edward N. *Awakening of Business.* New York: Doubleday, Page, 1916.

"The International Business College Association." *Harper's Weekly*, October 13, 1866, 654.

"The Invasion of the Business Schools." *Business Week*, May 7, 1966, 120.

Irwin, Neil. "The Great American Janitor Test." *New York Times*, September 3, 2017.

"It's Almost like Working." *Business Week*, August 4, 1962, 94–95.

Jacobs, James. "Nothing New about Deltasig Diversity," *Deltasig* 87 (Winter 1998): 2.

James, Edmund. "Commercial Education." In *Monographs on Education in the United States* 13, edited by Nicholas Murray Butler, 655–703. New York: J. B. Lyon, 1899.

———. "Relation of the College and University to Higher Commercial Education." *Publications of the American Economic Association*, 3rd ser., 2, no. 1 (February 1901): 144–65.

"Jane Von Bergen: Executive Q&A." *Philadelphia Inquirer*, August 20, 2017.

Jensen, Michael, and William H. Meckling. "Theory of the Firm: Managerial Behavior, Agency Costs and Ownership Structure." *Journal of Financial Economics* 3, no. 4 (October 1976): 305–60.

Jones, Barbara Britton. *Leading the Challenge of Change*. Chesterfield, MO: Consortium for Graduate Study in Management, 2016.

Jones, Edward. "Some Propositions concerning University Instruction in Business Administration." *Journal of Political Economy* (March 1913): 185–95.

Jones, William Carey. "The College of Commerce." *Arena* 23 (1900): 180–82.

Kennedy, William. "Wall Street and Academy Lane." *Independent* 117 (1926): 357–58+.

Kerr, Clark. "The Schools of Business Administration." In *New Dimensions of Learning in a Free Society*, 63–74. Pittsburgh: University of Pittsburgh Press, 1958.

Khurana, Rakesh. *From Higher Aims to Hired Hands: The Social Transformation of American Business Schools and the Unfulfilled Promise of Management as a Profession*. Princeton, NJ: Princeton University Press, 2007.

Ki, Youn. "Large Corporations and the Rise of Finance in the United States." PhD diss., University of Chicago, 2015.

Kilpatrick, James. "Why Students Are Hostile to Free Enterprise." *Nation's Business*, July 1975, 11–12.

Kinzer, Robert H. and Edward Sagarin. *The Negro in American Business: The Conflict between Separatism and Integration*. New York: Greenberg, 1950.

Kipping, Matthias, and Lars Engwall, eds. *Management Consulting: Emergence and Dynamics of a Knowledge Industry*. Oxford: Oxford University Press, 2002.

Kotlowski, Dean J. *Nixon's Civil Rights*. Cambridge, MA: Harvard University Press, 2001.

Krugman, Paul. "How Did Economists Get It So Wrong?" *New York Times*, September 6, 2009.

Labaree, David. *The Problem with Ed Schools*. New Haven, CT: Yale University Press, 2004.

Lamon, Eva Virginia. "An Investigation of the Aims and Objectives of Commercial Education with Special Emphasis on Conditions in Ohio." Master's thesis, Ohio State University, 1929.

Lanchester, John. "Money Talks: Learning the Language of Finance." *New Yorker*, August 4, 2014.

Landrum, Nancy. "US Business Schools Failing on Climate Change." *Conversation*, April 20, 2017.

Laughlin, J. Laurence. "Higher Commercial Education." *Atlantic* 89 (1902): 677–86.

Léautey, Eugène. *Enseignement Commercial et les Ecoles du Commerce en France et dans le Monde Entier.* Paris: Librairie Comptable et Administrative, 1886.

Lederman, Doug. "Less Academically Adrift." *Inside Higher Ed*, May 20, 2013.

Lee, Andre, John Clark, Claude Harris, and Donald Hassell. "Survey into Relevance in Three Top Business Schools, Blacks vs White." *AACSB Bulletin*, April 1973, 44–52.

Lee, Maurice W. "A Prologue to Some Diverse Views on Business Administration." In *Views on Business Education*, by American Association of Collegiate Schools of Business, 3–9. Chapel Hill: University of North Carolina at Chapel Hill School of Business Administration, 1960.

"Lending a Hand with Social Ills." *Business Week*, March 7, 1970, 106–7.

Levine, Arthur, ed. *Higher Learning in America, 1980–2000.* Baltimore: Johns Hopkins University Press, 1993.

Levine, David O. *The American College and the Culture of Aspiration, 1915–1940.* Ithaca, NY: Cornell University Press, 1986.

Lockley, Lawrence. "Business Education and the Humanities." *School and Society* 74 (1951): 417–20.

Loss, Christopher P. *Between Citizens and the State: The Politics of American Higher Education in the 20th Century.* Princeton, NJ: Princeton University Press, 2012.

Lough, W. H. "Reorganization of Instruction in Finance in University Schools of Business." *Journal of Political Economy* 29 (1921): 654–62.

Louviere, Vernon. "A New Way for College Students to Learn from Businessmen." *Nation's Business*, July 1975, 41.

"Low Marks in Ethics." *Business Week*, September 28, 1968, 64+.

Lyon, Leverett. *Education for Business.* Chicago: University of Chicago Press, 1922.

MacDonald, Steven. *Business and Blacks: Minorities as Employees and Entrepreneurs.* Princeton, NJ: Dow Jones Books, 1968.

MacKenzie, Ossian. "The Development of AACSB Standards." In *The American Association of Collegiate Schools of Business, 1916–1966*, 84–145. Homewood, IL: Richard D. Irwin, 1966.

Mangan, Katherine. "Survey Finds Widespread Cheating in MBA Programs." *Chronicle of Higher Education*, September 19, 2006.

Marens, Richard. "The Second Time Farce: Business School Ethicists and the Emergence of Bastard Rawlsianism." In *The Oxford Handbook of Sociology, Social Theory, and Organization Studies: Contemporary Currents*, edited by P. S. Adler, P. du Gay, G. Morgan, and M. Reed, 447–66. New York: Oxford University Press, 2014.

Marshall, Alfred. *Principles of Economics.* London: MacMillan, 1890.

Marshall, L. C., ed. *The Collegiate School of Business.* Chicago: University of Chicago Press, 1928.

Marshall, Leon. "The Relation of a School of Commerce to the Practical Problems of Business." In *Conference on Commercial Education and Business Progress*, 84–86. Urbana-Champaign: University of Illinois, 1913.

Mason, Edward S. "The Harvard Department of Economics from the Beginning to World War II." *Quarterly Journal of Economics* 97 (1982): 383–433.

"The MBA Itch Is Mostly a Myth." *Business Week*, September 26, 1970, 30.

McCabe, Donald. "MBAs Cheat. But Why?" *Harvard Business Review*, April 13, 2009.

McCraw, Thomas, and Jeffrey Cruikshank. *The Intellectual Venture Capitalist: John H. McArthur and the Work of the Harvard Business School, 1980–1995.* Cambridge, MA: Harvard Business Review Press, 1999.

McCrea, Roswell. "The Place of Economics in the Curriculum of a School of Business." *Journal of Political Economy* 34 (1926): 219–27.

McDonald, Duff. *The Golden Passport: Harvard Business School, the Limits of Capitalism, and the Moral Failure of the MBA Elite.* New York: Harper Business, 2017.

McGlade, Jacqueline. "The Big Push: The Export of American Business Education to Western Europe after the Second World War." In *Management Education in Historical Perspective*, edited by Lars Engwall and Vera Zamagni, 50–65. Manchester, UK: Manchester University Press, 1998.

McKenna, Christopher. *The World's Newest Profession: Management Consulting in the Twentieth Century.* Cambridge: Cambridge University Press, 2006.

McKersie, Robert. *A Decisive Decade: An Insider's View of the Chicago Civil Rights Movement during the 1960s.* Carbondale: Southern Illinois Press, 2013.

Mears, Eliot G. "The Teaching of Commerce and Economics." *American Economic Review* 13 (1923): 648–51.

"Mercantile Education." *Hunt's Merchant's Magazine* 10 (1844): 143–46.

"Mercantile Libraries." *Hunt's Merchant's Magazine* 29 (1853): 437.

Metzner, Henry E., and Edwin C. Sims, "Student Attitudes toward the Free Enterprise System." *Journal of Economic Education* 10 (1978): 46–50.

Miles, Edward W. *The Past, Present, and Future of the Business School.* New York: Palgrave Macmillan, 2016.

Miller, Jay W. *The Independent Business School in American Education.* New York: McGraw-Hill Books, 1964.

Miller, Jay W. and William J. Hamilton. *The Independent Business School in American Education.* New York: McGraw-Hill Books, 1964.

Mirowski, Philip, and Dieter Plehwe. *The Road from Mont Pelerin: The Making of the Neoliberal Thought Collective.* Cambridge, MA: Harvard University Press, 2009.

Moon, Hyeyoung, and Christine Min Wotipka. "Education, 1881–1999: Historical Trajectory and Mechanisms of Expansion." In *Globalization and Organization: World Society and Organizational Change*, edited by Gili S. Drori, John W. Meyer, and Hokyu Hwang, 121–36. Oxford: Oxford University Press, 2006.

"The Moral History of U.S. Business." *Fortune*, December 1949, 143–46+.

Moran, Gwen. "Women Now Make Up 40% of Students at Top MBA Programs." *Fortune*, November 9, 2015, http://fortune.com/2015/11/09/women-mba-40-percent/.

Moran, Robert, and Susan Snyder. "Temple Finds More Misreporting." *Philadelphia Inquirer*, July 25, 2018.

"A More Useful Public Library." *World's Work* 25 (1913): 504–5.

Morgan, Mary S., and Malcolm Rutherford. "American Economics: The Character of the Transformation." In *From Interwar Pluralism to Postwar Neoclassicism*, edited by Mary S. Morgan and Malcolm Rutherford, 1–26. Durham, NC: Duke University Press, 1998.

Morgan, Mary S., and Malcolm Rutherford, eds. *From Interwar Pluralism to Postwar Neoclassicism.* Durham, NC: Duke University Press, 1998.

Morrissey, Rick. "Past Imperfect." *Chicago Tribune*, November 30, 1997.

Moskowitz, Milton. "The Best Business Schools for Blacks." *Journal of Blacks in Higher Education* 2 (Winter 1993–94): 49–58.

Mussey, R. D. "Business as a Learned Profession." Address at Washington Business College, June 18, 1873. Washington, DC: Chronicle Publishing, 1873.

National Association of Corporation Schools. *Second Annual Convention. Papers, Reports, Bibliographies and Discussions.* New York: Trow Press, 1914.

National Survey of the Higher Education of Negroes, vol. 2. Washington, DC: Government Printing Office, 1942.

Nesbit, Robert C. *Urbanization and Industrialization, 1873–1893.* vol. 3 of *The History of Wisconsin*, edited by William Fletcher Thompson. Madison: State Historical Society of Wisconsin, 1985.

Nevins, Raphael, and Andrew Merryman. "The Search for Black Management." *MBA*, April/May 1969, 8–14+.

"The New Business Student." *Newsweek*, October 12, 1970, 76.

New Dimensions of Learning in a Free Society. Pittsburgh: University of Pittsburgh Press, 1958.

Norton, Charles. "Commercial Education." *Educational Review* 18 (1899): 417–24.

Norton-Taylor, Duncan. "The Business Schools: Pass or Flunk?" *Fortune*, June 1954, 112–14+.

Novack, Janet, and Edward DeAngelo. "Community Relations Reap Frustration, Hope." *Daily Pennsylvanian*, April 24, 1975.

Nowell, Gadis. "Black Businesses and Black Managers: Some Preliminary Findings." *Western Journal of Black Studies* 2 (1978): 151–57.

Oak, V. V. "Business Education in Negro Colleges." *Crisis* 45 (June 1938): 264–65+.

——. "Our Aimless Business Education." *Crisis* 44 (September 1937): 175–76+.

Olegario, Rowena. *A Culture of Credit: Embedding Trust and Transparency in American Business* Cambridge, MA: Harvard University Press, 2006.

"Opportunities for Negroes in Management." *Chicago Tribune*, October 27, 1965.

Owens, Martha J. "How to Get a Business Education." *Chautauquan* 22 (1895–96): 213–16.

Pamp, Frederic. "Liberal Arts Training for Executives." In *Toward the Liberally Educated Executive*, edited by Robert Goldwin and Charles Nelson, 44–45. White Plains, NY: Fund for Adult Education, 1957.

Panschar, William. "Businessmen, Educators, Move to Enlist Black Grads." *Indiana Business Review* 44 (May/June 1969): 12–16.

Parker, Martin. *Shut Down the Business School.* London: Pluto Books, 2018.

——. "Why We Should Bulldoze the Business School." *Guardian*, April 27, 2018.

Parsons, Floyd W. "Harvard Teaching Business the Way It Teaches Law." *World's Work* 46 (1923): 166–73.

Patten, Simon. *The Social Basis of Religion.* Philadelphia: J. P. Lippincott, 1914.

——. "University Training for Business Men." *Educational Review* 29 (1905): 217–33.

Pierce, Joseph. *Negro Business and Business Education.* New York: Harper, 1947.

Pierson, Frank. *The Education of American Businessmen* New York: McGraw-Hill Books, 1959.

Plehn, Carl. "Address." *Merchants' Association Review*, December 1899.

Podolny, Joel. "The Buck Stops (and Starts) at Business School." *Harvard Business Review*, June 2009.

"Popularity Swamps B-schools." *Business Week*, December 15, 1956, 193–94.

Porter, Lyman, and Lawrence McKibben, *Management Education and Development: Drift or Thrust into the 21st Century* New York: McGraw-Hill Books, 1988.

Prickett, A. L. *The Collegiate Schools of Business in American Education*. Cincinnati, OH: South-Western Publishing, 1944.

"Private Business Schools and Colleges and Universities." *School and Society* 24 (1926): 200–201.

Proceedings of the Fifth Meeting of the International Business College Association Held in Cincinnati, Ohio. Milwaukee, WI: Cramer, Aikens and Cramer, 1873.

Proceedings of the Second Annual Convention, Papers, Reports, Bibliographies and Discussions. New York: National Association of Corporation Schools, 1914.

"Progress in Marketing Research." *Journal of Marketing* 2 (1938): 236.

Readings, Bill. *University in Ruins.* Cambridge, MA: Harvard University Press, 1997.

"The Relationship between Departments of Economics and Collegiate Schools of Business." Supplement, *American Economics Review* 18, no. 1 (1928): 73–84.

Reuben, Julie A. *The Making of the Modern University: Intellectual Transformation and the Marginalization of Morality.* Chicago: University of Chicago Press, 1996.

Roca, Esther. "Introducing Practical Wisdom in Business Schools." *Journal of Business Ethics* 82, no. 3 (October 2008): 607–20.

Rooksby, Jacob. *The Branding of the American Mind: How Universities Capture, Manage, and Monetize Intellectual Property.* Baltimore: Johns Hopkins University Press, 2016.

Rothblatt, Sheldon, and Bjorn Wittrock, eds. *The European and American University since 1800.* Cambridge: Cambridge University Press, 1993.

Rubin, Robert, and Erich Dierdorff. "How Relevant Is the MBA? Assessing the Alignment of Required Curricula and Required Managerial Competencies." *Academy of Management Learning and Education* 9 (2009): 208–24.

Rutledge, R. E. "The Merritt Business School." *Junior-Senior High School Clearing House* 8 (May 1934): 545–47.

Saltmarsh, John. *Scott Nearing: An Intellectual Biography.* Philadelphia: Temple University Press, 1991.

Sapienza, Samuel, "Wharton's Venture into Non-profit Management Course." *MBA*, January 1972, 109–10.

Sass, Steven. *The Pragmatic Imagination: A History of the Wharton School.* Philadelphia: University of Pennsylvania Press, 1982.

———. "An Uneasy Relationship: The Business Community and Academic Economists at the University of Pennsylvania." In *Economists and Higher Learning in the Nineteenth Century*, edited by William J. Barber, 225–40. New Brunswick, NJ: Transaction Books, 1993.

Schoenfeldt, Lyle F., Don McDonald, and Stuart Youngblood. "The Teaching of Business Ethics: A Survey of AACSB Member Schools." *Journal of Business Ethics* 10 (1991): 237–41.

Schrecker, Ellen. *The Lost Soul of Higher Education: Corporatization, the Assault on Academic Freedom, and the End of the American University.* New York: New Press, 2010.

Schulman, Bruce, and Julian Zelizer, eds. *Rightward Bound: Making America Conservative in the 1970s*. Cambridge, MA: Harvard University Press, 2008.

Schwedtman, F. C. "An Experiment in Practical Commercial Education in the National City Bank of New York." In *National Education Association of the United States—Addresses and Proceedings, 1916*, 329–35. Chicago: University of Chicago Press.

Scott, William. "Training for Business at Wisconsin." *Journal of Political Economy* (February 1913): 127–35.

"Scott Nearing." *Wharton Magazine*, July 2007, 46.

"Seasoning B-schools with a Dash of Liberal Arts." *Business Week*, July 18, 1959, 112–13+.

Secrist, Horace. "Round Table Conference on the Aims and Methods of Bureaus of Business Research." Supplement, *American Economic Review* 13, no. 1 (1923): 223–26.

Sedlak, Michael, and Harold Williamson. *The Evolution of Management Education: A History of the Northwestern University J. L. Kellogg Graduate School of Management, 1908–1983*. Urbana: University of Illinois Press for Northwestern University, 1983.

"Sees Bottom of Slump." *New York Times*, February 20, 1931.

Seventeenth Annual Report of the Commissioner of Labor: Trade and Technical Education. Washington, DC: Government Printing Office, 1902.

Severin, Steven. "Wharton Community Program Helps Disadvantaged Residents." *Daily Pennsylvanian*, February 26, 1982.

Sharman, J. R., and Maxine Shaw. "Education of Business and Professional Leaders." *American Sociological Review* 5 (1940): 381–83.

Sheehan, Robert. "New Report Card on Business Schools." *Fortune*, December 1964, 148–50.

Sholl, Don. "MBA Association Debates Need for University Involvement." *Daily Pennsylvanian*, February 7, 1969.

Siegfried, John J., and Benu Bidani, "Differences between Economics Programs Located in Liberal Arts Colleges and in Business Schools." *Journal of Economic Education* 23 (1992): 181–88.

Siegle, Peter. *New Directions in Liberal Education for Executives*. Chicago: Center for the Study of Liberal Education for Adults, 1958.

Silk, Leonard. *The Economists*. New York: Basic Books, 1976.

"The Sloan Foundation." *Newsweek*, May 15, 1939, 23.

Smith, E. Newton. "Commercial Education." *Education* 37 (1916): 51–61.

Smith, Guy-Harold. *The First Fifty Years of the College of Commerce and Administration*. Columbus: Ohio State University Press, 1966.

Stauffer, Thomas, ed. *Agenda for Business and Higher Education*. Washington, DC: American Council on Education, 1980.

Stewart, Jane. "National Association of Corporation Schools." *Journal of Education*, July 9, 1914, 39–40.

Stewart, Matthew. *The Management Myth: Why the Experts Keep Getting It Wrong*. New York: W.W. Norton, 2009.

Stimson, Henry A. "The Need for Advanced Commercial Education." *Forum* 29 (April 1900): 240–44.

Stone, Arlington J. "The Dawn of a New Science." *American Mercury* 14 (1928): 446–55.

Stronk, Mary. "Modest Growth in the Number of Blacks in Business Schools." *MBA*, January 1972, 41–42.

Student's Guide to the Theoretical Department Eastman National Business College. Poughkeepsie, NY: Isaac Platt, 1868.

Student's Guide to the Theoretical Department of United States College of Business and Finance. New Haven, CT: Tuttle, Morehouse and Taylor, 1865.

"Stumping the Deans." *Business Week*, May 8, 1965, 106+.

Sturdivant, Frederick D. "The Limits of Black Capitalism." *Harvard Business Review*, January/February 1969, 122–28.

Summers, Lawrence. "Milton Friedman," *Time*, December 25, 2006.

"Survey Says Black Students Are Getting a Fair Shake at the Nation's Leading Business Schools." *Journal of Blacks in Higher Education*, no. 15 (Spring 1997): 24–25.

"Tax Bill Doctors." *Business Week*, March 1, 1941, 30.

Taylor, Aaron N. "Diversity as a Law School Survival Strategy." American Lawyer, Law .com. Accessed March 19, 2017. http://pdfserver.amlaw.com/nlj/Diversity-as-Survival _Strategy.pdf.

"They Prescribe More Education Less Business." *Business Week*, October 31, 1959, 84–85+.

Thwing, Charles Franklin. *The American and the German University: One Hundred Years of History.* New York: Macmillan, 1928.

Tooze, Adam. *Crashed: How a Decade of Financial Crises Changed the World.* New York: Viking, 2018.

"Top Students Sell Business Short." *Business Week*, September 9, 1967, 134.

Towle, Herbert L. "Business Cycles and Business Men." *Scribner's Magazine* 99 (1936): 365–67.

"Training Their Own Employees." *Outlook*, September 6, 1913, 10–11.

"Upswing in the M.B.A. Market." *Nation's Business*, May 1974, 34–35.

Van Overtveldt, Johan. *The Chicago School: How the University of Chicago Assembled the Thinkers Who Revolutionized Economics and Business.* Chicago: Agate, 2007.

Vanderlip, Frank. *Business and Education.* New York: Duffield, 1907.

Veblen, Thorstein. *The Higher Learning in America.* New York: B. W. Huebsch, 1918.

Vecchio, Diane C. *Merchants, Midwives, and Laboring Women: Italian Migrants in Urban America.* Urbana: University of Illinois Press, 2006.

Veysey, Laurence. *The Emergence of the American University.* Chicago: University of Chicago Press, 1965.

Viner, Jacob. *Essays on the Intellectual History of Economics.* Edited by Douglas A. Irwin. Princeton, NJ: Princeton University Press, 1991.

Vinocour, S. M. "The Trend Is toward the Trained." *National Business Woman*, 1957, 16–17.

Waldo, Frank. "The New Movement in Commercial Education." *Century Magazine* 66 (1903): 798–99.

Wanamaker, John. "The John Wanamaker Commercial Institute—A School Store." *Annals of the American Academy of Political and Social Science* 33 (1909): 151–54.

Washburn, Jennifer. *University, Inc.: The Corporate Corruption of American Higher Education.* New York: Basic Books, 2005.

Weaver, Findley. "Functions of a University Bureau of Business Research." *Southwestern Social Science Quarterly* 19 (1938): 46–52.

Weiss, Debra Cassens. "Women Could Be Majority of Law Students in 2017; These Schools Have 100-plus Female Majorities." March 16, 2016. http://www.abajournal.com/news/article/women_could_be_majority _of_law_students_in_2017_these _schools_have_100_plus.

Whalen, Edward. *Responsibility Center Budgeting: An Approach to Decentralized Management for Institutions of Higher Education.* Bloomington: Indiana University Press, 1991.

"Wharton Copes with Its Identity Crisis." *Business Week*, June 23, 1973, 49, 51.

"Wharton School Course Will Open in September to Women Matriculates." *Daily Pennsylvanian*, February 22, 1954.

Wharton, George. "Business Men at School." *Outlook* 87 (1907): 303–6.

What Business Education Means in Peirce School. Philadelphia: Peirce College, 1910.

Wheelan, Thomas. "Top Management's Perspective of Business Education: A Preliminary Summary Report." In *Proceedings of the 32nd Annual Meeting of the Academy of Management*, 289–91. New York: American Academy of Management, 1972.

Wheeler, Harry A. "The Public Concern in Improved Business Administration." In *Conference on Commercial Education and Business Progress*, 11–17. Urbana-Champaign: University of Illinois, 1913.

Wheeler, John. "The Development of AACSB Standards." In *The American Association of Collegiate Schools of Business, 1916–1966*, 19–83. Homewood, IL: Richard D. Irwin, 1966.

"When B-schoolers Act as a Company Consultant." *Business Week*, July 28, 1975, 36–37.

"Where Executives Are Building a Better Image for Business." *Nation's Business*, June 1975, 79–81.

Whitney, Eugene. "Business Education at the Crossroads." *Journal of Business Education* 45 (May 1970): 312–13.

"Why Women Need Their Own MBA." *Business Week*, February 23, 1974, 102+.

Willey, Malcolm. *Depression, Recovery and Higher Education.* New York: McGraw-Hill Books, 1937.

Wilson, William P. *The World's Trade and the United States' Share of It.* Philadelphia: Philadelphia Commercial Museum, 1899.

Wolfe, A. B. "The Undergraduate Economics Curriculum." *Journal of Political Economy* (January 1913): 1–17.

"Wooing the Disenchanted." *Newsweek*, June 19, 1967, 76–77.

Woolley, Edward Mott. "How Our Colleges Teach Business." *Collier's*, March 11, 1922, 5–6+.

Wooster, Harvey Aldon. "University Schools of Business and a New Business Ethics." *Journal of Political Economy* 27 (1919): 47–63.

"The Worrisome Boom in Second-Rate B-schools." *Business Week*, March 6, 1978, 82+.

Wyllie, Irvin G. "The Businessman Looks at the Higher Learning." *Journal of Higher Education* 23 (1952): 295–300+.

Youngman, Anna. "Retrenchment in Relief Outlay Is Asked to Cut Deficit." *Washington Post*, September 29, 1934.

Zimmerman, Jonathan. "Uncle Sam at the Blackboard." In *To Promote the General Welfare: The Case for Big Government*, edited by Steven Conn, 44–64. New York: Oxford University Press, 2012.

Zuckerman, Gregory, and Bradley Hope. "The Quants Now Run Wall Street." *Wall Street Journal*, May 21, 2017.

INDEX